A ROADSIDE C
ROCKYMOUNTAIN
NATIONAL PARK

Beatrice Elizabeth Willard & Susan Quimby Foster

Johnson Books: Boulder

*In memory of
Ruth Ashton Nelson,
pioneer botanist of
Rocky Mountain National Park
and dear friend*

Book and cover design by Robert Schram
Cover art by William Scott Jennings

First Edition
  2   3   4   5   6   7   8   9

ISBN: 1-55566-027-4
LCCCN: 89-85046

Printed in the United States of America by
Johnson Publishing Company, Inc.
1880 South 57th Court
Boulder, Colorado 80301

TO THE VISITOR

There is a spirit in Rocky Mountain National Park that
captures the heart and the imagination. It dwells in the
glowing sunsets that paint the evening sky, intensified by
the darkened outline of mountain peaks. It is also found in
the sweet birdsong of the ruby-crowned kinglet and the
rasping bugle of an amorous bull elk. This essence is
conveyed in sparkling mica crystals in the morning
sunshine and through the soothing caress of a cold mountain stream on weary feet that have carried the hiker aloft
to mountain summits.

The seven *roadside guides* in this book will help you
explore and enjoy the marvels of nature visible from the
roads in Rocky Mountain National Park and along its
boundaries. In preparing each guide, we have integrated
information from the disciplines of geology, biology,
geomorphology, glaciology, ecology, anthropology, archae-
ology, history, and hydrology in order to interpret what you
will see and experience in the Park.

The glacial and ecological processes that have shaped
this magnificent landscape are described so that you can
better understand how the mountains and their features
came to be. People whose lives have become woven into
the Park's cultural history are introduced to give you a
sense of the human role—both past and present—in
discovering, influencing, interpreting, and protecting this
remarkable place.

We hope your visit to Rocky Mountain National Park
will bring you pleasure, unanticipated discoveries, and a
sense of belonging to this beautiful land.

Bettie E. Willard
Susan Q. Foster

Sprague's stages on Big Thompson Road. F.H. Chapin 1888, N.P.S.

Key to illustration credits:
    BEW — Beatrice E. Willard
    SQF — Susan Quimby Foster
    NPS — Rocky Mountain National Park collection
    DOW — Colorado Department of Wildlife
    DFA — D. Ferrel Atkins
    RMNP Collection — special art commissioned by the
            Park

TABLE OF CONTENTS

1 **DEER RIDGE TOUR**

View high peaks and glacial features, see the effects of a catastrophic flood, and observe diverse wildlife—bighorn sheep, elk, deer, coyote, birds, small mammals—in their natural habitat.

2 **BEAR LAKE ROAD**

Explore a glacially-formed lake, glacial moraines, set amid forests, meadows, and the highest peaks in the Park. Learn about early settlers of the Park area and glimpse their experiences in it.

3 **TRAIL RIDGE ROAD—EAST**

Climb Trail Ridge through three life zones, see mountain scenery at close range, experience the open, rolling tundra in an Arctic climate. Follow a route used by Native Americans for thousands of years.

FOREWORD

In this 75th Anniversary Year of Rocky Mountain National
Park, it is gratifying that a guide to assist visitors in
experiencing what is along the Park roads is published. It
was about 30 years ago when I first met Bettie Willard. She
had just started her research on the alpine tundra in the
park. Over the intervening years, her understanding of the
park is not only of much greater depth, but more all
encompassing. Susan Foster teaches seminars on pond and
stream ecology with Rocky Mountain Nature Association.
Between them they have written a guide that can be
valuable to every visitor to the Park.

Here is a guide that can totally change the experience
from an "Oh Wow!" look at the passing scenery to a real
understanding and appreciation. All that is required is the
willingness to slow down—and learn. For the many visitors
who come to Rocky repeatedly, this guide is so filled with
information that even the most frequent and familiar users
will be surprised at what they didn't know.

Whether you are one of the two thirds of Park visitors
who never leaves your car, or are just using the Park road
as access to the trailhead, this roadside guide can enrich
your experience. For Rocky Mountain National Park is
much more than just a pretty place, it is an adventure. To
truly experience the park takes both knowledge and appreciation. Here is one of the tools. It is especially fitting that
this guide is coming out in the Park's 75th anniversary year.

James A. Thompson
Superintendent
Rocky Mountain National Park

ACKNOWLEDGMENTS

It is a joy to acknowledge the help of many people in accomplishing this book. Foremost among them are Mrs. Ruth Ashton Nelson, whose enthusiasm for Rocky Mountain National Park was expressed from Bettie Willard's first acquaintance with her in Europe in 1954. Ruth shared generously her long years of association with the Park, from her childhood memories visiting the Park from 1905 on to information clerk to botanist and resident of Estes Park. It was her intimate sharing of knowledge with Bettie Willard over many years that planted the seed for this book.

Equal but different in contribution is Dr. D. Ferrel Atkins, long-time friend and seasonal naturalist in Rocky Mountain National Park. His constant, staunch encouragement, numerous reviews of the manuscript, in-depth knowledge, and photographs of Rocky Mountain National Park have made him a real bulwark to this project.

Park Superintendent James B. Thompson, Assistant Superintendent Donald Brown, Management Assistant Frank Fiala, Chief Naturalists Glen Kaye and Jim Mack, Assistant Chief Naturalists Skip Betts and Michael Smithson, and Park Biologist David Stevens all made valuable contributions of information and reviews of the manuscript. Naturalists Carol Beidleman and Judy Rosen, Curator Lynne Swaine, and volunteer Walt Reynolds made significant contributions to its realization.

Long-time friend and executive secretary to the superintendent, Helen Keutzer, gave unstintingly of her time in transmitting messages and of her home while research was progressing. Curt Buchholtz, Director of the Nature Association, shared information and moral support. Assistant Regional Director Homer Rouse and his assistants helped by ferreting out details about the National Park Service.

It was of great value to be able to use historic and natural history photos contained in the Park collections. Especially appreciated was the painting by William Scott Jennings, 1985 Artist in Residence, that is used on the cover of the book. We are very thankful to Ann H. Zwinger and Frances Collin for their willingness to allow us to use a variety of excellent drawings from both *Land above the Trees* and *Beyond the Aspen Grove* to grace our pages. Other contributors of illustrations are Dr. John Andrews, Dr. D. Ferrel Atkins, Dr. Peter Birkeland, Bill Border, Dr. William C. Bradley, Perry Conway, and Robert Haines.

Enda Mills Kiley and her husband Bob spent untold hours in expanding facets of Enos Mills's life and work. They also clarified details about Tahosa Valley and shared Mills's photos of the Park area for use in the book—a wonderful opportunity. All photographers and artists are acknowledged in the credit lines on illustrations.

Mel Bush of the Estes Park Area Museum and Lennie Bemis of the Estes Park Library were very helpful in filling in gaps. Bob Haines assisted in reviewing the manuscript.

For her unflagging conviction that the book should be completed, we are deeply grateful to Dr. Sandra H. Cooper. She also executed a masterful editing of the entire manuscript and field tested it.

Several scientific professionals contributed reviews of the manuscript related to their particular knowledge of the Park:

- Dr. William A. Braddock, Professor of Geology, University of Colorado, Boulder, shared his recent investigations of the Park geology with us and reviewed the manuscript for geological accuracy;

- Dr. William C. Bradley, Professor of Geology, University of Colorado, Boulder, reviewed the many references to geomorphology of the Park;

- Dr. Curt Buchholtz, Executive Director of the Rocky Mountain Nature Association and author of *A History of Rocky Mountain National Park*, checked the references to history throughout the manuscript;

- Dr. David J. Cooper, Wetland and Arctic ecologist, made his insightful review of ecological sections;

- Dr. John A. Emerick, Professor of Ecology, Colorado School of Mines, examined references to ecology and biology of the Park in light of his current investigations within the Park;

- Dr. Richard F. Madole, Glacial Geologist, U.S. Geological Survey, Denver, shared information about glacial deposits in and around the Park.

To all these experts, we are deeply grateful for their efforts.

Others who made a variety of contributions are: Pat Cahn, who read and commented on the manuscript at a formative stage; Katharine Welch, who field-tested the manuscript and made insightful comments about facilitating use of the manuscript; Kurt Wunnicke, who tested the early road logs and made constructive alterations; as well as assisting in proofing the galleys; Victoria Barker, who road-tested the early logs and contributed ideas; Jean Goldberg, who edited the initial manuscript and made helpful suggestions; Joan Michener Foote, who reviewed the manuscript, sharing her life-long knowledge of the Park; Ben Foster, who provided suggestions for map design and endless encouragement; and Mary Marcotte, who gave unstintingly of the secretarial skills in preparing the manuscript.

We are particularly appreciative of the creative intercessions provided by Donald C. McMichael in necessary legal transactions. His thoughtful, encouraging work enabled us to go forward. We also acknowledge Doris B. Osterwald's contributions during initial data gathering phases and her original interest in publishing the book.

To Barbara Johnson Mussil, Michael McNierney, and the staff at Johnson Publishing Company go our untold gratitude for their patience and professional assistance in producing this book. Robert Schram, book designer, has added greatly by his arrangement of text and illustrations.

We acknowledge that any errors in this manuscript are our own, not Johnson Books or that of any other person involved in the endeavor. We shall happily receive comments from knowledgeable persons who have additional information.

Our desire is to produce a useful, meaningful book, therefore we eagerly solicit comments about the format of the book and how is actually functions in practice. Please mail comments to Johnson Books, 1880 South 57th Court, Boulder, Colorado 80301.

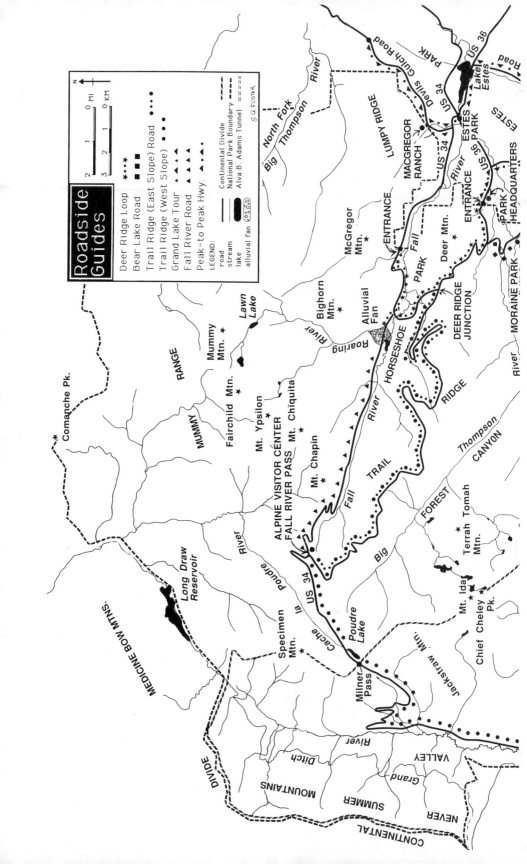

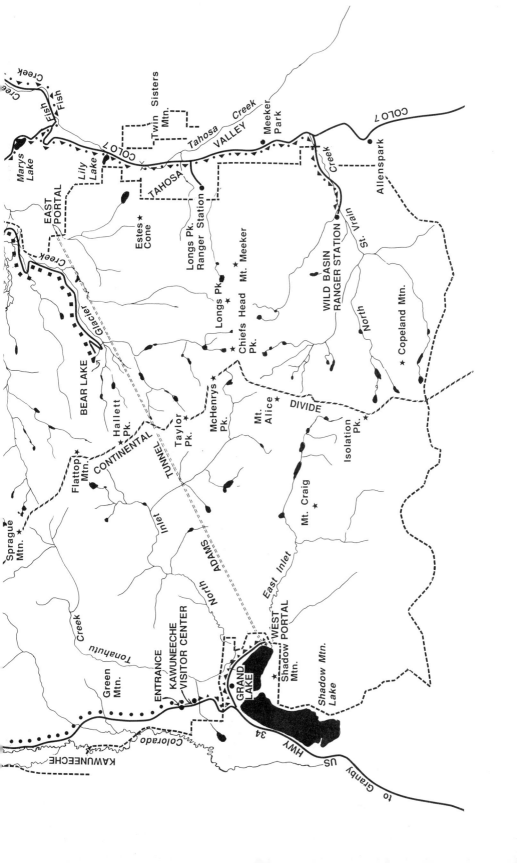

HOW TO USE THE ROADSIDE GUIDES

We recommend that you read the roadside guide of your choice and examine the accompanying map before driving the route. Mark places in the log that particularly interest you. You are your own tour director—free to linger and free to proceed. However, a half-day (three to five hours) is needed to utilize each roadside guide to its fullest. Trail Ridge and West Slope guides combined require a full day. Plan for time to enjoy a hike, sidetrip, and a picnic.

When you reach a designated stop, park, set the emergency brake, and lock the car, taking valuables with you when you leave it. Walk to the vantage points suggested in the guide. We hope you will see the wonders of Rocky Mountain National Park from a new perspective as you use the roadside guide.

Before proceeding to the next stop, note its distance, and set your trip odometer or note the mileage. This is especially important where the next stop is not indicated by a road sign. You will sometimes find material that is indented and set off by lines immediately following the distance to the next stop. This material contains a brief description of interesting features encountered in transit, for which there are no convenient stopping places.

Each roadside guide is in the same format:

- A large-scale map indicates numbered stops, mileages between stops, and other special features of each road guide.

- Names of places and natural features are in *italics*.

- Scientific terms also are in *italics* and defined in the text.

- These symbols are used for facilities at stops:

  📞 telephone   🚻 restroom   ▲ boardwalk

  🚶 hiking   ⛷ skiing   🍁 nature trail

⌗ picnicking	? information
🐎 horseback riding	⊘ Tundra Protection Zone
♿ wheelchair access	▨ research exclosure
🛏 lodge	⊤ interpretive sign
🍴 restaurant	🏪 store
🚐 shuttle bus	🐟 fishing

- A map of Rocky Mountain National Park is on pages x and xi.

- A map of the glaciers in the Park is on page 14.

- A list of facilities inside the Park is on page 304.

- The index contains names of places, natural features and processes, people, plants, and animals.

All roadside guides can be used when driving in either direction, except for Old Fall River Road, which is one-way. TO USE A ROADSIDE GUIDE IN REVERSE of the way it is written:

1. Turn to the beginning of the guide you wish to use. Read the theme page and scan the map.

2. Turn to the last page in that guide and read any material that is indented and enclosed in a box.

3. Drive to the place indicated as the last stop in that guide; read the description.

4. When you are ready to proceed, note the mileage to the stop with the next lower number (this is given at the right margin at the end of the section you just read). Reset your trip odometer, or check your mileage. The mileage given on the roadside guide maps will confirm mileages between stops for you.

5. Drive to the stop with the next lower number, after reading material in the box describing features to be seen on the way. Remember that RIGHT AND LEFT DIRECTION will be reversed from those given in the guide.

6. When you arrive at the next stop, turn to the page where the description of that stop begins and continue this procedure.

7. In the Trail Ridge Road and West Slope Road guides, specific statements are inserted for those who are driving these roads in reverse. Watch for notations to "Eastbound Visitors."

Driving Suggestions

Driving in the mountains may be a new experience for some readers. For those visitors, we make the following recommendations:

1. ***Enter the park with a full tank of fuel.*** There are ***no*** service stations within the Park.

2. ***Observe posted speed limits.*** They are designed to enable you and others to be able to see and experience the Park safely and at a relaxed pace.

3. ***Travel in early morning or late afternoon.*** At these hours, wildlife is more likely to be active and the lighting is especially beautiful. Traffic can be nearly bumper-to-bumper during midday in summer-time.

4. ***Downshift to lower gears*** when going up or down steep grades. This will reduce stress on the engine and minimize the chances of the brakes and engine overheating. ***Downshift your automatic transmission manually.*** A good rule-of-thumb is to go down hill in a lower gear than you used to go up.

5. ***Tap your brakes*** gently and repeatedly when going down hill. Constant pressure on the brake pedal causes brake pads to wear, overheat, and possibly to fail completely. ***Make sure*** you do not descend in overdrive.

6. When stopping at turnouts and parking areas, ***be sure to signal and watch for oncoming traffic.***

Sounding the horn on blind corners is quite accept-
able to alert oncoming drivers of your presence.

7. Always *set the emergency brake* when stopped.

8. *Lock your car when it is left unattended.* Always
keep valuables out of sight; consider taking them
with you when possible.

9. *Be sure to drive in your own lane,* whether you
are going up or down hill. Many drivers tend to
cross the center line in an attempt to avoid the
outside edge of the roadway. The road is well
designed and safe, but you must stay in your own
lane.

10. *Do not expect peak performance from your
car,* particularly if it is tuned for lower elevations.
Driving in a lower than normal gear keeps rpms up
and helps prevent overheating. Your car may stall or
act as if it is not getting enough gas. Pumping the
accelerator pedal floods the carburetor and makes
matters worse.

On warm days, some cars get vapor lock in the fuel
line. If this happens try to get your car off the road, if at all
possible; then wait for your engine to cool. But do not
drive onto meadows and the tundra in an effort to get off
the road. The fuel vapor should cool rapidly if you place a
wet cloth around the outside of the carburetor.

Precautions

1. Bring more than adequate *wind and rain gear* on
all trips into the Park. This is especially important on
Trail Ridge, Fall River, and West Slope roads, which
take you above treelimit. Summer daytime temperatures at these altitudes usually are only in the 50s
(10°C). The record high to date in the alpine tundra
is 63°F (17°C)!

2. Summer storms produce thunder, lightning, hail,
snow, and high winds. They are frequent and sudden occurrences, but are usually short in duration.

Thunderstorms can be very dangerous, particularly above treelimit. Fatalities from lightning do occur. If a storm develops, stay off ridges and peaks. Keep away from trees, boulders, isolated buildings, and metal objects. Your car is the safest place to be in a thunderstorm. A tingling sensation at the base of the neck or scalp, and hair standing on end with static electricity are both signs that lightning is about to strike near you. ***Move rapidly to your car.*** Do not stand still, no matter what. If you are unable to return to your car, squat and wrap your arms around your knees, keeping your head low. ***Do not lie or sit on the ground.***

You can estimate how far a lightning strike is from you by counting the seconds between the flash and the accompanying thunder. ***It takes five seconds for the sound to travel one mile***; that is much closer than you want to be to a lightning strike!

3. There is 40 percent less oxygen in the air above 8,000 feet (2,438,) than there is at sea level. You may experience ***altitude sickness***—with symptoms of headache, dizziness, mild nausea, or shortness of breath. Breathing into a paper or plastic bag for five minutes reduces these symptoms.

   To avoid altitude sickness, refrain from strenuous activity for a few days after arriving in the Park. It is always wise to ***move slowly above treelimit***. Eat lightly and drink lots of fluids. Alcoholic beverages tend to aggravate the symptoms. If annoying symptoms persist, return to a lower elevation. People who have a history of respiratory or heart problems should check with a physician before traveling to high elevations. Small portable oxygen flasks are available at local drug stores.

4. ***Avoid sunburn.*** The thin air at high elevations is less capable of filtering out the sun's harmful ultraviolet radiation. Over-exposure can be reduced by wearing a long-sleeved shirt, long pants, and a brimmed hat. Sunscreen with a rating of at least 15 is recommended.

5. ***Mountain streams can be dangerous.*** Their currents are much stronger than they appear. Slippery rocks, rapid velocities, and cold temperatures have been responsible for numerous drownings. Be cautious when fishing or when children are playing near streams. Sudden thundershowers can raise stream levels rapidly. If a storm persists in your vicinity, it may create a flash flood, so ***move to high ground.***

6. ***Do not drink water from streams and lakes.*** Carry your own water bottle filled with tap water. Stream or lake water can be purified by boiling it for 10 or more minutes. Natural waters throughout the Rocky Mountains are contaminated with bacteria, as well as a microscopic organism called *Giardia lamblia.* Both can cause debilitating intestinal disorders. *Giardia* is transmitted into water supplies by cysts contained in human, domestic animal, and wildlife feces. Dogs and cats can catch and transmit *Giardia.*

7. ***Prevent forest fires.*** Be very careful with fire when camping or picnicking. Extinguish all flaming and smoking materials thoroughly. Never discard coals, ashes, or cigarettes on the ground or from a car window. Dowse all campfires with water.

8. ***Place all trash in trash cans.*** In this climate, organic wastes, such as orange peels, egg shells, and paper can take over 100 years to decompose. Picnickers and all backcountry users must ***carry out all trash***. Where toilet facilities are unavailable, ***bury*** human and animal wastes eight inches deep in the soil, at least 100 feet from the nearest lake or stream. Used toilet paper should either be burned or carried out.

9. ***Wood ticks*** appear in the spring as soon as vegetation starts to leaf out in the Lower and Upper Montane zones. These pesky parasites may be active in forested and shrubby areas as early as February and remain active into late summer. They are rare in the Subalpine zone and above treelimit—above 9,500 feet (2,896 m).

Wood ticks transmit Colorado tick fever and the more serious Rocky Mountain fever. Insect repellents discourage them, and trousers and long-sleeved shirts may prevent skin contact.

The best precaution is to check frequently for ticks on your clothing, hair, and body, since it takes several hours for a tick to attach. Undress in a shower or tub, or on a tarpaulin OUTSIDE your tent. Inspect clothing carefully before putting it back on. Destroy ticks, but do not crush them with your fingers.

If a tick attaches itself to you, disinfect the area. Grasp the tick firmly with tweezers close to its head. Gently remove it by pulling it upward and out from the skin. Never twist or jerk on it. Localized swelling, enlarged lymph glands, or a fever in the days or weeks following a tick bite should be discussed with a physician.

INTRODUCTION

WELCOME TO ROCKY MOUNTAIN NATIONAL PARK

Climb the mountains,
Get their good tidings

Nature's peace will flow into you
As sunlight flows into trees;

The winds will blow their freshness into you
And the storms their energy

And cares will drop off like autumn leaves.

— John Muir, (*Our National Parks,* 1887)

These words of the eminent American naturalist, John Muir, have meaning to visitors in Rocky Mountain National Park, as well as to those in the Sierra Nevada of California, where Muir explored extensively. A pleasure to behold and a challenge to climb, mountains in the park unfold in all directions—beautiful and mysterious, yet beckoning. Fascinating lakes, streams, waterfalls, rocks, forests, flowers and wildlife await all who venture there.

Ever since people arrived in North America, they have been drawn to the Rocky Mountains. The footpaths, campsites, ambush walls, and tipi rings used by prehistoric peoples in their travels through the Rockies date back some 11,000 to 12,000 years.

The attractions of the mountains were diverse. Native Americans traversed the Park hunting for food, trading their goods, and socializing with other tribes. The earliest American pioneers trapped animals for valuable fur pelts or explored the Rockies looking for more direct routes between the nation's coasts. Others mined the mountains for precious metals, harvested the region's timber resources, or homesteaded its valleys.

The mountains offered adventure to those who climbed their heights and stalked their bountiful game animals. By the early 1870s, the Front Range of the

Colorado Rockies was enticing its first tourists. Among them was Victorian Englishwoman Isabella Bird who came to Estes Park on horseback and climbed Longs Peak in 1873. She reported in her journal, "...wild fantastic views opening continually, a recurrence of surprises; the air keener and purer with every mile, the sensation of loneliness more singular."

Overwhelmed with a sense of anticipation as she approached the Continental Divide, she wrote that "mountain fever seized me, and, giving my tireless horse one encouraging word, he dashed at full gallop over a mile of smooth sward at delirious speed."

Today, more than 2.7 million visitors throng annually to Rocky Mountain National Park. We, who number among these modern-day adventurers, approach the Park in much the same spirit of anticipation as did Isabella Bird.

The Lay of the Land

Rocky Mountain National Park is located 62 airline miles (99 km) northwest of Denver. It encompasses 414 square miles (107,225 hectares) of pristine forest, meadow, and tundra. Within the Park, there are 113 named peaks above 10,000 feet in elevation (3,048 m). The highest point is Longs Peak, 14,255' (4,345 m); the lowest point is 7,630' (2,326 m) on the Big Thompson River at Beaver Point. There are about 150 lakes and 476 miles (761 km) of streams within the Park boundary.

The visitor to "Rocky" will find 57 miles (91 km) of paved roads (nine miles [14 km] of which cross the alpine tundra) and 14 miles (22 km) of gravel roads. Trail Ridge Road is the highest continuous paved road in the United States. For those who wish an invigorating and solitary experience, there are 355 miles (568 km) of hiking trails.

Rocky Mountain National Park lies astride the Front Range, one of more than a hundred ranges that make up the Rocky Mountains in the United States alone. Most of these ranges trend north-south; a few lie on an east-west axis. Between the mountain ranges are intermountain basins—a distinctive signature of the Rocky Mountains. They were created when pieces of Earth's crust lowered as

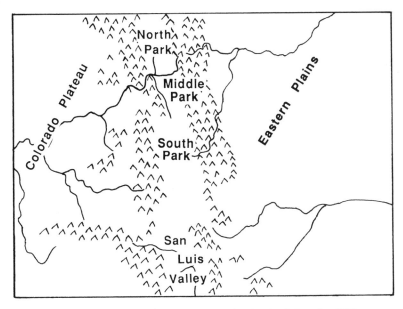

Rocky Mountain ranges and intermountain basins in Colorado. SQF

the mountains rose. Some of these basins continue to sink and all are accumulating sediments.

Several intermountain basins in the Rocky Mountains are called "parks," a term originating from the early French trappers' word "parque," meaning enclosure. "Mountain park" has come to describe large, grassy, level areas surrounded by high mountains. Estes Park, Moraine Park, Horseshoe Park, and parts of Kawuneeche Valley are typical mountain parks, but they are not structural intermountain basins. North Park and South Park are true intermountain basins.

What Made These Mountains?

The geologic story of Rocky Mountain National Park is a dynamic one spanning perhaps two billion years—nearly one half of Earth's history. This saga began at a time when part of the Earth's crust that would become North America was beneath the seas.

Over a very long period of time, layers of mud and sand, products of the erosion of pre-existing continents, accumulated on the ocean floor. These materials alternated

Estes Park, showing the expanse of grass with scattered trees. BEW

with layers of calcium carbonate produced by seawater and the cells of primitive marine algae and bacteria.

Compressed by their own immense weight, these strata were gradually transformed into *sedimentary rocks* known as shales, sandstones, and limestones. Interbedded with them were lavas that were periodically extruded into the ocean basins.

About 1.7 billion years ago, a continental plate containing North America collided with another plate. This contact gave rise to powerful, but intermittent, forces that compressed, contorted, faulted, and baked the pliable marine sediments. Altered both physically and chemically, they became *metamorphic rocks* known as *gneisses, schists, marbles,* and *quartzites.*

During this period of *metamorphism,* molten material upwelling from deep inside the earth pushed into the contorted metamorphic rocks and worked its way into cracks and fissures. Upon cooling, the *magma* formed *intrusive, igneous rocks* called *granite* and *pegmatite.* They are common throughout Rocky Mountain National Park and distinctive as light-colored bands in the sheer faces of high peaks. In some locations, the pegmatites contain crystals of *quartz, mica,* and *feldspar* over three inches wide, formed as the magma cooled exceedingly slowly.

About 1.4 billion years ago a second period of intrusion of molten rock occurred. This event created large and distinctive masses of pink granite rocks seen today in the Longs Peak Complex, in Lumpy Ridge, and along Trail Ridge in *dikes* and *sills* that appear as conspicuous, contrasting stripes in the faces of Mt. Ida and Mt. Ypsilon and in rock outcrops called *tors* located along Trail Ridge's Tundra World Trail.

Certainly, mountains rose above the seas perhaps several times during this extended period, but they were worn down by erosion.

Sediments removed from them accumulated several miles thick in adjacent basins. Relatively little is known about this region during the long period from 1.4 billion to 510 million years ago.

By about 510 million years ago, the region had been eroded to very flat terrain. The land sank beneath the seas again. Metamorphic and granitic rocks, once the roots of mountains, were buried a mile deep in layers of marine sediments that accumulated for over 400 million years.

As a consequence of new collisions of continental plates, midway in this period, about 300 million years ago, a new mountain system was uplifted several thousand feet above the ocean. We know about these *Ancestral Rocky Mountains* because rocks formed from products of their erosion are now found tilted against the eastern edge of the Front Range and along the flanks of the West Elk Range southwest of the Park. These rocks are distinctive pinkish-red, coarse-grained sandstone and conglomerate called the Fountain and Maroon formations.

More recently, streams have cut through these formations in a number of places, leaving distinctive and photogenic features such as Red Rocks west of Denver, Garden of the Gods west of Colorado Springs, the Flatirons west of Boulder, and the Maroon Bells near Aspen.

The Ancestral Rockies eventually were reduced by erosion to a rolling lowland surrounded by shallow seas; they remained in this form for tens of millions of years. This featureless landscape was bordered by large beaches and sand dunes that later became salmon-colored Lyons

6

Sandstone. Named for the place it was first described near Lyons, Colorado, this formation is quarried extensively for its handsome building stone.

Marine waters advanced and retreated across the land repeatedly, sometimes creating lagoons where fishes and

The mountain building cycle includes stages of: A. erosion and deposition; B. folding and faulting; C. volcanics, metamorphism, and graben formation; and D. erosion and deposition. SQF

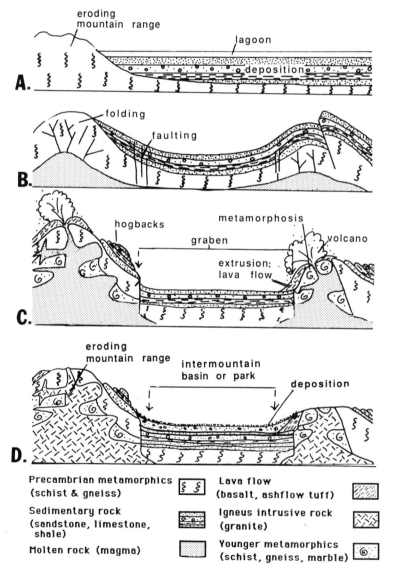

shellfish thrived. Several types of dinosaurs lived near these lagoons, where they grazed on lush vegetation or stalked prey.

Footprints and bones of these lumbering giants are found in the Morrison Formation, named for its type locality in the foothills due west of Denver. Although there once were layers of the Fountain, Lyons, and Morrison formations hundreds of feet thick covering all the Southern Rocky Mountains, erosion has removed most of these sedimentary rocks. They were completely stripped from the area of Rocky Mountain National Park.

Geologic timeline for Rocky Mountain National Park. SQF

ERA	PERIOD	EPOCH	YRS. AGO	GEOLOGICAL EVENT
CENOZOIC	QUATERNARY	HOLOCENE "Little Ice Age"	Present Time 10,000	Climate cools
		PLEISTOCENE "Great Ice Age" and Interglacial Periods	27,000 70,000 100,000 105,000 127,000 160,000 600,000 2,000,000	Pinedale Glaciations ? Bull Lake Glaciations ? ? Pre-Bull Lake Glaciations ?
	TERTIARY	PLIOCENE	6,000,000	Final uplift of Rockies to above 12,000 ft.
		MIOCENE	26,000,000	Uplift of mountains continues
		OLIGOCENE		
		EOCENE	38,000,000 54,000,000	Volcanic activity Erosion
		PALEOCENE	65,000,000	Laramide Revolution
MESO-ZOIC	CRETACEOUS		136,000,000	Seas invade area and retreat
	JURASSIC		190,000,000	
	TRIASSIC		225,000,000	
PALEOZOIC	PERMIAN		280,000,000	Uplift of Ancestral Rockies
	PENNSYLVANIAN		320,000,000	
	MISSISSIPPIAN		345,000,000	
	DEVONIAN		395,000,000	Seas invade and retreat repeatedly
	SILURIAN		430,000,000	
	ORDOVICIAN		500,000,000	
	CAMBRIAN		570,000,000	
PRECAMBRIAN	PROTEOZOIC		1,300,000,000 1,450,000,000 1,700,000,000	Intrusion of Iron Dike Intrusion of Granite Schist and Gneiss created
	ARCHAEOZOIC		2,500,000,000 4,600,000,000	Origin of the Earth

8

About 110 million years ago, the Ancestral Rockies became totally submerged in the ocean once again. Marine muds and sands accumulated over a mile deep on top of the old mountain stubs, eventually forming the Dakota Sandstone and the Pierre Shale.

The Dakota Sandstone forms the light-colored, nearly-vertical hogbacks at the foot of the mountains. Gray-to-tan Pierre Shale lies beneath several communities on the plains. Small, highly altered patches of Pierre Shale remain atop the northern Never Summer Mountains within the Park.

The Age of the Earth
(4.6 billion years)
Represented as the passing of 12 hours of time

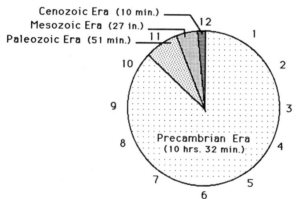

Geological Activity in Rocky Mountain National Park:

Precambrian Era (87.7 % of time on Earth)

Deposition, metamorphism, mountain building and erosion

Paleozoic Era (7.1% of time)

Invasion by seas, deposition, uplift, erosion, invasion by seas, and uplift of the Ancestral Rockies

Mesozoic Era (3.8% of time)

Erosion of Ancestral Rockies, invasion by seas, and formation of Modern Rockies (Laramide Orogeny)

Cenozoic Era (1.4% of time)

Erosion of Modern Rockies, regional uplift, erosion, and Ice Ages

Geological time expressed in percentage of whole. SQF

9

The Laramide Orogeny

Climaxing this 40-million-year period of submersion under the seas, the land underwent another period of regional uplift over a broad belt from Alaska to Mexico. As the North American continent separated from the European continent about a 100 million years ago, it drifted west, sliding up over the edge of the crustal plate carrying the Pacific sea floor. This collision triggered a period of even more intense mountain building—the Laramide Orogeny, 70 to 50 million years ago.

Mountain ranges resulting from this uplift took the form of rows and rows of vast, broad domes. Known as the "Laramide Revolution" (one of the few uprisings in which not one shot was fired) this mountain-building period, or *orogeny*, is named for the Laramie region of southern Wyoming.

The ancient Precambrian metamorphic and granitic rocks in this region were faulted, folded, and thrust upward, sliding over younger rocks in some locations. This activity created rows of north-south trending, massive blocks—the Rocky Mountain Ranges we know today. Some sections of bedrock were down-faulted and folded, forming intermountain basins.

During a 10-million-year respite in the Laramide Orogeny, erosional forces of wind, rain, and frost relentlessly rounded and furrowed the mountains. In the Park area, deposits of sedimentary rock up to 10,000 feet thick were entirely stripped away, exposing the Precambrian metamorphic/granitic mountain core. In fact, this process probably reduced the mountains to an elevation of about 4,000 feet above sea level. It also created a second trademark of this mountain system—large expanses of high-elevation, nearly horizontal erosional surfaces.

In true revolutionary style, this erosional period ended in a blaze of fireworks lasting two million years. Volcanic eruptions periodically clothed the land with *volcanic ashflow tuff, breccia, pumice,* and patchy *lava flows* that cooled rapidly to form *andesite, obsidian,* and *rhyolite.* Along the northern crest of the Never Summer Mountains on the Park's northwestern boundary, numerous volcanic eruptions came from *intrusive stocks* between 28 and 26 million years ago.

Buoyant, hot ashflows obliterated valleys, including Cache la Poudre, as well as Milner and LaPoudre Passes. They also partially filled the Kawuneeche Valley. One flow extended eastward and accumulated several hundred feet deep on Trail Ridge. This rock was later exposed in Lava Cliffs by glacial quarrying.

Sixteen to 21 million years after this volcanic display, the mountains were again uplifted. More faulting occurred, thrusting upward pieces of the undulating erosional surfaces on Trail Ridge, summits of the Mummy Range, and the Continental Divide. The highest of these erosional surfaces within the Park is the horizontal summit of Longs Peak.

Regional uplift also increased the gradient of rivers and accelerated their erosional activities. Streams incised deep, narrow, V-shaped canyons on each side of Trail Ridge, in the Mummy Range, and south of Longs Peak. An immense valley was cut along a fault running the full length of Kawuneeche Valley. In addition, five westward-trending valleys were created within the Park.

Glaciers—Sculptors of Mountains

Over the last six million years, the formerly sub-tropical climate cooled and dried into a semi-arid, *continental climate*. Extended periods during the most recent 1.7 million years have been cold and wet; alternating with them have been warmer, drier times. During periods of cooling, snow accumulated at the heads of mountain valleys, compressing into ice masses so deep they did not melt during summers. Gradually, they became huge, moving rivers of ice called *glaciers*. The *Great Ice Age* had begun!

The valleys of every major river system in the Park contained sizeable glaciers. They quarried headward in the valleys, steepening mountain slopes and scooping out magnificent cliff-bound, amphitheatre-like basins by pluck-ing rocks from the faces of the mountains. As they flowed from the *cirques*, glaciers carved giant *Cyclopean steps* and

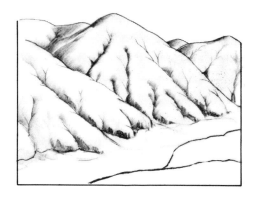

Pre-glacial landscape

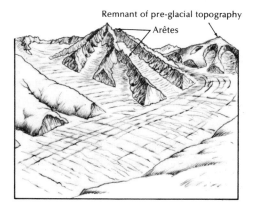

Remnant of pre-glacial topography

Arêtes

Glaciation

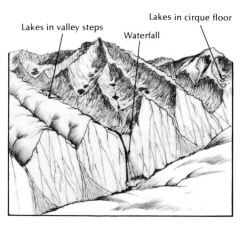

Lakes in valley steps

Lakes in cirque floor

Waterfall

Post-glacial landscape

Glacially-carved features and glacial deposits. After P. Birkeland

INTRODUCTION

12

scooped out basins in bedrock. These mountain-sculpturing processes carved most of the awe-inspiring ranges, peaks, lake basins, and valleys we see in Rocky Mountain National Park.

In the middle reaches of valleys, these rivers of ice transformed V-shaped canyons into U-shaped troughs with steep slopes and flat floors. Chunks of rock frozen in the ice scraped long grooves and nicked halfmoon-shaped hollows in bedrock. Ice containing finer silt and sand polished rock surfaces to a nearly glass-like sheen.

The climate warmed and dried at intervals within this two-million-year period. During these times, glaciers melted, retreating into their high basins and eventually disappearing. As they receded, they dropped rock debris in *moraines* along their margins. These materials were reworked by the braided rivers issuing from the snouts of glaciers, resulting in the *outwash terraces* and *kettles* scattered throughout Rocky Mountain National Park. Large moraines dammed rivers and formed lakes in Horseshoe and Moraine parks and at Grand Lake. Only Grand Lake remains. The other lakes have either filled with sediments or have drained. Exposed lakebeds created flat valley floors containing deep layers of relatively fine sediments. They have been invaded by lush wetland plants, including grasses, sedges, and willows.

The Great Ice Age was marked by at least three major periods of glaciation, alternating with warmer, drier interglacial periods. It is thought that the first series of major glaciers occupied these mountain valleys between 220,000 and one million years ago. Little is known about this *Pre-Bull Lake glaciation*, as it is called, because nearly all evidence of it has either been buried by more recent glacial debris or stripped away by erosion. The Pre-Bull Lake period encompasses both the Nebraskan and Kansan Continental glaciations.

The *Bull Lake glaciers* followed the Pre-Bull Lake glaciations. They reached their peak around 150,000 years ago, when the Illinoian Continental glaciers covered the northern part of the Midwest and East. The name "Bull

Lake" is derived from the place east of the Wind River Mountains in Wyoming where glacial debris of this age were first identified.

The most recent Great Ice Age glaciers were at their largest about 20,000 years ago. This glacial stage was responsible for much of the quarrying in cirques and deepening of valleys in the Park. It also created many moraines and outwash terraces highly visible in the landscape today. Called the *Pinedale stage*, it is the Rocky Mountain equivalent of the Wisconsin Continental glaciation.

Some sense of the scale of Rocky Mountain National Park glaciers can be gained by considering that Pinedale ice flowed 13 miles down the Big Thompson River Valley from its source near Forest Canyon Pass. Its terminus was in eastern Moraine Park. This glacier was 2,000 to 2,500 feet deep in Forest Canyon. Earlier Bull Lake glaciers appear to have been somewhat longer and deeper.

We are presently living in the *Holocene Interglacial Period* that started 10,000 years ago. Much of this period has been warm and dry, but there have been at least five cooler and moister periods responsible for small glaciers restricted to high cirque basins. The fifth mini-glacial period spanned the last 300 to 500 years and ended around 1920. Little Ice Age glaciers quarried sections of old cirques and deposited small moraines within them.

Glacial stages and interglacial periods, in the southern Rocky Mountains. SQF/BEW

EPOCH	YRS. AGO	GEOLOGICAL EVENT
HOLOCENE	1,650 - 1,030	Climate warms "Little Ice Age" Earlier small ice ages
	— 10,000 —	
PLEISTOCENE	12,000 70,000	Pinedale Glaciations
"Great Ice Age" and Interglacial Periods	? 150,000	Bull Lake Glaciations
	? 220,000 1,000,000	? Pre-Bull Lake Glaciations ?

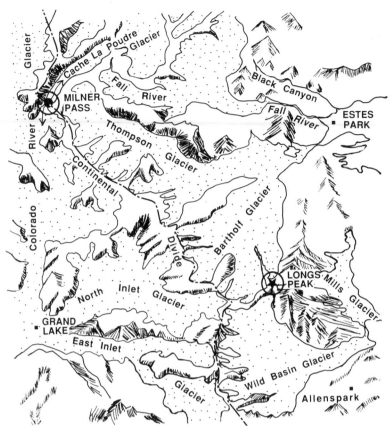

Location and extent of the Pleistocene glaciers of the Park. SQF after S. Trimble/B. Haines

Seven mini-glaciers still occupy east-facing cirques in the Park. The largest, Andrews Glacier, is between Otis and Taylor peaks on the Continental Divide. It is out of view to all but those who hike to it.

Weather in Rocky Mountain National Park

The weather in the Park is typical of continental localities—hot and quite dry in summer, cold and moderately wet in other seasons. One major moisture source for the East Slope of the Park is fall, winter, and spring upslope storms. They originate in the Gulf of Mexico and are pulled inland by high pressure systems northwest of Colorado. These heavy, wet storms deposit moisture that is very important to spring and summer plant growth.

During fall, winter, and spring, moisture-laden Pacific air masses from the Gulf of Alaska sweep over the state. As they move east, they deposit their moisture on the West Slope of the Rockies in the form rain and snow.

By the time Pacific air masses reach the Rockies' East Slope, they are quite dry. Warm chinook winds announce the arrival of Pacific air masses on the plains. Temperatures rise as much as 40 degrees Fahrenheit (22.2 degrees Centigrade) in a just few hours. Chinook winds melt snow rapidly, and evergreen trees are severely stressed by water evaporating from their needles.

Winds associated with Pacific fronts have been clocked at over 173 miles per hour (278 kilometers per hour) on Longs Peak and at 155 miles per hour (249 kilometers per hour) on the eastern end of Trail Ridge. Even higher velocities are sometimes experienced along the base of the mountains, especially near Boulder.

Common storm patterns in Rocky Mountain National Park region. SQF

A. Warm, moist air moves north from the Gulf of Mexico bringing "up slope" storms to the Front Range.
● Rocky Mountain National Park

B. "Pacific front" storms, originating in the Gulf of Alaska, are stripped of moisture as air masses pass over the Sierra Nevada and Rocky Mountains.

C. The Southern Rockies receive precipitation as air masses originating from tropical storms in the Pacific Ocean move northeast across the continent.

D. Air masses arising in the Arctic engulf the middle of the continent in dry, frigid, still air.

During the summer growing season, frequent thunder-showers are important sources of additional moisture on both slopes. As much as one tenth of an inch of rain can result from each storm, and nine or more storms can form in a day. They are accompanied by lightning, which endangers human life and ignites forest fires. Lightning also serves a beneficial role in producing nitrate, a plant nutrient. Nitrate results when electrical charges in the atmosphere cause oxygen and nitrogen to combine and come to earth in raindrops.

Waves of bitter cold Arctic air, called "Alberta Clippers," occasionally drift down from Canada. They grip the Park in frigid stillness for days at a time. Temperatures are often lower on the plains, where cold air draining from the mountains accumulates.

In spite of occasional extremes in the weather, Colorado has a relatively mild, stable climate. The state averages 300 days of sunshine per year, although the high mountains are more frequently cloud-covered than are the lower elevations.

Living Things of the Past

Many fascinating plants and animals have inhabited the Rocky Mountain region. Some have become extinct, but they share ancestry with species we see today. Gigantic dinosaurs once lumbered slowly and laboriously over the lowland landscape in what was a tropical climate during the Mesozoic Era, 200 to 70 million years ago.

More recently, 40 to 30 million years ago in the mid-Cenozoic Era, towering forests of redwood trees thrived in a cooler, subtropical climate. An invaluable fossil record of these trees, together with rarely preserved delicate insects, flowers, and leaves is found in paper-thin shale layers encompassed by Florissant Fossil Beds National Monument west of Colorado Springs. The only fossils within Rocky Mountain National Park are shells of marine animals in Pierre Shale found on the summits of some of the Never Summer Mountains.

As the climate continued to cool during the late Cenozoic Era, tiny alpine plants developed many adaptations

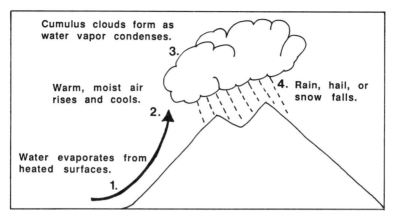

Cumulus clouds form as water vapor condenses.

3.

Warm, moist air rises and cools.

2.

4. Rain, hail, or snow falls.

Water evaporates from heated surfaces.

1.

Conventional thunderstorms. SQF

that allowed them to thrive in spite of the cold environment. These plants gave rise to *alpine tundra* communities.

Alpine tundra plants probably grew in isolated locations on mountaintops during the Great Ice Age. These sites are believed to have included elevated regions like Trail Ridge above the glaciers, as well as many of the lower mountain summits. Tundra also occupied high intermountain basins similar to the Laramie Basin in Wyoming and South Park in Colorado, and the high eastern prairies south of the continental glaciers' reach. The trees, shrubs, and flowering herbs that were unable to tolerate cold climates gradually retreated to lower elevations and southern latitudes.

While glaciers were grinding away in the high mountain valleys, mammoths, mastodons, camels, tiny horses, giant sloths, bison, and saber-toothed tigers roamed the region. All these animals except the bison became extinct during the last 100,000 years for reasons not yet fully understood. Modern bison continued to live in the Rocky Mountains and on the Great Plains until their numbers were decimated by Western pioneers. Bison were reported to have been hunted by Native Americans on the tundra-covered summits as well as in the valleys of the Park.

As the glaciers receded and the climate warmed, Engelmann spruce, subalpine fir, and limber pine recolonized the mountains, reaching the present limit of trees at 11,400 feet elevation in the Park. The trees provided shelter

Alpine tundra on Trail Ridge. J. Larson, NPS

to shrubs, flowers, mosses, and lichens that were less hardy than their tundra cousins. In the drier and warmer low elevations of the park, ponderosa and lodgepole pine, Douglas-fir, and aspen became established; they are found there today.

Life Zones in Rocky Mountain National Park

As you drive across Rocky Mountain National Park, horizontal bands of different vegetation types are superimposed upon the rugged landscape. These patterns result from responses of plants to temperature, wind, and precipitation at different elevations. Changes in plant species herald the transition from one life zone to another.

For example, as you approach the Park, you encounter the Short Grass Plains life zone if you come from the east, or the High Desert life zone if you come from the west, and higher up, the Lower Montane life zone. When you drive over Trail Ridge, you pass through the Upper Montane, Subalpine, and Alpine life zones. These three life zones are seen at a glance from Horseshoe Park, as you gaze from the valley floor to the mountain tops.

Lower Montane Life Zone: As you leave the High Plains and climb above 6,000' elevation (1,829 m), you enter open forests of ponderosa pines with shrubs and grasses covering the ground between them. This is the Lower Montane life zone where Douglas-fir trees also rise in spires from cool, north-facing canyon walls. Rocky Mountain juniper and mountain mahogany dot dry, sunny slopes up to 7,800' (2,377 m). Plains cottonwoods and boxelders shade the stream banks.

To the traveler approaching the Park from western Colorado's plateau country, this zone is characterized by scrubby junipers mixed with pinyon pine on south-facing slopes and Douglas-fir on the cooler, wetter north-facing slopes. Some areas of fine soils support extensive stands of western sagebrush, rabbitbrush, and greasewood. Dwarf forests of scrub oak clothe the slopes where there has been extensive disturbance. An occasional large ponderosa pine towers above the oaks.

Upper Montane Life Zone: Below the elevation of Rocky Mountain National Park (about 7,800' elevation [2,377 m]), lodgepole pine and aspen mark your entrance into a higher, cooler climate. These two species form dense forests of slender trees wherever older forests have been disturbed, especially by forest fire. Narrow-leafed cotton-woods, Colorado blue spruce, and several kinds of shrubs fringe the streams in the Montane zone.

Ponderosa pine continue to form open, park-like stands on south-facing slopes. Rocky Mountain juniper and mountain mahogany are replaced by a variety of low shrubs. Dense Douglas-fir forests give north-facing slopes a green, velvety appearance.

In the Upper Montane life zone, large, open areas carpeted with grasses and flowers contrast with surrounding forests. Such mountain parks are laced with meandering rivers. Their associated wetlands provide nutritious forage for hoofed animals.

Subalpine Life Zone: Above 9,100' elevation (2,774 m), ponderosa pine and Douglas-fir forests grade into forests of subalpine fir and Engelmann spruce. Lodgepole pine and aspen continue to grow, healing the landscape where fire and other disturbances have occurred.

Lush wetlands cut open swaths through dense forests, especially along water courses on valley floors. They also form verdant rings around lakes and ponds. In summer

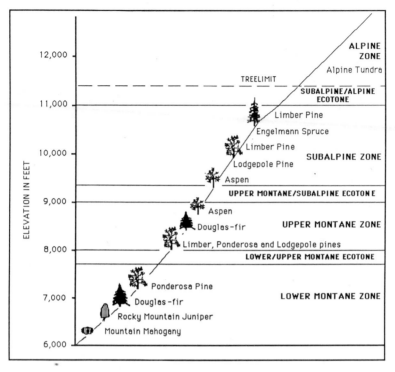

Life zones in the Rocky Mountains. SQF/BEW after J.W. Marr 1962

months, bright wildflowers festoon these areas. Nesting birds and wildlife abound in thickets of bog birch and willows.

Above 11,000' elevation (3,352 m), the Temperate and Arctic-Alpine climates intermingle in a region called *tree-limit*. Trees become shrub-like, migrating "tree islands" in expanses of low tundra. Above treelimit, Temperate climate yields to Arctic climate, and alpine tundra plants hug the ground like a carpet.

Alpine Life Zone: Tundra occurs throughout the world at any elevation or latitude where Arctic or Alpine climates prevail (except ice-bound Antarctica). Alpine tundra in Rocky Mountain National Park is very similar to the tundra in other parts of the world. In fact, 42 percent of the tundra plant species growing in the Park also occur in the Alps and cover thousands of square miles in the lowland arctic regions of Alaska, Canada, Siberia, and Scandinavia.

| LIFE ZONE | AIR TEMPERATURE | | WIND VELOCITY | GROWING | PRECIPI- |
	Annual Range	Annual Mean	Annual mean	DAYS	TATION
ALPINE above 11,200 ft. (3,414 m.) elev. Dwarf herbs & grasses Fell fields Turfs Marshes Grasslands	62° to -18° F. 16.7° to -27.8° C.	26° F. -3.3° C.	18 m.p.h.	45 days	26 in. 66 cm.
SUBALPINE 11,200-9,100 ft. (3,414 - 2,774 m.) Engelmann spruce Subalpine fir Aspen Lodgepole Limber pine	75° to -14° F. 23.9° to -25.6° C.	34° F. 1.1° C.	10 m.p.h.	87 days	26 in. 66 cm. average snow: 60 in. 152 cm.
UPPER MONTANE 9,100-7,800 ft. (2,774 - 2,377 m.) Ponderosa pine Douglas fir Aspen Lodgepole pine Limber pine	89° to -7° F. 31.7° to -21.7° C.	42° F. 5.6° C.	7 m.p.h.	100 days	21 in. 53 cm. average snow: 11 in. 28 cm.
LOWER MONTANE 7,800-6,000 ft. (2,377 - 1829 m) Ponderosa pine Douglas-fir Rocky Mt. juniper shrubs	96° to -3° F. 35.6° to -19.4° C.	47° F. -3° F. 8.3° C.	7 m.p.h.	137 days	20 in. 51 cm. average snow: 12 in. 30.5 cm.

Climatic factors by life zones. BEW after J.W. Marr, 1962

Nonetheless, the extensiveness and diversity of alpine tundra in Rocky Mountain National Park far exceed that found in other U.S. national parks. This distinction is attributable to a combination of factors unique to this park:

1. There are vast areas of high, gently rolling surfaces on Trail Ridge, in the Mummy Range, and all along the Continental Divide.

2. Deep, rich soils have developed on these areas over several million years, because they were untouched by glaciers. Tundra plants have helped to hold this soil in place.

3. Frequent thunderstorms act as built-in sprinkler systems, irrigating tundra communities.

4. There has been very little concentrated human impact on the Park's tundra. Domestic sheep and cattle were never grazed in high country. Despite recent damage from hikers and horses, the tundra looks very much the way it did when the first Native Americans set foot on it.

Early Human Activities in the Region

Prehistoric peoples have wandered through and lived in the Colorado Rocky Mountains for the last 11,000 to 12,000 years. When the climate was damp and cold, they lived in the intermountain basins and on the Great Plains. When the climate was dry and warm, they moved into the mountains, where water and food were more plentiful and summer temperatures more comfortable.

Trail Ridge is named for its use as a major route across the mountains by Native American peoples. Known as *Taieonbaa*—the Child's Trail—it offered open, nearly level terrain and soft tundra under foot. It was an ideal place to search in all directions for big game.

The eastern portion of Rocky Mountain National Park was once part of the immense Louisiana Purchase. It was acquired from the French in 1803 by President Thomas Jefferson for two million dollars. Interestingly, the precise boundaries of the purchase were unclear, partly due to some last minute exchanges made between Spain and France just prior to the purchase.

European fur trappers harvested pelts throughout the Rocky Mountains. Most of them were transients who left little evidence of their presence. U.S. frontiersman, Indian agent, and soldier Kit Carson built a cabin in Tahosa Valley on the eastern edge of the Park.

More modern forms of economic activity have had only minimal impacts on the Park's ecosystems. There was a minor spurt of mining activity at Lulu City, Dutchtown, Gaskil, Prospect Canyon, and near Longs Peak in the last third of the 1800s. Enthusiasm declined quickly when mineral deposits proved to be unproductive.

Cattle ranching and limited crop farming took place at elevations below 9,000 feet. Logging in Hidden Valley, Hollowell Park, and Wild Basin produced lumber for ranch and resort construction in the Estes Park vicinity. Logging operations in the Kawuneeche Valley met the needs of dude ranches and the developing Grand Lake village.

By the 1870s, people around the world began to hear about the spectacular scenery in this place called Estes

Native American hunters on the tundra. Bill Border 1982 RMNP Collection

INTRODUCTION

Park, Colorado. Many came to see it for themselves and a few stayed, intrigued by the notion of ranching, farming, and residing in the valleys. Most settlers soon found housing tourists was profitable. They built rustic lodges that grew into the dude ranches so popular in the early 1900s.

The Medicine Bow Forest Reserve (later renamed Colorado National Forest) was established by proclamation of President Theodore Roosevelt in 1905 as one part of a vast new national forest system. H. M. Wheeler opened the first Medicine Bow National Forest office in Estes Park in 1907.

Founding of Rocky Mountain National Park

Wheeler was the first to suggest creating a "wildlife reserve" in the mountains near Estes Park. This idea was promoted by Enos A. Mills, a local naturalist, writer, and innkeeper. Soon Mills was joined by many other local citizens, including Freelan O. Stanley, a prominent inventor and local hotel owner. Together, they established the Estes Park Protective and Improvement Association to preserve the region's exceptional scenery and abundant wildlife.

Enos Mills became the preserve's most vocal proponent, advocating protection of a 1,000-square-mile area. A 20-year resident of the Estes Park area, Mills had observed and interpreted the region's natural history in great detail. His enthusiastic appreciation for Nature's gifts deeply moved guests at his Longs Peak Inn.

President Theodore Roosevelt commissioned Mills in 1909 to tour the country, promoting the concept of preservation of wild lands. Mills did this, utilizing knowledge he had gained during his earlier travels in every state in the union. He was also inspired by his friend, John Muir, the nationally known California naturalist.

The Colorado Mountain Club, led by James Grafton Rogers, energetically promoted the concept of a national park in Colorado. As early as 1910, Congressman Edward Taylor of Fort Collins prepared a bill to create Estes National Park and Game Reserve. The bill finally reached the U.S. Congress in 1913.

Other supporters soon rallied around legislation proposing a park extending from Longs Peak south through

Assembling in the rain for dedication ceremony. First Director of the National Park Service, Stephen Mather, and his assistant Horace Albright were in attendance. Fall River Canyon is in the background. Fred Clatworthy, NPS

Mt. Evans to Pikes Peak. Ultimately, only a small fraction of land in this grand proposal was established as a park, in spite of two years of resolute political lobbying. On January 18, 1915, Congress passed the bill creating Rocky Mountain National Park—the tenth national park in the country and the world. President Woodrow Wilson signed it into law on January 26. The first Park superintendent, C.R. Trowbridge, arrived less than six months later to set up an office. He also hired rangers to enforce restrictions on cattle grazing and game hunting.

On September 4, 1915, several hundred Park support-ers and dignitaries assembled in Horseshoe Park to dedi-cate the National Park. This was a momentous day for Enos Mills, who had campaigned so steadfastly for the Park—"another jewel (in) the crown of the Nation."

The National Park Concept

National Parks were first conceived and established in the United States. The concept arose when early explorers of

Closeup of dedication: Robert Sterling Yard, E. Mills, inventor and local philanthropist F.O. Stanley, Congressman Edward Taylor, Mrs. Mary Belle King Sherman, President of the National Federation of Garden Clubs, Governor George Carlson, September 4, 1915, in Horseshoe Park. Fred Clatworthy, RMNP Collection

the Yellowstone area concluded that everyone, not just a privileged few, should be able to enjoy the wonders and beauty of that place. They recommended to the U.S. Congress that Yellowstone be set aside as a permanent reserve, an inspiration that became a reality in 1872.

Conceptualized as landscapes of superlative and unique grandeur, each national park is created by an act of Congress. These acts state the specific features for which each park is being set aside.

National parks differ from national monuments and national historic sites. National monuments are selected for their exemplary scientific or archaeological features. National historic sites are established to commemorate places of particular historic significance. Monuments and historic sites are created by either an act of Congress or by Presidential proclamation.

As of 1988, there are 353 designated sites within the United States, 53 of which are national parks. Many other countries around the world have taken up the national park idea.

Fostering the New Rocky Mountain National Park

The Congressional mandate creating Rocky Mountain
National Park stated that this parcel of land should be,
"dedicated and set apart as a public park for the benefit
and enjoyment of the people . . . being primarily aimed at
the freest use . . . for recreational purposes by the public
and for the preservation of the natural condition and scenic
beauties. . . ."

Over the past 75 years since the Park's founding, the
federal government has managed the land in this spirit. It
has acquired private property within the Park boundaries
whenever owners have been willing to sell it. The National
Park Service has also removed structures and reestablished
conditions on the land conducive to returning it to its
natural character and functions.

To date, these actions have brought into public use
and protection over 94 percent of the 11,000 acres of
private property within the Park boundary. Restoration has
been done with such great care that it is difficult to detect
former land uses.

Policies of National Parks

Creating a national park embodies two objectives. The first
is to preserve natural and historical objects including
wildlife, scenery, and ecosystems. The second is to
promote the enjoyment of these resources by the public.
These two objectives have been harmonized by Park staff
applying ever-deepening understanding, dedication, and
imagination to their implementation. Even so, conflicts
occasionally arise between the objectives of preservation
and public enjoyment. Fire management, use of horses and
pack animals, and camping in the backcountry are just a
few of the many issues that have required careful management planning.

Another example is that feeding wild animals in
national parks was accepted practice until about 25 years
ago. Visitors were encouraged to attract small and large
wild animals with food. This seemed a humane practice
because animals did not have to search for food and visitors were able to see them at close range. However, long-

28

term research has shown that wild animals are healthier when kept to their natural diets. At the least, they are protected from eating plastic, paper, and other harmful foods.

Wild animals may also cause physical injury and can transmit disease to humans. National park policies now prohibit feeding wildlife. This ensures that the animals will remain wild and healthy and that the integrity of national park areas will be retained.

Regulations of Rocky Mountain National Park

Over 2.7 million people visit Rocky Mountain National Park each year. As the number of visitors has increased, signs, trails, fences, and mass transit have become necessary to minimize damage to the Park's ecosystems. Despite the number of visitors, this area remains more natural today than most other mountainous areas of Colorado.

Current regulations and information about amenities in Rocky Mountain National Park are provided in the brochure given visitors at entrance stations.

When this guide was published, the Park regulations were:

1. *Dogs, cats, and other pets* are not allowed on trails or away from roadways. When in the national park, pets must be on a leash at all times.

2. *Do not feed or touch wild animals.* Store all food in a locked car or hang food in rodent-proof bags from trees out of the reach of bears. *Do not keep food in tents.*

Hunting and harassment of wildlife are prohibited. Stalking wild animals for photographs frightens them and makes them less available for other visitors to see.

3. *Picking wildflowers and plants is prohibited.* Removing, disturbing, damaging, or destroying natural features, including rocks, is illegal.

4. *Fishing requires a valid Colorado state fishing license.* Only artificial lures may be used. Children under 12 years of age may use bait in all waters open to fishing in the Park. Check with Park rangers for catch limits and other restrictions.

5. *Camping is restricted to designated areas.*

6. *A permit is required for all overnights in the back-*

country. There are restrictions on the use of pack animals.

7. *Fires* may be built only in picnic areas and campsites with grates.

8. *Vehicles must remain on roads or in parking areas.* Prior permission is required to leave vehicles or other personal property unattended longer than 24 hours.

9. *Hitchhiking within the Park is prohibited.*

10. *Trail bikes, snowmobiles, and all other vehicles are restricted to roads.*

11. *Firearms are to be kept unloaded.*

12. *Remove all your own trash* from picnic and campsites and dispose of it in trash cans.

13. *It is illegal to have open alcoholic beverages* in a vehicle on Park roads and in parking areas.

Rocky Mountain National Park—a Biosphere Reserve

In 1975 Rocky Mountain National Park received another singular honor. It was named the 21st biosphere reserve in a world-wide system of areas designated by the United Nations Man and Biosphere Programme. To date 221 biosphere reserves have been set aside in 63 countries for the purpose of observing and monitoring changes in natural ecosystems, especially those resulting from human activities.

"Climb these mountains" . . . by whatever means you choose.

Drive, winding your way at the pace of the first cars,
      especially at dawn or dusk;
    savoring every muted color, texture, sound, and
        shadow of this ancient, yet young landscape.

Listen for its many wild sounds—-
    a hermit thrush's plaintive call at sunset,
      the refreshing splash of rushing streams,
        a soft undercurrent of wind in the treetops,
    an occasional thrilling howl of a coyote,
      the bugle of a bull elk, the hoot of an owl.

Smell the spicy aroma of sage released by the noon
      sunlight,
    the sweet perfume of wild roses or alpine
      forget-me-nots,
    the essence of real pine needles on a warm day—
      all so different from scents sold in bottles.

Feel the textures of rocks,
    of flower petals and leaves,
      of bark on trees;
    the differences between spruce and fir needles,
      luxuriant, varied tundra carpets,
        and glacial polish on bedrock.

Read the many stories told by squirrels, birds,
    tundra, forests, meadows,
      glacial cirques and moraines,
        clouds, sky, stones.

Walk with early people—and Park naturalists—
    or just by yourself
      up canyons,
        over ridges,
          along lakes and rivers of the Park.

Or *just sit back* on a rock and gaze
    at sky and hills
        clouds and birds
    in delicious, relaxed abandon.

Then, many times in the future,
    you will recall these vivid images,
        especially when you need a change of scene,
          peace of mind,
            a comforting thought.

                Beatrice E. Willard, 1986

Glimpse wild animals and mountain vistas from spacious meadows and forested moraines.

*T*HIS ROUTE ON THE EASTERN
side of Rocky Mountain
National Park passes through exemplary, mature ponderosa pine and Douglas-fir forests, montane meadows, and wetlands. At dawn or dusk, discover wildlife that lured early Native Americans here. Listen for the crack of a twig signaling the step of a deer, the bugle of an elk in fall rut, the soft swoosh of a hawk as it dives for a meadow mouse.

Along Deer Ridge Tour, beautiful and awe-inspiring views appear in all directions. They encompass Longs Peak, high summits of the Continental Divide, and the Mummy Range.

The road parallels and crosses massive piles of rocky debris called moraines left behind by Great Ice Age glaciers. From the wide, flat floor of Horseshoe Park, glimpse the U-shaped Fall River Canyon carved by glaciers.

In the upper end of Horseshoe Park, evidence of the recent, devastating Lawn Lake Flood is vivid. This is a rare opportunity to examine the power water has had on shaping the landscape. Both a new alluvial fan and a lake were created by this catastrophic event.

DEER RIDGE TOUR

Tassel-eared Abert's squirrel. Perry Conway, 1980

In addition to Deer Ridge Tour's scenic interest, it is the eastern approach to Trail Ridge, Bear Lake, and Old Fall River roads. It also intercepts the ancient Ute and Fall River trails followed by Native Americans for at least 11,000 years as they traversed the mountains from the plains west to intermountain basins.

Deer Ridge Tour once was the only road on the East Slope of Rocky Mountain National Park. World travellers, including Englishwoman Isabella Bird and early western photographer William Henry Jackson, passed over it on foot and on horseback in the 1870s. Decades later, when it was known as the "High Drive," many others, including inventor Freelan Stanley and Kansas editor/publisher William Allen White drove it in early automobiles. Today, Deer Ridge Tour continues to reward the visitor.

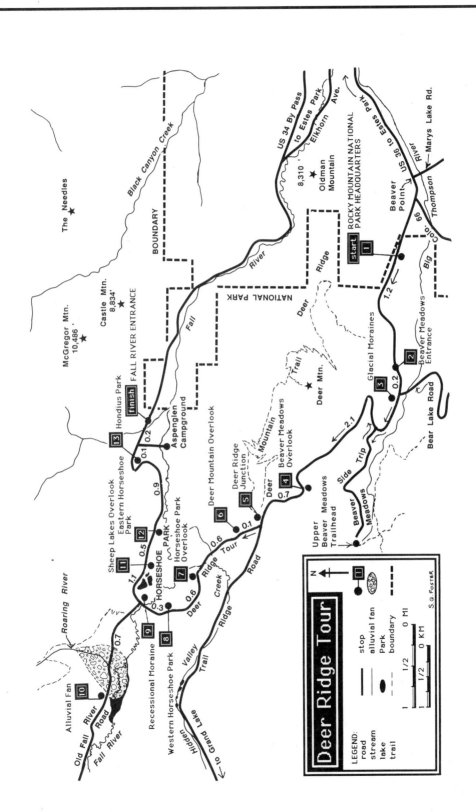

DEER RIDGE TOUR

STARTING POINT: *Rocky Mountain National Park Headquarters and Visitor Center on U.S. Highway 36 west of Estes Park*

ENDING POINT: *Fall River Entrance, Rocky Mountain National Park on U.S. Highway 34 west of Estes Park*

DISTANCE: *9.9 miles*

Getting Started: Deer Ridge Tour follows two roads—U.S. Highway 36, which enters the Park through the Beaver Meadows Entrance, and U.S. Highway 34, which enters the Park through the Fall River Entrance. Because these routes converge on Deer Ridge, we have used its name for this roadside guide. Early in the Park's history, the route was called the "Highdrive." To reach Stop 1 take U. S. Highway 36 *2.5 miles* west from the intersection of Elkhorn Avenue and Moraine Avenue in downtown Estes Park.

1 ROCKY MOUNTAIN NATIONAL PARK HEADQUARTERS & VISITOR CENTER
7,840' (2,390 m) 🛗 🚻 ♿ ❓ 🖥

The *Park Headquarters* was designed by Taliesen Associated Architects, Ltd. and was opened in 1967. In true Frank Lloyd Wright style, it fits well into its natural surroundings both in color and design. It is part of the National Park Service Utility Area, which is an Historic District listed on the National Register of Historic Places.

Stop at the Visitor Center to view the 22 minute *Park Orientation Film,* which is shown continuously, except in winter. Information about the Park and its interpretive activities, maps, and books are also available. The central office for camping reservations is reached by a footpath to a small building just east of Headquarters.

After visiting Park Headquarters, walk to the west end of the parking area, where you can see to your left *Longs Peak* and neighboring summits, hereafter referred to as the

Longs Peak Complex. Nearby and farther to the right, the
pyramid-shaped mountain is *Eagle Cliff Mountain,* 8,906'
elevation (2,715 m). Across the road, the forest-covered
ridge with four rocky knobs is *Deer Mountain,* 10,013'
elevation (3,052 m). The tour you are about to take winds
around this mountain before reaching Fall River Entrance.

Surrounding Park Headquarters and extending westward past Deer Ridge Junction is an outstanding example
of a mature Upper Montane *ponderosa pine forest.* In the
Rocky Mountains, these beautiful trees are found most
often at elevations between 6,000' and 9,300' (1,830 m and
2,830 m) on dry slopes that face south and receive intense
sunlight. The dark reddish-brown ponderosa bark has an
aroma of vanilla, butterscotch, or pineapple, depending on
the tree and your sense of smell.

Vast expanses of Colorado mountains were covered
with forests like this until they were logged prior to 1920.
Dense stands of younger lodgepole and ponderosa pines
have replaced most of the mature ponderosa pines that
were cut at that time.

Below the parking area are low, rounded shrubs with
dark green leaves called *bitterbrush*—or antelope brush.
This is one of several shrubs that cannot live in the shade
of more closed forests. In winter, bitterbrush twigs are a
reddish-brown color that contrasts with the muted tones of
the snowy landscape.

Muledeer prefer bitterbrush twigs to most other available foods. Because they are constantly being pruned, the
shrubs are compact in size. They would grow much wider
and taller—to a height of four to six feet—if the deer chose
to dine elsewhere.

Watch for dark squirrels with tufts on their ears; they
range in color from gray to black. These tassel-eared squirrels, also known as Abert's squirrels, are found only in
ponderosa pine forests. Active throughout the winter,
tassel-eared squirrels feed on pine seeds, small twigs, and
fungi; they build their bulky nests high in the pines. This
squirrel species is closely related to the Kaibab squirrel that
lives on the North Rim of the Grand Canyon.

Stop 2 is in 1.2 miles

Ponderosa
pine cone
and needles.
Ann Zwinger

Bitterbrush
leaves and
flowers. NPS

Please SET YOUR ODOMETER TO 0.0 BEFORE LEAVING THE HEADQUARTERS PARKING AREA. Turn left from the parking area to continue Deer Ridge Tour.

BEAVER MEADOWS ENTRANCE

As you approach Beaver Meadows Entrance, spectacular ice-carved peaks along the Continental Divide come into view. In June and July, meadows around the entrance station are awash with the color of wildflowers—yellow arnica, yellow cinquefoil, blue penstemon, white miners candle, and many others. Earlier in the spring, lavender pasque flowers, white candytuft, and lilac-pink Easter daisies dot the hillsides.

The Park entrance fees help support Rocky Mountain National Park, as well as other parks that do not collect fees. Additional funds, far in excess of these fees, are appropriated annually by the Congress to meet the Park's operating expenses. Prior to 1939 when the fee system was first adopted, park rangers counted cars instead of collecting money.

Stop 3 is in 0.2+ miles

In *0.2 miles*, you will pass the JUNCTION with BEAR LAKE ROAD. The *Bear Lake Roadside Guide* is the next chapter.

GLACIAL MORAINES
(no sign)

Immediately beyond the Bear Lake Road Junction, pull right onto the paved shoulder next to a huge gray *boulder* of banded *gneiss*. Freezing and thawing of water has cracked the boulder since it was carried down valley and deposited here by the Thompson Glacier over 150,000 years ago. Large patches of grey-green *lichen* nearly cover its surface. Lichens are remarkable for their slow rate of

Drawing of lichens on rock. Ann Zwinger

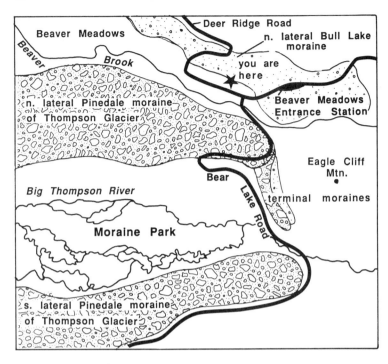

Spatial relationship between Bull Lake and Pinedale age glacial moraines in Beaver Meadows and Moraine Park vicinity. SQF

growth—approximately one millimeter in 100 years under the present climate.

To the right and beyond the boulder, trending parallel to and close to the road, is a low ridge composed of rocky rubble. This is a *lateral moraine* left by a glacier of the Bull Lake glaciation. The rusty-brown soil on the moraine is the result of iron oxidizing over a very long time span.

Tan *Richardson ground squirrels* make their homes in the soft morainal soil. In spring, they pop out of their holes and sit up very straight—resembling tent pegs—while they survey their world.

Across the road, the higher, densely forested, ridge is another *lateral moraine* that was left by the much more recent Pinedale Glacier 20,000 years ago. Both the Bull Lake and Pinedale glaciers originated along the Continental Divide.

At the foot of the younger moraine is a stand of white-barked *aspen* marking the course of *Beaver Brook*. Their trunks are scarred for four to six feet above the ground, making them look like they are wearing dark grey knee-socks. The scars develop after elk and deer feed on aspen bark in winter when other food plants are in short supply or are covered with snow.

At this time, beaver are not living along the creek. However, mule deer and elk may be viewed in this meadow in early morning and evening.

Stop 4 is in 2.1 miles at Beaver Meadows Overlook.

Sidetrip of *3.0 miles* roundtrip to
BEAVER MEADOWS TRAILHEAD
(no sign) 🚻 🪧 🚶

To take this sidetrip, turn left *0.4 miles* beyond Stop 3 onto the graded dirt road after rounding the next large right curve. This road winds through delightful *Upper Beaver Meadows* to the trailhead for the *Ute Trail*. You can follow the Ute Trail up Windy Gulch and onto Trail Ridge, where it intersects Trail Ridge Road at Ute Crossing.

Beaver Meadows is a good area to watch for wild game, especially in early morning and at twilight. Sit very quietly and wait patiently for the animals to appear; going in search of them will only frighten them away. Training spotlights on wildlife is illegal in the National Park.

Interspersed with the meadows are wetlands created by melting snows, rain, and high groundwater. This area was homesteaded in the late 1800s; its meadows were irrigated and cut for hay. For thousands of years before homesteading, Native Americans found this valley an attractive place to camp and hunt. Several bitter tribal battles were fought here within the last 200 years.

When you reach the trailhead, look for a fenced *exclosure* across the stream. It is a plot of land protected for the purpose of studying the effects of deer and elk grazing.

By comparing the growth of plants within the plot to the growth of plants outside it over many years, scientists are able to determine how vegetation changes as a result of animal grazing. Similar studies throughout the Park and elsewhere have shown that elk are a significant influence on the environment.

As deer and elk browse on young twigs, new shoots, and tender bark outside the exclosure, they effectively eliminate new aspen growth. Inside the plot, you can see many young aspen growing closely together. These spindly, immature trees sprouted from roots belonging to the older trees nearby. Reproduction from roots ensures that aspen can regenerate once grazing pressure is removed. If aspen depended only on seeds to reproduce, these stands of trees would have been eradicated long ago by animals that browse on them.

Large alders and willows line the stream along the parking area. Small cone-like fruits hang from the branches of the alder.

As you return to Deer Ridge Road, pull into a small picnic area on the right in *0.4 miles* from the trailhead. You can see another exclosure here that contains both dry sageland and wetland. The difference between fenced and unfenced vegetation is dramatic.

This sidetrip ends when you return to Deer Ridge Road. Turn left to continue Deer Ridge Tour.

Between Beaver Meadows Road and Deer Ridge Junction, the road climbs through a mature ponderosa pine forest. A few aspen, limber pine, and Douglas-fir grow among the pines. The occasional dead ponderosa pine trees were killed in the late 1970s by the *ponderosa pine beetle,* a parasitic insect common throughout the Rocky Mountains.

42

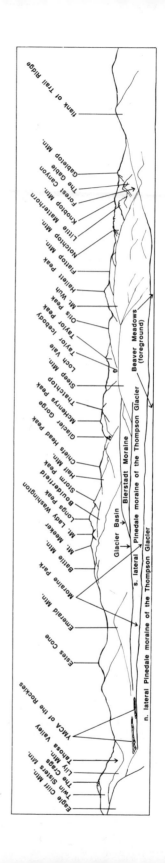

View south of Longs Peak and the
Continental Divide from near
Beaver Meadows Overlook. SQF

DEER RIDGE TOUR

Mixed in with the bitterbrush is low, greenish-grey *western sagebrush* that is especially abundant on south-facing mountain slopes. This entire forest-shrub complex is essential winter habitat for deer.

You may glimpse a tassel-eared squirrel darting through the trees. Frisky mating rituals take place in February and March; baby squirrels appear six weeks later.

 BEAVER MEADOWS OVERLOOK
8,720' (2,658 m) 🚻

Stop at the first paved turnout on the left, well before the blind curve. Walk to a large interpretive sign at the upper end of the turnout.

Longs Peak, the highest point in the Park, is named for Major Stephen Harriman Long. In 1820 this young U.S. Army officer led an exploratory expedition along the base of the Colorado Front Range in search of agricultural lands for settlement in the newly acquired Louisiana Purchase. Long was so discouraged with the appearance of the semi-arid High Plains that he called the region the "Great American Desert."

Native Americans called Longs Peak and neighboring Mt. Meeker the "Two Guides." French-speaking fur trappers adopted another name, "Les Deux Oreilles"—the Two Ears.

With the help of the sketch, locate the parallel, flat-topped, forested ridges beyond Beaver Meadows. These are *moraines* left by the Thompson Glacier 20,000 years ago. The Thompson Glacier originated up valley out of view to the right. Imagine an immense river of ice strewn with rocks and gravel nearly filling the trough-like valley between these two moraines. As it moved and melted, the glacier dumped its burden of debris along its margins, creating the moraines.

The road cuts through towering, weathered granite outcrops that have been exposed by erosion. Upon close scrutiny, tiny crystals of mica, quartz, and feldspar can be seen in the 1.4 billion-year-old rock.

At the upper end of the turnout, look downslope at several large hollows in the granite. These are *weathering*

Upper Montane ponderosa pine forest on south side of Deer Ridge. NPS

pits that have developed over thousands of years due to water dissolving minerals in the granite. In this same outcrop, several small ponderosa pine are growing. They are so stunted that they resemble bonzai trees.

To your right beyond the three large ponderosa pines, you can see the forested east end of Trail Ridge rising at the head of Beaver Meadows. Many Parks Curve on Trail Ridge Road is visible on the ridge's right flank.

Stop 5 is in 0.7 miles

5 DEER RIDGE JUNCTION
8,937' (2,724 m) (Junction U.S. 34 and U.S. 36)
Deer Mountain Trailhead

Pull off on the right before the junction at Deer Mountain Trailhead. More parking is located beyond the right turn onto Deer Ridge Road.

Around the turn of the century, Deer Ridge Junction was homesteaded by E. O. Schubert. In 1917 O. W. Bechtel operated a rustic open-air counter where he sold Park

Deer Ridge Chalet about 1940. The viewing tower was built in 1933.
NPS, DFA file

mementos and refreshments. *Deer Ridge Chalet* grew from
this simple enterprise into a popular stopping place for visitors. It offered a full range of services, including a viewing
tower and miniature railroad. This attraction was located on
the grassy area to your right.

By the early 1950s, traffic at Deer Ridge Junction had
become so congested that the road needed widening. The
Schubert family sold the property to the federal government, and the buildings were removed during the spring of
1960. The National Park Service sprayed the area with
hydromulch to hasten the establishment of plants.

It is remarkable that natural processes have erased
nearly all physical evidence of this sizeable resort. This is
especially impressive, considering the constraints that a dry,
south-facing ridgetop at this elevation imposes on plant
growth. Please *stay on the trail* to help protect this revege-
tated area.

Turn right to continue Deer Ridge Tour. If you entered
the Park through the Fall River Entrance, *turn left to continue.*

Stop 6 is in 0.1+ miles

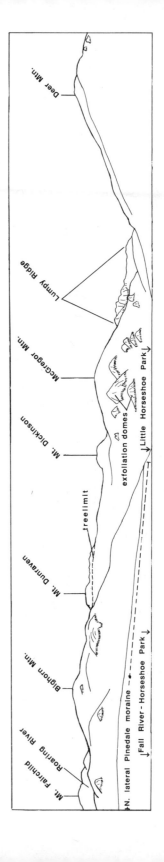

Mountains seen from Deer
Mountain Overlook. SQF

DEER RIDGE TOUR

DEER MOUNTAIN OVERLOOK
(no sign)

Pull off on the right. Straight ahead above the road rise *Mount Ypsilon,* 13,514' elevation (4,119 m), and *Fairchild Mountain,* 13,502' elevation (4,115 m), in the Mummy Range. Mount Ypsilon is named for the Greek Y created by snow that lingers in large cracks on its face. Glaciers have carved into it, exposing banded metamorphic rock in its cirque headwall. Fairchild Mountain was named for a former governor of Wisconsin.

The numerous rocky knolls on the lower mountains to the right are *exfoliation domes,* made of granite that was once covered by thousands of feet of metamorphic and sedimentary rocks. The domes formed as the overlying rocks eroded away, releasing the exposed granite from tremendous stress. The rock responded by cracking into concentric slabs that resemble the rings of an onion in their arrangement.

Below you is *Little Horseshoe Park*—a small meadow nestled between the moraine of Fall River Glacier and Deer Ridge. Occasionally, in early morning or evening, you can spot elk there. In the fall mating season, you can hear them bugle to attract prospective mates.

Farther to the right is the cool, moist, north flank of *Deer Mountain,* 10,013' elevation (3,052 m). It is forested with a dense stand of Douglas-fir that contrasts sharply with the forest of scattered ponderosa pine through which you just drove. Mosses and ground lichens grow abundantly in the shade of Douglas-fir forests.

Directly across the road are a number of *Douglas-fir trees*. Many of them are dying from an infestation of western spruce budworm. Budworm caterpillars feed on the tender tips of Douglas-fir and spruce needles. Since this is a natural process resulting from parallel evolution between tree and insect, the National Park Service does not interfere. The western spruce budworm does not attack ponderosa or lodgepole pines.

Douglas-fir wood is tough and strong, making it an

excellent construction material. In the Pacific Northwest where the climate is more moist and less windy, they obtain heights sometimes exceeding 250 feet.

Evergreen forests are the home of the *chickaree,* a small gray to black squirrel with rounded ears and a bushy tail. It scolds intruders with a repeated chatter. Also known as the Douglas squirrel, it remains active throughout the winter.

Stop 7 is in 0.6 miles

Exfoliation domes. SQF

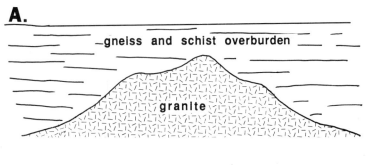

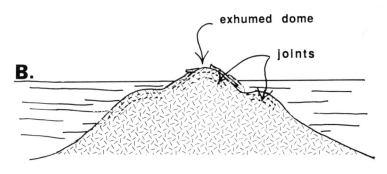

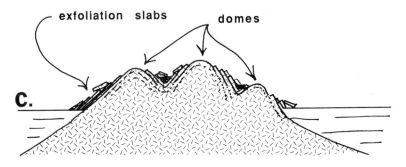

49

Below Deer Mountain Parking Area, the road cuts through extensively weathered Precambrian bedrock, which is rusty brown in color. On the left in *0.3+ miles* from Stop 6, you can see glacial debris that was deposited on top of the Precambrian bedrock by the Fall River Glacier. The debris has grayish, rounded rocks mixed with brownish-gray sand and silt.

 HORSESHOE PARK OVERLOOK
(no sign)

Drive into a parking area on your right. Begin your explorations by walking onto the rock promontory. You are standing on *gneiss* and *schist*—two common metamorphic rocks that once were ocean sediments before they were bent, pressed, and baked into their present form. Grey, green, and black lichens cover much of the rock surface, and *waxflower* bushes grow out of its cracks.

Five species of trees surround the parking area: aspen, Douglas-fir, and lodgepole, ponderosa, and limber pines.

Chipmunks and *golden-mantled ground squirrels* are common in summer. The chipmunks remain active all year, but the golden-mantled ground squirrels hibernate in winter. Both animals have learned to beg brazenly, even to grab your food if you are not wary. *FEEDING THE ANIMALS IS AGAINST PARK REGULATIONS.* It discourages instinctive foraging for natural foods that are more healthful for the animals. The rodents bite people and may have fleas that carry bubonic plague.

Large birds, including black ravens, black and white magpies, grey, black, and white Clark's nutcrackers, blue Stellar's jays, and gray jays, also gather here to beg for food. Small birds, including mountain chickadees, hop among the trees. Dark-eyed juncos forage on the ground. Their white outer tail-feathers are clearly displayed in flight.

Below you is *Horseshoe Park.* Flowing lazily across its floor is *Fall River,* a fine example of a meandering stream. Its *oxbows*—especially apparent downstream—looked like horseshoes to early settlers. Along the river, willow

Douglas-fir cone and needles. NPS

wetlands provide important bird and wildlife habitat. Across the valley are all four *Sheep Lakes,* which you will visit soon.

Notice how flat the floor of Horseshoe Park is. Had you stood here some 10,000 or 11,000 years ago, as prehistoric people likely did, you would have looked down on a large lake. It formed as water from the melting glaciers was dammed down valley by a terminal moraine.

Straight across the valley, notice the large exfoliation domes on *Bighorn Mountain,* 11,463' elevation (3,494 m). Find the horizontal tree-covered ridge draped along the mountain's base and extending up and down the valley. This is a *lateral moraine* left by a recent Fall River Glacier.

The spectacular *Mummy Range* rises upvalley. Treelimit creates an obvious line between Subalpine forest and Alpine tundra on the mountain flanks. Recent research indicates that treelimit was only about 1,300 feet above the valley floor during the peak of the last major glacial period. Since the glaciers melted, it has migrated an additional 1,200 feet up the slopes to around 11,400 feet elevation.

Had you been here around 6:30 a.m. on July 15, 1982, you would have witnessed the devastating *Lawn Lake Flood*. Across and up the valley is an *alluvial fan* (best seen from the rock outcrop) that was deposited within two hours by raging flood water from Roaring River.

The flood originated in the Mummy Range at Lawn Lake, 10,987' elevation (3,349 m), four miles upstream. In 1911 this small, natural lake was enlarged by an earthen dam to store irrigation water for use on the plains around Loveland.

The lead caulking that welded a pipe in the dam deteriorated and seeping water began to erode the old earthen structure. Early on July 15, 1982, the dam failed, releasing a wall of water 25 to 30 feet high. It rushed down Roaring River at nine miles per hour, toppling trees, tumbling massive boulders, and scouring the riverbed.

Just before the mass of debris-ladened water reached Horseshoe Park, it cut through the North Lateral Moraine and dropped over the valley wall into Horseshoe Park. The flood dumped a tremendous load of debris on the valley floor, forming a new alluvial fan. The alluvium dammed Fall River, forming a new lake, which is out of view.

Lawn Lake Flood from Horseshoe Park Overlook. 8:15 A.M. DFA

Fortunately, Stephen Gillette, a Park contractor, was near the Lawn Lake Trailhead that morning and heard the roar of the floodwaters. He called the national park dispatcher on the phone at Lawn Lake Trailhead at 6:22 AM to issue the first warning. The dispatcher alerted officials in the town of Estes Park who contacted the local radio station. Residents were urged to evacuate the downtown area and to stay away from Fall River. When the raging flood waters reached Elkhorn Avenue at 8:45 AM, everyone in the center of town had reached high ground.

Unfortunately, the flood claimed the lives of three campers. Property damage in Estes Park amounted to more than $26 million. Repairs of roads, bridges, trails, and camping facilities cost the National Park Service another $5 million.

Stop 8 is in 0.6 miles

Between here and Stop 8, you will pass through a *hillside wetland* growing on a moraine. Water from beaver ponds along Hidden Valley Creek on the other side of this moraine seeps through the porous glacial debris. Since most wetlands are flat, this one is unusual in its hilly setting.

This luxuriant wetland displays colorful wildflowers in July and August when yellow coneflowers, blue delphinium, scarlet Indian paintbrush, and other plants bloom in profusion. Deciduous aspen and balsam poplar trees grow among lush shrubs of willows, alders, and river birch. Scattered through the wetland on your right are tall, beautifully tapered trees with bluish needles; these are *Colorado blue spruce*—the state tree. Blue spruce trees require soils with high moisture content.

---

8 | WESTERN HORSESHOE PARK
8,522' (2,598 m) 🚻

Pull into the large parking area on the right. At dawn and dusk, Western Horseshoe Park is the best location to view *elk* grazing and, in autumn, to hear the males bugle their mating calls. Mature bulls make deep, melodious sounds while the young bulls generate high-pitched dissonant noises. An effective way to experience these wonderful beasts is to remain quiet and still, waiting for them to appear. This may take an hour or two, but it is well worth your time. Walking into the meadows drives the animals away. You are well advised to keep your distance from elk for your own safety, especially during the fall rut. They stand five feet at the shoulder and weigh over 1,000 pounds (454 kilograms).

Bull elk duel for herd dominance by rushing contenders, posturing, and sparring ritualistically with one another. When convincingly displayed, shining antlers and dark body markings can intimidate a rival.

Elk have inhabited the plains and mountains of Colorado for millions of years, but it was not until after the great Pinedale glaciers had melted 13,000 years ago that adequate vegetation developed in the valleys of the Park to support large herds. Prehistoric man came soon after to hunt the elk, as well as bison, bighorn sheep, pronghorn antelope, and deer.

Elk, called "wapiti" by Algonquin Indians, are relatively inactive animals, spending most of the day feeding or resting and a small fraction of it walking about. In groups of more than seven or eight, as they usually are seen, at least one animal is alert with its head up at any given time, looking for predators.

Willard H. Ashton, who came to Estes Park from Massachusetts in the early 1900s, fell in love with the Rocky Mountains. In 1907 he built *Horseshoe Inn* across the road on the flat area; it accommodated 115 guests. Ashton also built and managed a rustic backcountry lodge at Lawn Lake. In 1931 Horseshoe Inn was purchased by the federal government and removed, with the intent of restoring the natural appearance and functions of the land.

Ashton's older daughter, the late Ruth Ashton Nelson, first visited Estes Park with her family in summer 1905 at the age of eight. After she graduated from Mt. Holyoke College, she returned to study the local plants. Her book

View of Horseshoe Inn with Mummy Range behind it to the northwest. Although Willard H. Ashton had Frank Lloyd Wright prepare a design for the hotel, that building was never actually built. The tall ponderosa pines you see today are the same ones shown in this photo. Mt. Chiquita and Mt. Ypsilon are beyond the inn. Estes Park Museum, NPS

Plants of Rocky Mountain National Park was first published in 1933. It is now in its third edition.

Down the valley, a large *willow wetland* occupies a major part of Horseshoe Park. Wetland ecosystems are very rich in bird life. They are populated in summer by mountain bluebirds; American robins; Wilsons and Macgillivrays warblers; Lincolns, fox, and song sparrows; dusky flycatchers; broad-tailed hummingbirds; warbling vireos; redwing blackbirds; and Swainson's thrushes.

A U. S. Geological Survey study of the Lawn Lake flood concluded that loss of life and damage to property in Estes Park would have been far greater had it not been for these extensive wetlands in Horseshoe Park. The wetlands reduced the speed of the flood wave from nine miles per hour to two miles per hour. The wetlands absorbed the water long enough to allow people downstream to reach safe ground. After leaving Horseshoe Park and toppling Cascade Lake Dam, the floodwaters reaccelerated to seven miles per hour and bore down on Estes Park.

In addition to their value in flood control and as wildlife habitat, wetlands cleanse ground and surface

55

Path and arrival time of Lawn Lake Flood. SQF after Costa 1982

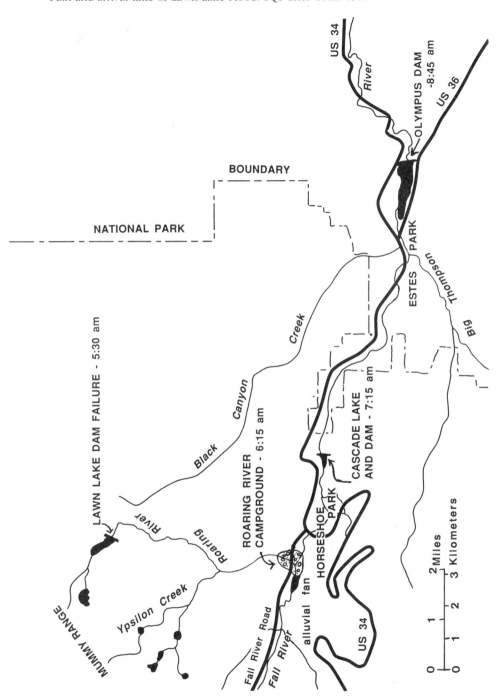

DEER RIDGE TOUR

waters by concentrating and holding sediments, heavy metals, and pollutants. It is estimated that only three percent of the nation's land area originally was wetlands. Realizing that 40 percent of the acreage of these ecosystems had been destroyed by human activities by 1956, Congress conferred protective status on our remaining wetlands in 1972.

Stop 9 is in 0.3+ miles

On the left between here and Fall River, watch for piles of *tree stumps* and other *woody debris* deposited by the 1982 Lawn Lake flood. Notice how the flood shredded the wood by tumbling it in the raging water. Between this debris and the river are mini-dunes formed of sand left by the flood and later shaped by the wind.

Dedication ceremony at Rocky Mountain National Park. NPS

9 RECESSIONAL MORAINE
(no sign)

After crossing the river, turn right into a parking loop opposite Old Fall River Road. To the north across the road, craggy *Bighorn Mountain* is now at close range. A bighorn sheep herd spends the summer on its upper slopes and farther north into the Mummy Range. In winter the herd ranges down Fall River valley nearly to Estes Park.

Next to the parking area is a low, grassy hill. This is a small moraine left by the last Fall River Glacier about 17,000 years ago when the glacier was stationary for a time.

A cluster of shrubs in the middle of the moraine marks the route of the first road through this area. When the road was rerouted in 1960, the original contour of the moraine was restored.

Stop 10 is in 0.7+ miles

> Stop briefly as you leave the moraine parking loop. Notice the small terrace across Deer Ridge Road to the right of the ponderosa pines. This was the site of the *dedication ceremony* on September 4, 1915, marking the formal creation of Rocky Mountain National Park.

10 ROARING RIVER ALLUVIAL FAN

Proceed straight across Deer Ridge Road onto *Old Fall River Road*. Opened in 1920, this was the first route built across the northern Front Range connecting Estes Park and Grand Lake. The Old Fall River Road winds through a high mountain valley, bringing you into intimate contact with nature. This trip requires half a day using the *Old Fall River Roadside Guide* found on page 226 in this book.

Follow the Old Fall River Road a short distance up valley until you cross the alluvial fan composed of boulders, sand, and dead trees. Turn right into the parking area.

A paved trail starts here, crosses the alluvial fan, and ends *0.2 miles* away at the parking area on the east side of the fan.

The alluvial fan was created on July 15, 1982, as a result of the failure of the Lawn Lake dam five miles upstream and over 2,000 feet above the valley floor. The Roaring River certainly lived up to its name that fateful day! It became a muddy, rampaging torrent carrying a maximum flow volume of 18,000 cubic feet per second. It was so forceful, it cut a V-shaped gorge into the glacial moraine that hugs the valley wall above you. This erosion obliterated Horseshoe Falls that once cascaded gracefully down the slope.

The boulder-ladened water raced toward Horseshoe Park, where it slowed abruptly and dumped its debris into a broad, cone-shaped pile called an *alluvial fan.* The largest material—boulders, tree trunks, and roots—came to rest in the upper part of the alluvial fan. The smaller particles—sand, silt, and clay—were carried out onto the flat valley floor where they dammed Fall River, creating a new lake.

People convening for dedication of Rocky Mountain National Park, September 4, 1915. NPS

The alluvial fan covers 42 acres and contains 364,000 cubic yards of material. This volume is equivalent to that contained in 132 single-story homes, each with 2,000 square feet of floor space. Some boulders exceed the size of a large car and weigh an average of 452 tons.

Numerous plants have invaded the alluvium. This process is monitored by Park botanists, who are documenting the plant species and the sequence in which they appear on this new surface. To date, these pioneers include two alpine species!

In spite of the fact that this flood was triggered by the failure of a man-made structure, it provides a graphic example of the power of nature. Flash floods are natural processes that frequently deposit alluvial fans at the mouths

Distribution of materials in alluvial fan formed by Lawn Lake Flood. SQF after Blair, 1987

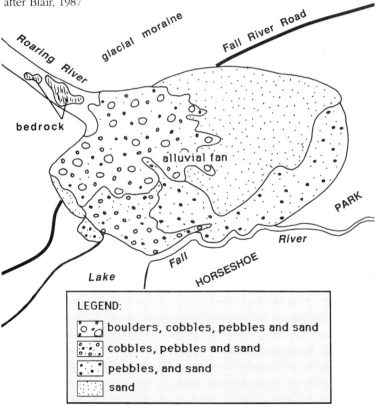

LEGEND:

boulders, cobbles, pebbles and sand

cobbles, pebbles and sand

pebbles, and sand

sand

of steep valleys throughout the western mountains and deserts.

The Lawn Lake Flood was estimated to be a once in 10,000-year event, unequalled by any other event since the most recent Great Ice Age glaciers melted. The likelihood of a comparable natural catastrophe occurring during the next few thousand years is very low.

Around the eastern Alluvial Fan parking area, flood debris suffocated most root systems, leaving only a few surviving Engelmann spruce. Some of the standing dead aspen have been converted to summer nesting "condominia" by birds, including wrens, flickers, sapsuckers, woodpeckers, and violet-green swallows.

Stop 11 is in 1.1+ miles

Turn left as you exit the Alluvial Fan parking area and return to Deer Ridge Road. When you reach it, turn left again to continue the tour.

SHEEP LAKES OVERLOOK
(no sign) **?**

Turn right into Sheep Lakes parking area. During the summer, an information booth here may be staffed by a park naturalist.

The parking area is built on a natural flat surface called a *glacial outwash terrace*. It was formed by braided streams issuing from the most recent melting glacier. Over time, these streams distributed glacial debris into many thin layers, as they moved back and forth across the valley floor.

Scan the meadow carefully for *bighorn sheep, mule deer, and elk.* These large mammals may be some distance away, even across the river. It is always a thrill to see wild animals, but tracking them is best done using binoculars or a camera with a long lens.

Bighorn sheep are attracted by salt deposits in the soil. If there are no sheep in the meadow, you may be able to spot them on the hillside across the road. During midday, they rest in the shade of trees. Bighorn sheep, the Colorado state animal, is also the symbol of the Colorado Division of Wildlife.

Before 1800 there were two million bighorn sheep in the lower 48 states, most of which were concentrated in the Rockies. The flocks have declined since the mid-1800s as a result of hunting, lungworm, pneumonia, scabies, and competition with elk, cattle, domestic sheep, and horses.

Only about 400 of the original bighorn sheep population remain in the Park. There are two flocks—one in the Mummy Range and another in the Specimen Mountain/ Never Summer Mountains area. Their populations are slowly increasing.

Concern has grown for the herds' future, as harrassment from hikers, photographers, and road traffic has increased. The National Park Service has taken several steps to ensure the animals' well-being. Domestic cattle grazing has been prohibited in the Park since 1915. The bighorn sheep's summer range and lambing area near Specimen Mountain is closed to hikers. Traffic on Deer Ridge Road is strictly regulated to guarantee the right-of-way to bighorn

Visitors admire Sheep Lakes in 1889. Note that large aspens grew along the far shore. Since then they have died from the combined effects of drought and browsing wild animals. NPS

sheep as they move between the slopes of Bighorn Mountain and Horseshoe Park.

In 1977 the flock was augmented by 20 animals imported from the Pikes Peak area. The goal was to reduce genetic inbreeding in the native flocks and to restore migration of animals between summer range and winter range at lower elevations. This project has been so successful that animals have since been transplanted from here to sites in the Big Thompson Canyon.

From the right (west) end of the parking area, you can see *Sheep Lakes*. As the last glacier retreated, large debris-ladened chunks of ice broke loose and came to rest here. The ice mass melted, creating cavities into which overlying debris slumped. Such depressions, when filled with water, are called *kettle lakes*. They have no surface drainage and may go dry during droughts.

Rising above the lakes is *Fall River Canyon* with Trail Ridge on the left and Mt. Chapin, 12,454' elevation (3,796 m), and Mt. Chiquita, 13,069' elevation (3,983 m), on the right. To the left on the hillside beyond the lakes, you can see the lower switchback of Trail Ridge Road. Below the

Rocky Mountain bighorn sheep at salt lick in Horseshoe Park. BEW

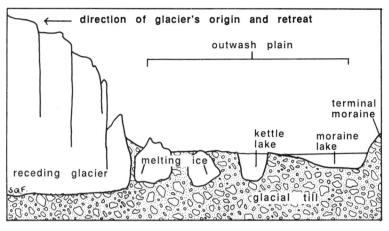

Kettle and moraine lakes form as glaciers recede. SQF

switchback, aspen groves delineate the unusual hillside wetland through which you drove after leaving Stop 8.

Stop 12 is in 0.5+ miles

WARNING—DO NOT PARK BETWEEN THE RED STRIPES PAINTED ON EACH SIDE OF THE ROAD FOR THE NEXT 0.1 MILE. This is the preferred road crossing for bighorn sheep. *Please give the sheep the right-of-way.*

12 EASTERN HORSESHOE PARK

Pull right into a parking area that offers views of Horseshoe Park and the beautiful glaciated *U-shaped canyon of Fall River.* If this pullout is full, there is another one just down the road.

Across the valley are the distant summits of Longs Peak and Mt. Meeker rising beyond Deer Ridge. To their left, *Deer Mountain* looms above Fall River.

Had you been here toward the end of the Great Ice Age, you would have been on the shore of a large, shallow lake. The terminal moraine that dammed it is the group of low, forest-covered hills extending north from the base of Deer Mountain. This ancient lake gradually filled with glacial debris and river sediments. Water eventually rose over the top of the moraine, breaching it, and draining the lake.

In early summer, diverse *montane plants* flower in the dry meadow on either side of the wet sedge-willow wetland. Scattered throughout the meadow at different times in summer, you can see red and yellow gaillardia; yellow sulfur flower, gumweed, sunflower, and shrubby cinquefoil; white yarrow, evening primrose, and bedstraw; pink wild rose; and blue penstemon. This seemingly undisturbed meadow was irrigated and hayed by Pieter Hondius, Sr., between 1876 and 1886.

The hill across the road topped with large, rounded boulders is the *lateral moraine* of the Fall River Glacier. This moraine is so young that boulders still show scratches and grooves etched on their surfaces when they were rubbed against bedrock at the bottom of the glacier. Given more time, weathering and lichen growth will gradually obscure these features.

The height of the moraine shows that the Fall River Glacier was at least 50 feet deep at this point. The forest growing on the moraine is dominated by long-needled ponderosa pines mixed with a few Douglas-fir.

Stop 13 is in 0.9 miles at Hondius Park

Shrubby cinquefoil and penstemon. Ann Zwinger

An OPTIONAL STOP is in *0.2 miles* near the site of the
FORMER CASCADE LAKE.

Turn into a long narrow pullout on the right in *0.2 miles*
and walk to its lower end. Fall River is flowing through the
empty basin of former *Cascade Lake,* the first reservoir in
the Estes Park water system. It was built in 1908 to pipe
water to the hydroelectric power plant that furnished electricity to the town and the Stanley Hotel.
Cascade Lake Dam was washed out by the 1982 Lawn
Lake Flood. Upon its sudden failure, it released a wall of
water into Aspenglen Campground just downstream, drown-
ing a camper. Fall River cut gullies deep into the meadow
here as the water accelerated. Evidence of the flood is still
visible along the river down valley.

In the lower end of Horseshoe Park, the road crosses
several low, forested ridges that are *recessional moraines*
left by the last Pinedale Glacier. The glacial debris is
exposed in roadcuts.

The former home of *Dave Stirling,* a well-known Estes
Park landscape artist, is the only house on the left in *0.4
miles*. Stirling painted in the region from 1921 until his
death in 1971 at the age of 84. He called his studio
"Bugscruffle Ranch." It is now owned by the federal government.
Beyond the Stirling house, the road curves down and
around the toe of the lateral moraine of the Fall River
Glacier.

13 HONDIUS PARK
8,320' (2,436 m) (no sign)

Stop in a pullout on the right. This small meadow is named
for Pieter Hondius, Sr., an immigrant from the Netherlands
who owned this parcel in the late 1800s.
The west end of the meadow lies between *moraines*
left by two different stages of the Fall River Glacier. The
older *Bull Lake Moraine* is the tree-covered, rocky hill
across the road to the left. It is forested with ponderosa
pine, scattered juniper, and limber pine.

The Bull Lake Glacier filled the valley to considerable depth. Its terminal moraine is located immediately beyond the Fall River Entrance. The National Park Village is built on top of the moraine.

The roadcut to your left exposes soil that developed on the Bull Lake Moraine during the last 150,000 years. It is composed of loose, light-brown topsoil; fine-grained, unsorted sand, gravel, and pebbles; and large boulders. Weathering and lichens have nearly erased glacial grooves and scratches from the boulders.

Across the meadow and behind you, the densely forested low hill is the larger, but younger, Pinedale Moraine across which you just drove. *Colorado blue spruce* grow along its base.

A few *aspen trees* in the upper end of the meadow remain from a large grove that grew here until the late 1950s. These and many other aspen groves in the Park have been damaged by the combined effects of heavy game browsing and drought. You can see many fallen dead aspen lying in the meadow—evidence of the grove's much greater size 50 years ago.

When Joel Estes settled in Estes Park in 1859, elk, deer, antelope, and bison roamed the lush, grassy parklands in vast herds. Estes began grazing cattle in 1860 and soon other ranchers followed his lead. By 1900 the only grasses that survived were limited to areas fenced off from live-stock grazing.

The elk were doomed when their rich winter range was overgrazed and their herds overhunted. Elk carcasses were transported to Denver by the wagonloads in the 1860s and 1870s. Elk were virtually eliminated from this part of Colorado by 1880, according to early settler, Abner Sprague, who claimed to have seen the last elk that year.

All natural animal populations are kept in equilibrium by predation and disease. When these two controls are not operating, numbers in a healthy deer or elk herd can increase by 25 percent each year, doubling the population in less than three years.

Until 1960, hunters received bounties for killing wolf, coyote, mountain lion, lynx, bobcat, and bear to assuage fears that they would prey upon livestock. Predators were nearly eliminated from Colorado by the early 1900s. Consequently, game populations skyrocketed. To compound the problem, elk hunting was prohibited in the Estes Park area in 1913 by the state government.

Later in the same year, 49 elk were imported to the region from Yellowstone National Park and the Jackson Hole Elk Refuge by the Estes Park Protective and Improvement Association. Nearly half of the animals survived their first winter, expanding to a herd of 34 animals by 1917. In the absence of hunting and natural predation, the elk population grew to 200 by 1926. Deer increased from 63 animals in 1917 to 3,000 in 1926.

Plants within the Park showed signs of serious overbrowsing by 1930. The animals had exceeded the carrying capacity of the vegetation; their range outside the Park, now in private ownership, was already over-grazed by livestock.

Ever since Rocky Mountain National Park was founded, the National Park Service has searched for the

Old Fall River Road Entrance Station, originally located in Horseshoe Park, in 1925. NPS

best way to balance numbers of elk and deer with available food. Partially successful remedies have included special hunting seasons near the Park, transplanting the animals, and selectively shooting them. Some people have suggested reintroducing natural predators, such as gray wolves.

Each of these remedies has produced a cry of protest from some sector of the public. At present, the National Park Service is allowing elk and deer populations to fluctuate normally. It also cooperates with the Colorado Division of Wildlife to establish special hunting seasons to harvest animals when they migrate outside the Park. Populations within the Park appear to be stable at present as a result of predation and this hunting policy.

In 0.1+ miles, is the side road to Aspenglen Campground.

On the hill to your left is
BIGHORN RANGER STATION.
These three log buildings are constructed in the National Park Service Rustic Architectural Style. They are over 50 years old. One historian recently described the significance of the rustic style:

> "Rustic Architecture . . . allowed the development of necessary park facilities without needless disruption of the natural scene. . . . At its best, rustic architecture produced buildings of rare and distinctive beauty. A unique expression of 20th century American architectural thought, the pre-1942 rustic buildings of the National Park Service are a priceless heritage. . ."

In *0.2 miles,* you will pass *Fall River Entrance Station.*

The original Fall River Entrance Station was west of Sheep Lake. In 1926 the Park boundary was changed, and the entrance station was moved to its present site. The logs from the original building were reassembled here.

Sheep Lakes and Fall River Canyon flanked by Trail Ridge on left and Mummy Range on right. BEW 1959

Explore glacial valleys and climb toward mountains sculptured by glaciers

*A*S YOU EMBARK UPON YOUR *adventures in Bear Lake country, imagine glaciers filling its valleys, sculpting its mountains, and heaping rocky debris on its valley floors. Visualize these rivers of ice forming long ridges 400 to 700 feet above the valley floor, carrying rocks of many sizes, shapes, and types quarried from the mountain peaks. See in your mind's eye the cracked, chaotic surfaces of these rivers of ice that moved ever so slowly from mountain faces to valley floors.*

The glaciers' diverse handiwork will be evident throughout your journey. Moraines left in their wakes dammed flowing water, creating lakes, such as the one that once occupied and accumulated sediments on the floor of Moraine Park. Since that lake drained, its lake-bed soils have come to support wetland plants of great value to wildlife.

Extensive outwash terraces in Tuxedo Park and Glacier Basin were fashioned by braided rivers gushing from melting ice. You will find rounded pebbles and cobbles that were tumbled and smoothed by moving water. The rivers dispersed stones and fine materials into thin

BEAR LAKE ROAD

layers—one on top of another—until these broad benches took form.

At the end of the road is Bear Lake, a glacial jewel set in a rock basin chiseled out by moving ice. It is the only subalpine glacial lake in the park that can be reached by car. Above Bear Lake is a U-shaped glacial valley where four more lakes nestled in high basins are accessible only by foot trails that traverse massive bedrock benches.

Views from Bear Lake display the profound and astonishing influence glaciers have had on this mountain landscape. You will see magnificent amphitheatres called cirques that were carved by glaciers along the Continental Divide and Longs Peak. Their sheer headwalls rise to meet gently sloping expanses of unglaciated alpine tundra on the mountain tops. Plastered against a few headwalls are remnants of recent glaciers, appearing now like perennial snowfields. Below the cirques lie series of polished giant stairs composed of metamorphic rock smoothed by flowing ice.

A Subalpine forest has become established since the glaciers melted some 13,000 years ago. Most trees in the Bear Lake area and along the road have replaced those destroyed some 90 years ago by a large forest fire. You will have several opportunities to observe how nature heals a landscape ravaged by fire.

Time has erased most signs of early settlers active in this area during the late 1800s. Several ranches provided rustic accommodations, complete with mountain tours for adventurous visitors who came to experience the Park's dramatic scenery and physical challenges.

The National Park Service, encouraged by the U.S. Congress, adopted a policy in the 1930s to restore the Park to its natural form and function. To accomplish this, the federal government has gradually acquired private property and removed many buildings. As a result, few structures remain to illustrate the colorful history of this region.

Hallett Peak framed by ponderosa pines from glacial outwash terrace at entrance to Glacier Basin Campground. NPS, Grater 1945

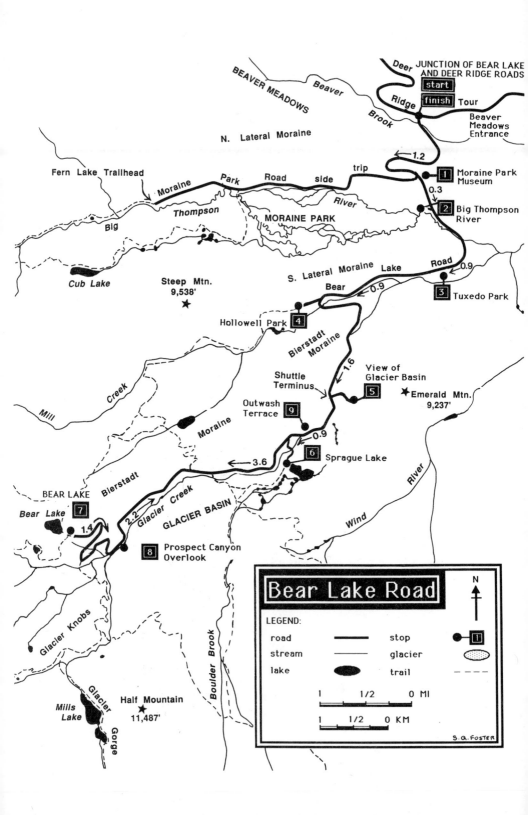

BEAR LAKE ROAD

STARTING POINT: *Junction of Bear Lake Road with the Deer Ridge Tour*

ENDING POINT: *Bear Lake 9,475 feet elevation (2,888 meters)*

DISTANCE: *9.2 miles*

Getting Started: Bear Lake Road starts 0.2 miles west of the Beaver Meadows Entrance to the Park on Deer Ridge Tour (U.S. Highway 36), and 2.8+ miles east of Deer Ridge Junction on Deer Ridge Tour.

Remember to set your trip odometer to 0.0 at the intersection.

Stop 1 is in 1.2+ miles at Moraine Park Museum.

As you turn onto Bear Lake Road, look immediately on the left for Beaver Brook. In spring the meadow along this intermittent stream sports patches of yellow golden banner. In early summer yellow cone flowers, yellow/red gaillardia, and blue penstemon bloom here. Elk and deer frequently graze in this meadow during early morning and evening on grass, herbs, and in winter, on aspen bark.

In *0.5 miles* from the junction, the road climbs around the eastern end of a long gentle hill. It is a *lateral moraine* that was deposited about 20,000 years ago by the Thompson Glacier.

Beyond the crest of the hill, a mature ponderosa pine forest grows on the south-facing slope of the moraine. Farther down the road, you will see ponderosa pines that were killed in the late 1970s by a natural parasite, the ponderosa pine beetle.

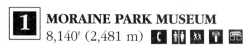

1 MORAINE PARK MUSEUM
8,140' (2,481 m)

Turn left into the parking area for *Moraine Park Museum*.
Exhibits, tapes, a 15-minute film, and books inside the
museum will introduce you to Moraine Park's colorful
human history, as well as to Rocky Mountain National
Park's wildlife and glacial history. Several naturalist-led
walks start here.

This log building was built in 1923 as a social center,
assembly hall, and tearoom for Moraine Lodge by Imogene
McPherson. Its opening was an occasion of great festivity in
the Moraine Park community. "Mother" McPherson, as she
was fondly known, assumed this homestead claim in 1899,
while a guest at Spragues Hotel. Her popular and friendly
lodge operated until 1928 when Mrs. McPherson was killed
in an accident. The family sold the property in 1936 to the
federal government. It is now on the National Register of
Historic Places.

Moraine Park—the beautiful, wide, flat valley of the
Big Thompson River—lies between two conspicuous glacial
moraines. You just drove over one of them; the other
moraine is the large, forested hill that rises beyond the
river. These *moraines* were deposited here by the Thompson Glacier 20,000 years ago.

The glaciers quarried and plucked rocks from high
ridges, peaks, and valleys and ferried them along as they
moved down valley. The rock debris was dumped along
the edges of the ice, forming these long ridges.

Beyond Moraine Park are mountains of the Longs Peak
complex and the Continental Divide, which become even
more awe-inspiring as you approach Bear Lake. These
peaks exhibit glacially sculptured cliffs below their
summits.

If you had been standing here 12,000 years ago, you
would have looked down on a lake that covered the floor
of Moraine Park. Meltwater from the *Thompson Glacier* was
trapped behind the terminal moraine that dammed it.

Moraine Lodge social center about 1924. Its proprietor, "Mother" McPherson as she was fondly known, assumed this homestead claim in 1899 while staying at Spragues Hotel on an extended visit. NPS.

Eventually, the Big Thompson River eroded through the moraine, releasing the impounded water. The fine lake-bed sediments now support many wetland and meadow plants. Notice how the trees stop at the edge of the meadow where the soil becomes too wet and finegrained for them to grow.

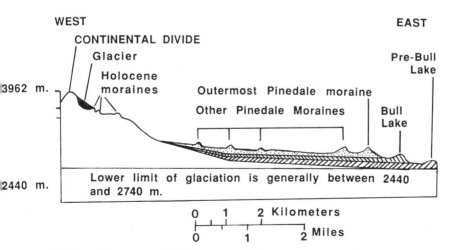

Relationship among glacial features of different ages. SQF after R. Madole, 1979.

78

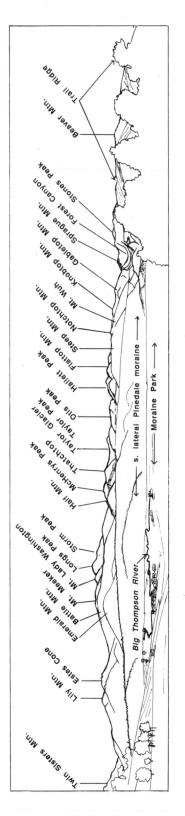

View from Moraine Park museum. SQF

BEAR LAKE ROAD

Along the upper edge of the parking lot you can see unsorted morainal debris at close range. Several rocks in the moraine have flat sides and are angular, in contrast to the evenly rounded cobbles found in streams. These flat surfaces were created when the rocks were frozen in the bottom of the glacier and ground against bedrock as the glacier moved.

Moraine Park was first settled in 1875 by Abner Sprague, his father, and brother, who homesteaded and ranched on part of the valley floor. Their first rustic cabin was about three-quarters of a mile up valley from here. Within a decade, the Spragues had so many requests for lodging that they expanded their house and eventually built a hotel.

By 1890 two sizeable communities had developed in Moraine Park. One was in the vicinity of Spragues Hotel in the center of the valley, out of view. The other community, remnants of which you see from here, was called "Moraine Park" after its post office was established in 1880. It contained several lodges, stores, and numerous summer homes that were built around the Chapman Ranch. Many of its seasonal residents after 1900 were associated with the University of Kansas. The summer residents of these two communities enjoyed grocery delivery from Estes Park.

Rocks embedded in glacial ice became flattened on one side by abrasion against bedrock. SQF

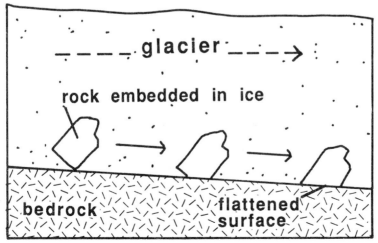

Debris on surface of a glacier. John Andrews

All of these structures were built before the Park was created in 1915. A few remaining summer homes are still owned by members of the original families. Today there are only small traces of the three large resorts and a golf course that were removed from this lovely meadow by 1962. The landscape has restored itself quite remarkably in the last quarter century.

Stop 2 is in 0.3+ mile at the Big Thompson River

> After you leave the parking area, set your trip odometer as you turn left onto Bear Lake Road. Immediately, you will see another road junction on your right. This is Moraine Park Road, a 2.7-mile side trip. We suggest that you save it for your return trip. The description of Moraine Park Road begins on page 105 of this roadside guide

Moraine Park Store and Post Office, built by Abner Sprague in the late 1870s and operated by his mother. This photo was taken after a heavy snow in 1913. NPS

BIG THOMPSON RIVER
(no sign) 🏕 🚶

Turn right into a parking area by the river. This is a pleasant place to fish or to take a gentle walk. *Do not climb on the boulders along the river.* Several people have lost their footing on slippery rocks and have drowned.

The origin of the name "Thompson" seems obscure, but the Arapaho Indians told Oliver Toll and Shep Husted in 1914 that they called this river "haatja-noont-neechee," meaning "where the pipes were made." The Indians hauled pipestone from 50 miles away over the Continental Divide and carved their ceremonial pipes here beside the Big Thompson River.

Notice the large shrubs of river birch and smaller willows that border the river. Unusual balsam poplar trees (growing near the bridge) have aromatic pointed leaves. From 1880 to the 1920s, the Moraine Park Post Office was located just across the river, as were numerous summer residences.

BEAR LAKE ROAD

Mrs. Chapman's home and buggy. The Chapmans settled here around 1895 on land originally homesteaded by the Sprague family. This home was well-furnished with Victorian-style furniture. The Chapmans also built small cabins and rented them to early visitors. NPS

Look up the Big Thompson River to the mouth of *Forest Canyon* and the massive mountain beyond it—*Stones Peak,* 12,922' elevation (3,939 m). To its right is the forest-covered east end of *Trail Ridge*. Farther to the right on the skyline rises the *Mummy Range* and rock-domed *Deer Mountain,* 10,013' elevation (3,052 m).

Even farther to the right and nearby are several houses. The nearest one, sporting a rock-faced porch, was built in 1908 by Professor Olin of the University of Kansas. It is now named the *William Allen White Cabin* for its second owner. This cabin and the cluster of small buildings around it are listed on the National Register of Historic Places.

William Allen White was a journalist, editor, political activist, and publisher of the Kansas *Emporia Gazette*. White first visited Moraine Park in 1889 while on college summer vacation. After returning many times to Moraine Park and to Longs Peak Inn, he purchased the cabin from Professor Olin in 1912. A recipient of two Pulitzer prizes, White entertained many important people here. After his death in 1944, the property was retained by his family until the federal government purchased it in 1973.

The main cabin is now used for an artist-in-residence program. Individuals who work on projects that will benefit the National Park can apply to stay in the White cabin. The main building sits on a recent, Pinedale-age *terminal moraine* left by the Thompson Glacier. The cabin above and to the right is on a much older Bull Lake-age *terminal moraine*. These moraines wrap around the base of Eagle Cliff Mountain and once dammed lakes in Moraine Park thousands of years ago.

Just to the left and behind the White cabin is a large, two-story, steep-roofed cabin known as "The Scottage." It was built in 1900 by Charles Chapman for Congressman Charles Scott, owner of a newspaper in Iola, Kansas. A close relative, Dorothy Scott, presently has an art studio in Estes Park.

Stop 3 is in 0.9+ miles

In *0.3 miles,* you cross the bridge over the Big Thompson River. Notice the huge, rounded boulders in its channel. Water has removed most of the fine glacial debris from around these boulders deposited by a recent glacier in a terminal moraine.

William Allen White and his wife, Sally, in their Moraine Park home, 1926. NPS

William Allen White and friends from the University of Kansas on
holiday at Sprague's Hotel in Moraine Park, 1889. NPS

3 | TUXEDO PARK
8,060' (2,457 m) (no sign)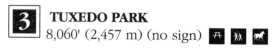

Pull left into the parking area above Glacier Creek; follow
the footpath that starts at the *lower* end of the parking area
onto the pine-covered flat.

"Tuxedo Park" may appear to be a strange name for
this open, boulder-strewn terrace. One can only guess
about the origin of the name: perhaps the early owner of
this valley, F. O. Stanley, dreamed of creating a luxurious
resort here similar to one by that name he had visited in
the East.

You are standing on a place where two glaciers
converged during the older Bull Lake glaciation, 140,000
years ago. A high *medial moraine* formed where the
glaciers met and it was left here as the glaciers melted.
Braided streams from the glaciers reduced the lofty
morainal ridge to a low *glacial outwash terrace* that forms
the floor of Tuxedo Park. This terrace extends downstream
to the Big Thompson River.

Many large, well-rounded boulders and cobbles
protrude from the light brown soil. They have been sitting

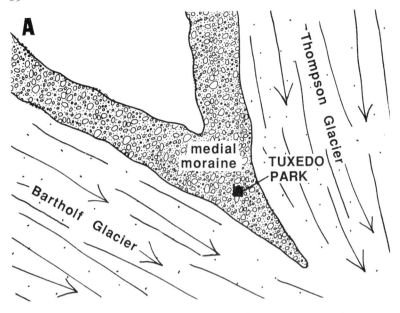

Bull Lake medial moraine was created about 140,000 years ago where Tuxedo Park stands today.

Following the Pinedale glaciation, a braided stream leveled the Bull Lake glacial materials 13,000 years ago. SQF

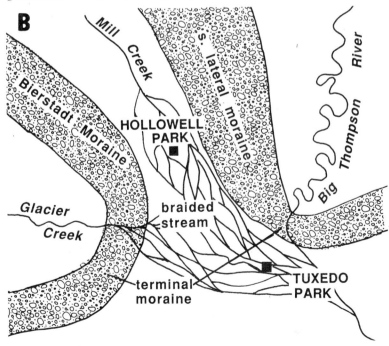

here for many thousands of years, as witnessed by the rocks' high degree of surface weathering and cracking, together with their nearly complete lichen cover.

Growing on the terrace are large ponderosa pines. Such a mature stand of widely spaced ponderosa pine is seldom found on flat terrain in the Rocky Mountains. Some of these trees could be more than 300 years old. Tassel-eared Abert's squirrels live only in forests of this type.

Growing among the pines are low, olive-green shrubs—*bitterbrush* or antelope brush—that are favorite browse of deer. Large shrubs of Rocky Mountain maple and American chokecherry line sections of the roadside from here to Hollowell Park.

The eastern part of this flat was a favorite camping site for Arapaho Indians.

Stop 4 is in 0.9+ miles

4 HOLLOWELL PARK
8,410' (2,563 m) 🚻 🏕 🚶

Turn right onto a side road just before the main road curves sharply left. Leave your car in the parking area and walk a short distance into the meadow on the trail that begins at the large information sign.

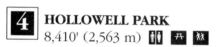

American chokecherry. NPS

Mill Creek flows through a typical *mountain wetland* of willows, birches, alders, grasses, dark green rushes, and wildflowers. Elk and deer may be seen here at any time of the year. Hiking trails to Mill Creek, Cub Lake, and Bierstadt Lake start here.

Across the meadow (south), you encounter another moraine—the densely forested ridge in front of Longs Peak that extends down the valley beyond the wetland. It is the *north lateral moraine* of the Bartholf Glacier, which flowed down from the Bear Lake area.

Turn around and look at the ridge (north) with the open forest beyond the parking area. This is the *south lateral moraine* of the Thompson Glacier. Both these moraines were deposited by glaciers about 20,000 years ago.

The forests on the moraines demonstrate the effect of *slope aspect* on forest growth. A dense Douglas-fir forest grows on the north face of the moraine across the meadow. In contrast, an open ponderosa pine forest with many shrubs and grasses occupies the south-facing slope of the other moraine.

Why is there such a distinct difference between forests that are so close to each other? The primary reason is the amount and angle of sunlight falling on the two slopes.

North-facing slopes receive very little direct sunlight during late fall, winter, and early spring; they *never* receive light at right angles to the slope. Consequently, snow accumulates and lies for long periods in these cool, moist areas. This creates a climate similar to that found on the southern coast of Alaska or the coast of Norway.

By contrast, south-facing slopes receive abundant sunlight all year long, especially in the winter, when the sun is low on the horizon. At that time of year, the sun's rays strike this slope at nearly right angles, delivering maximum energy per square foot of land surface. Consequently, snow on south-facing slopes generally melts after each storm. Air over these slopes is warm and dry. This produces a climate similar to that found in mountains of southwestern United States and in the Gobi Desert of China.

Slope aspect has a profound effect on the development of plant communities. SQF

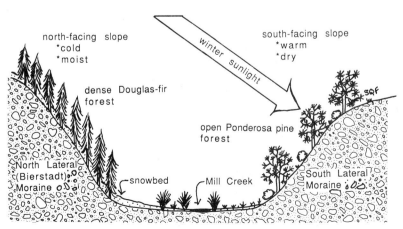

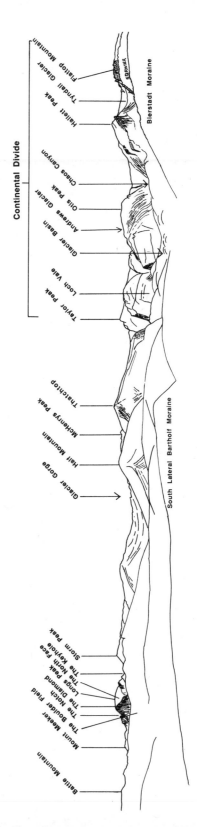

Continental Divide

Flattop Mountain
Tyndall Glacier
Glacier
Hallett Peak
Bierstadt Moraine
Chaos Canyon
Otis Peak
Andrews Glacier
Glacier Basin
Loch Vale
Taylor Peak
Thatchtop
McHenrys Peak
Hail Mountain
Glacier Gorge
South Lateral Bartholf Moraine
Storm Peak
The Keyhole
The North Face
Longs Peak
The Diamond
The Notch
The Boulder Field
The Meeker
Mount Meeker
Battle Mountain

Mountains seen from Glacier Basin.
To the right is the south side of the
Bierstadt Moraine, which you also
viewed in Hollowell Park. SQF

BEAR LAKE ROAD

Arapaho Indians camped here also and ran their horses in the meadow. This park takes its name from Guy C. Hollowell, a cattle rancher on the Colorado eastern plains who homesteaded this land for summer pasture in 1893. The name is spelled "Hallowell" on some maps, because his handwritten name on original surveys was misread.

Hollowell Park was the site of timber harvesting before the founding of the national park. Three sawmills were operated in the area: one at the junction of Mill and Bierstadt creeks belonged to early settler, Abner Sprague; another on Mill Creek was started in 1876. A third sawmill at Bierstadt Lake atop the large moraine to the south produced rough timbers for the construction of Stanley Hotel in Estes Park.

As you return to Bear Lake Road, notice three huge, cracked, and weathered boulders on your left. They were likely ferried here by a Bull Lake glacier some 140,000 years ago.

Stop 5 is in 1.6 miles

> Between Hollowell Park and Glacier Basin Campground, the road cuts through a *terminal moraine*. This ridge was formed by the *Bartholf Glacier*—the immense river of ice that occupied Glacier Basin.
>
> After you drive around the toe of this huge moraine, *Glacier Creek* will be in a deep gulch on your left. This cleft is where Glacier Creek cut through the half-mile wide terminal moraine.

5 VIEW of GLACIER BASIN

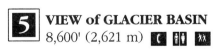

8,600' (2,621 m)

Turn left onto the side road that leads to Glacier Basin Campground. After crossing the creek, follow the road to the campground entrance station. Pull right next to the open flat area where you can see a spectacular view of high peaks. They are identified in the sketch on page 88.

Braided streams and outwash terraces in New Zealand. W.C. Bradley

BEAR LAKE ROAD

The flat in front of you is a *glacial outwash terrace* formed by rivers of meltwater flowing from the Bartholf Glacier. Gushing, braided streams repeatedly moved pebbles and cobbles back and forth across this area, rounding and sorting them as they were deposited in wide terraces.

Several *recessional moraines* stand out as low, rounded ridges in the campground. They were formed during temporary halts in the most recent retreat of the Bartholf Glacier.

In 1877 early pioneer, Abner Sprague, named this valley and its former glacier "Bartholf" for a family of seven he enjoyed during his childhood in Loveland. The name "Bartholf Park" was changed to Glacier Basin on the 1961 U.S. Geological Survey topographic map to reflect current usage.

Glacier Basin Campground is nestled among *lodgepole pines*. The pines, together with aspen, revegetate disturbed landscapes in the Rocky Mountains. Lodgepoles are often uniform in size because many of them sprout at once, especially following fires.

You are near the northeastern edge of the *Glacier Basin Burn* caused by a fire that escaped from picnickers three miles upstream in 1900. The forest fire spread rapidly throughout Glacier Basin.

In those days resources and manpower were not available to fight forest fires, so this one alternately smoldered and flared up for eight months, much the way some fires burned in Yellowstone National Park in 1988. Within a decade, lodgepoles and aspen grew tall enough to cover the charred ground. Now this burned area is one of the most beautiful valleys in the Park, partly due to the aspen trees.

When the pines are very closely spaced—as they are along the road from here to Bear Lake—they form what are called "doghair stands." Apparently early pioneers thought these forests of crowded, spindly trees looked like hair on the back of a giant dog. An excellent example of a doghair stand is on your right just before the bridge as you return to Bear Lake Road.

J.D. Stead and his wife about 1920 in Glacier Basin forest, burned in 1900. Hallett Peak and Flattop Mountain can be seen through the trees. NPS

In the Rocky Mountains, lodgepole pine forests are especially tolerant of human activity, as in campgrounds and picnic areas. Soil compaction caused by foot and auto traffic may actually benefit the trees by enhancing the capacity of the soil to hold moisture.

Ground cover in lodgepole forests is sparse because very little sunlight and moisture can penetrate through them to the forest floor. Few animals, other than the *chickaree squirrel,* live here due to limited food supply.

Stop 6 is in 0.9 miles

SHUTTLE BUS TERMINUS and PARKING AREA

Directly across from the junction of Bear Lake Road with the road to Glacier Basin Campground is the shuttle bus parking area. We strongly recommend that you park in the shuttle bus parking lot and *take the shuttle bus,* especially during the summer season, when buses run frequently. This is a comfortable and convenient way to see the magnificent scenery of Glacier Basin. The shuttle operates July through mid-September. Stops mentioned in this guide are announced by the bus drivers; they are also clearly labelled with signs. The shuttle does not stop at Sprague Lake Stop 6 or Prospect Canyon Stop 8.

6 SPRAGUE LAKE
8,710' (2,655 m)

Turn sharply left *in 0.6 miles* onto a side road and cross Glacier Creek. A trail encircling the lake is accessible to wheelchairs for half its distance. Another trail for hikers and horseback riders leads to Bear Lake. Horses can be hired at the livery stable. A backcountry camping area for handicapped persons is one-half mile beyond the lake.

From the far side of Sprague Lake you may see dramatic views of the Continental Divide reflected in the water. Morning is the best time for photos. Mallard ducks nest and rear their young along the shore of the lake in early summer. Beaver are active at dawn and dusk along Glacier Creek.

Low hills around the lake are recent recessional moraines left by the Bartholf Glacier. Notice the variety of rock types in these moraines, indicating the geological complexity of the mountains from which they were quarried by glaciers. The picnic area is located on a glacial outwash terrace.

Around the lake and in the picnic area are large ponderosa pines that survived the 1900 forest fire. A stately ponderosa in the central area near the lower end of the parking lot has had sections of its bark eaten recently by *porcupine.*

Patches of lodgepole pine indicate where fire or other ground disturbances have occurred. Below the parking area toward Glacier Creek is a sizeable stand of young Engelmann spruce. They appear to have grown here since the 1900 fire. Willows, river birch, and alders delineate wetlands along the creek and the lake shore.

This is a wonderful place to watch chipmunks, golden-mantled ground squirrels, Clark's nutcrackers, blue Stellar's jays, and gray jays as they move in to panhandle from visitors. National Park Service biologists have found that feeding these animals discourages them from collecting natural foods. Also, they bite people who handle them;

Original Sprague Lodge in 1905 with a Stanley Steamer parked beside it. Sprague sold this property to the federal government in 1932. He and later his nephew, Ed Stopher, continued to operate it until 1957, when the lease expired. "Con" Squires NPS

some carry fleas that transmit *bubonic plague*. Please restrain your desire to give them handouts.

Sprague Lodge was a very popular resort from 1914 through the summer of 1957. Abner Sprague built it and the fishing preserve after he sold his hotel in Moraine Park. Many well-known people were guests at the lodge, and various features in the Park bear their names. Sprague was an expert guide in the region for over 65 years. He wrote two voluminous journals about experiences with his guests and his adventures exploring the area.

Stop 7 is in 3.6 miles at Bear Lake

The drive from Sprague Lake to Bear Lake is particularly captivating in early June, when the young translucent green *aspen leaves* are illuminated by sunshine. Autumn is equally entrancing when winds fill the air with yellow and red aspen leaves. In winter aspen trunks without foliage are beautiful nonetheless, silhouetted against the stark landscape.

In the first *0.5 miles* during spring, you may see light purple pasque flowers and white candytuft blooming on open gravel terraces between the trees. Later, lilac cushion locoweed, yellow golden banner and wallflower, and white fairy daisies blossom. Low-growing clumps of evergreen *kinnikinnik* accent the flowers; leaves of this plant were smoked by Native Americans.

Bear Lake Road meanders along between the base of *Bierstadt Moraine* and Glacier Creek. Spectacular vistas of the Longs Peak massif, as well as Chiefs Head, Thatchtop, Taylor, Otis, Hallett peaks, and Flattop Mountain loom high on the skyline as the road climbs to Bear Lake.

In 1.0 mile, you pass *Bierstadt Lake Trailhead*. This small parking area is for those who wish to hike the short, but steep trail to *Bierstadt Lake*.

In 2.1 miles, you pass *Prospect Canyon,* Stop 8 on your return trip. In a few road cuts between here and Glacier Gorge, you can see a thin layer of glacial debris resting on metamorphic rocks that were planed off by glaciers.

In 2.8 miles, you drive around *Glacier Gorge Trailhead*. Trails lead from here to Alberta Falls, to lakes in Glacier Gorge and Loch Vale, the Longs Peak area, and down valley. During late summer, white yarrow, purple aster, and bracken fern brighten the roadside.

Kinnikinnik, a plant smoked by Native Americans, is related to several manzanitas found in the chaparral of California. NPS

BEAR LAKE ROAD

96

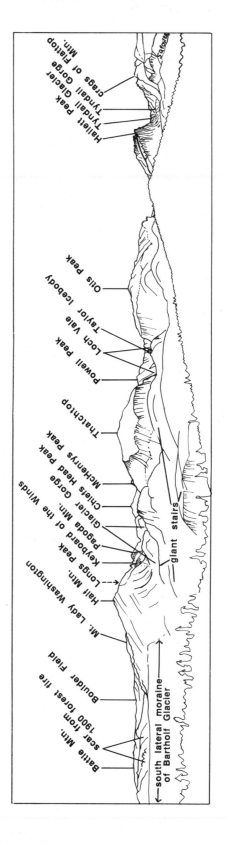

Prominent peaks and glacial features seen from Bear Lake Parking Area. SQF

BEAR LAKE ROAD

7 BEAR LAKE PARKING AREA
9,475' (2,888 m)

On a clear day, one feels very close to the mountain land-scape here. Walk to the log rail fence next to the parking area and take a moment to enjoy the spectacular view of the ice-sculptured peaks.

Imagine the large valley of Glacier Basin below you filled with the converging tributaries of the *Bartholf Glacier.* Ice several hundred feet deep covered this area 20,000 years ago. It flowed out into Glacier Basin and past Tuxedo Park—more than five miles downstream.

Along the skyline you can see three high basins called *cirques,* where Great Ice Age glaciers originated. Glaciers carve *cirque basins* at their origins by quarrying rocks from the mountainsides. Water freezing in cracks of bedrock gradually loosens pieces of the cliff-faces. Rock fragments either fall onto the glacier or are pulled from bedrock as the glacier moves down valley. The immense weight of glacial ice gouges rock chunks out of cirque floors, forming depressions that later may be occupied by *cirque lakes,* also called *tarns.* This quarrying process eventually steepens cirque walls into sheer cliffs.

The smooth slopes you see near the summits of Half Mountain, Thatchtop, and Mt. Otis were above the reach of glaciers. These undulating surfaces have undergone millions of years of weathering and erosion.

To your right is a glacially carved *U-shaped valley.* It is best seen from the median strip in the lower end of the parking area. *Tyndall Glacier* flowed down between Hallett Peak and Flattop Mountain during the Great Ice Age, sheer-ing off the flanks of both mountains and leaving the near-vertical cliffs you see today. At the same time, the glacier sculpted the *giant step* at the far side of Bear Lake.

Tyndall Glacier and *Taylor Ice Body* are remnants of *Little Ice Age glaciers* that formed during the last 350 years. *Andrews Glacier,* the largest active glacier in the Park, is out of sight behind Otis Peak on a tributary of Loch Vale.

These glaciers and ice bodies look like large snowfields today—mere hints of the size and depth of previous glaciers.

Bear Lake is set in a basin scooped out by glaciers and surrounded by bedrock cliffs and moraines. As you approach the lake, *Hallett Peak*, 12,713' elevation (3,875 m), rises precipitously on the left, and the crags of *Flattop Mountain*, 12,324' elevation (3,756 m), jut against the sky on the right.

William L. Hallett, for whom the peak was named, was a mining engineer from the East who climbed extensively in the area in the 1870s. Hallett moved west and established several large cattle ranches in Wyoming. His mountain home, one of the oldest buildings in Estes Park, still stands near Marys Lake. The Arapaho Indians fittingly called this peak *banah ah—nitsieux*, "Thunder Cloud Peak."

Take a leisurely walk around Bear Lake on the *nature trail*. Among the many interesting features awaiting you is a striking and famous view of Longs Peak from the north

Process that creates glacial cirques. SQF after Rink, 1986

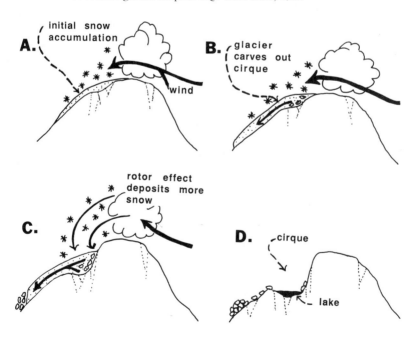

shore. You will find a National Park Service trail guidebook in a dispenser at the trailhead.

The *1900 forest fire* that burned throughout Glacier Basin started near Bear Lake when picnickers lost control of a campfire.

Bear Lake is in the *Subalpine life zone,* where subalpine fir and Engelmann spruce dominate mature unburned forests. *Engelmann spruce* that survived the 1900 fire stand today as slender sentinels above the rest of the forest. One very tall tree near the lake's outlet was found to be over 397 years old when cored in 1959 by Dr. Bettie Willard. *Limber pine* that survived the fire grow on rocky, wind-exposed ridgetops nearby.

Millions of visitors have walked around Bear Lake during the past century, causing considerable damage to delicate plants along the lake shore. In 1958 the National Park Service rerouted and paved the path, diverting visitors away from fragile areas. Most plants grew back within five to 20 years. With your cooperation, even rare wild plants will continue to grow near this trail.

The National Park Service also closed the lake to fishing in 1958. This action protects both lakeshore vegetation and a population of native *greenback cutthroat trout.* Bear Lake is one of several sites in the Park where this threatened native Colorado species has been restored.

U-shaped valley formed by glaciers flowing between Hallett Peak and Flattop Mountain. SQF

Greenback cutthroat were once the only trout species in the Colorado Front Range. It was nearly destroyed by interbreeding and competition with non-native trout species planted in the region over a century ago.

In 1975 non-native brook trout were removed from Bear Lake, and pure breeding greenback cutthroat were released into it. Six years later, more greenbacks were added. This population is now self-sustaining. You may observe fish spawning in the lake inlet and outlet during spring and early summer. The precipitous gradient of Glacier Creek isolates the population from non-native fish down stream.

Maps in the *nature trail pamphlet* and on the information station wall show the trails into nearby glacial cirques. The most popular area is the cirque containing Dream and Emerald lakes. Other trails lead to Lake Haiyaha, Flattop Mountain and North Inlet, Loch Vale and Glacier Gorge,

Bear Lake Lodge under construction at the shore of Bear Lake in 1920. Halletts Peak rises on the skyline with Otis Peak to its left. Evidence of 1900 fire is visible. Logs of burned trees were used in the buildings. NPS

Fern and Odessa lakes, and Bierstadt Lake. All have their own charm and unusual features.

As you leave Bear Lake, look up to your left at the *immense boulder* that the glacier deposited on top of the moraine across from the shuttle bus stop. It stands as silent testimony to the awesome power of moving ice. All the vegetation growing on the slope above the parking area was seeded by natural processes and has grown since 1956 when the parking area was built.

More discoveries await you on your *return trip to Deer Ridge Road.*

Stop 8 is in 1.4 miles

Glaciated peaks, cirques, and giant Cyclopean stairs come into view as you descend the road to Glacier Gorge Trailhead.

Tour bus on Bear Lake Road just above Glacier Gorge Parking Area about 1928. Glacier Gorge and giant Cyclopean steps are in background. NPS

8 PROSPECT CANYON OVERLOOK
9,010' (2,746 m) 🌲

Park on the right side of the curve at the rail fence. For a good view of Prospect Canyon, walk to the picnic site below the steps.

This site is called Prospect Canyon because a small horizontal tunnel or *adit* was cut into the cliff by a prospector named Albert Schwilke. He was looking for gold and silver in 1909. Schwilke built a cabin and sunk several shafts but failed to find much gold. He gave the property to the Park in 1916. The opening of this adit is directly across the creek from where you are standing.

Glacier Creek has eroded a narrow, deep, channel here along the major bedrock fractures. These fractures were created when the rock was deep within the earth's crust, where it was baked, bent, and stressed hundreds of millions of years ago. On top of the bedrock across Glacier Creek is a large *glacial erratic,* a boulder that was transported down valley and perched there by the last glacier.

Downstream, on the far side and above the creek, large streaks of orange *nitrate lichen* are growing on the cliff. Throughout the world, this lichen is found only where nitrates flow over rock surfaces for long periods of time. The nitrates come mainly from mammal and bird droppings.

From this vantage point, you see narrow tapered tips of Engelmann spruce rising from Prospect Canyon directly in front of you. These spruce either survived the 1900 fire or have grown since the burn. Near the picnic area is a *mountain ash* shrub—an uncommon plant in the Park.

The ridge on the skyline down valley is *Bierstadt Moraine.* It extends for more than a mile along the flank of the valley, cresting 600 feet above the road in several places. This moraine contains debris from at least two separate glacial periods.

This moraine and a lake nestled on its crest are named for Albert Bierstadt, a renowned western American landscape artist. Bierstadt was invited to Estes Park by the

British nobleman Windham Thomas Wyndham-Quin, better known as the Earl of Dunraven, to paint its spectacular landscape and to assist the Earl in choosing the site for his English Hotel. During his stay in 1876, Bierstadt captured several famous scenes of Longs Peak on canvas, one of which hangs in the Denver Public Library. It also adorns the cover of C. W. Buchholtz's book, *A History of Rocky Mountain National Park.*

In autumn an extensive *aspen forest* creates a showy display of brilliant yellow and gold on this slope of the moraine. These groves sprouted following the 1900 forest fire.

In the Rocky Mountains, aspen reproduce primarily by shoots that grow horizontally from their underground roots. Trees in groves like this one are both physically interconnected and biologically related. Because aspen leaves generally hang vertically from the branches, much more light and moisture reach the aspen forest floor than in coniferous forests. Numerous herbaceous plants thrive in the filtered light of aspen groves.

Aspen bark comes in several colors—white, grey-green, and soft gold. In the Front Range, white-barked trees

Stems on aspen leaves are flat, which makes them quake in the breeze. RMNP Collection

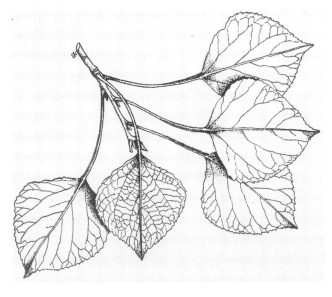

leaf out about two weeks earlier than trees with other bark colors. This makes them more susceptible to frosts in May and June.

Occasionally an especially severe spring frost kills all the leaves on white-barked aspen. When this happens, many side branches die and eventually drop off. Consequently, white-barked trees tend to have fewer lateral branches than other aspen trees. During the summer following such a frost, white-barked aspens may produce one or two leaves the size of dinner plates that hang vertically from the top of the tree—a bizarre sight, indeed!

Elk feeding on aspen bark down valley from Prospect Canyon have caused black scars to form on the tree trunks. Deep winter snows prevent elk from reaching the aspen that grow above Prospect Canyon.

As you return to the car, you can see a large shrub of Rocky Mountain maple on your left. Its small leaves have the characteristic pointed lobes of maples. In fall the maple leaves turn salmon pink.

Colorado columbine, the state flower, grows profusely in the partial shade of aspen trees. Ann Zwinger

Stop 9 is in 2.2 miles

Upon leaving Prospect Canyon, *drive slowly* and watch straight ahead. Just before the road curves, you can see a large jumble of rounded boulders on the moraine above the road. This highly unusual feature formed when meltwater flowing under the glacier washed fine materials out of the moraine. The remaining boulders collapsed into a heap against the slope are called *glacial flood debris*.

 OUTWASH TERRACE
(no sign)

Just past the entrance to Sprague Lake, pull off on the right side of the road into a small turnout. On your left is a flat grassy area into which the road has made a small cut. In the face of this cut are many small, egg-shaped rocks—the signatures of a *glacial outwash terrace*. It is similar in origin and form to the one you saw at Glacier Basin Campground, Stop 5.

In 4.2 miles is an opportunity for a *2.7 miles side trip* into Upper Moraine Park.

After you cross the Big Thompson River, *Eagle Cliff Mountain,* 8,906' elevation (7,715 m), is on your right. The original road entering Moraine Park skirted along the south base of this mountain just above the Big Thompson River. Restoration of the topography and revegetation have nearly erased most evidence of this road.

SIDE TRIP to UPPER MORAINE PARK
(2.7 miles one way)

Turn left onto the Moraine Park Road. *Moraine Park Campground* is located about *0.5+ miles* from Bear Lake Road on the gently rolling lateral moraine.

Just before the campground sign, turn left and descend the moraine. Within *0.1 miles,* you come to the site of *Stead's Ranch* and golf course. Abner Sprague sold his hotel to Jim Stead in the late 1890s. The Stead family operated it as the well-known Stead's Ranch until 1950, when Ed Stopher, a nephew of Abner Sprague, assumed its management. Stopher sold the ranch to the federal government in 1962 and the buildings were removed. The lodge

Braided streams flowing from receding glaciers create glacial outwash terraces. SQF

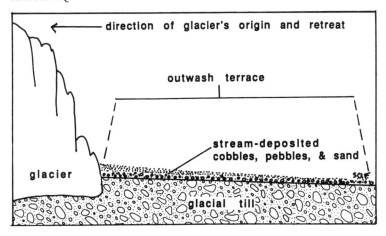

and cabins were on the slope of the moraine and the golf course was in the meadow at the foot of the hill.

After reaching the Big Thompson River, *0.8 miles* from the Bear Lake Road, look left for a large bedrock knob in the center of the valley. This resistant hump is a *roche moutonnee*. Several glaciers gliding up and over it smoothed its surface.

The meanders and beaver ponds along the Big Thompson River offer enticing fishing holes, and on a clear day, reflections of blue sky and puffy clouds. A mixture of willows, river birch, and alder line the riverbanks. Their branches are pruned repeatedly by deer and elk, which

Spragues Ranch and Hotel, 1895. Abner Sprague, a ninth generation American descended from Frances Sprague who landed in Plymouth in 1623, utilized his 240 years of pioneering heritage by farming and developing one of the earliest dude ranches in Rocky Mountain National Park. Abner took a great interest in the natural features of the region and is credited with many of the names attached to places within the Park. He especially enjoyed taking guests on excursions in his beloved mountains, which he did until he was over 70 years of age. He lived to be the ripe age of 93. NPS

feed on them in the winter. Numerous summer wildflowers bloom among the shrubs.

The road winds westward *1.6 miles,* passing a *livery stable* built near the site where Brinwood Inn once operated.

Cub Lake Trailhead is *1.8 miles* from the main road. This trail leads through flower-filled glades and past more glacially polished knobs to a secluded lake known for its yellow pond lilies.

In *0.3+ miles* beyond Cub Lake Trailhead, you will come to a picnic area, where the wide valley of Moraine Park narrows into a *U-shaped canyon* with sheer, glacially polished walls. Envision for a moment how this canyon looked when it was filled with 1,500' to 2,400' of slow-moving ice during three major glaciations, the most recent ending about 13,000 years ago.

Moraine Park Road terminates at *Fern Lake Trailhead.* This trail winds through glorious groves of balsam poplar, narrow-leafed cottonwood, aspen, willow, birch, and alder, where many wildflowers bloom from June to September.

Haying in meadows in Moraine Park in the late 19th century. Natural mountain grasses are highly nutritious. NPS

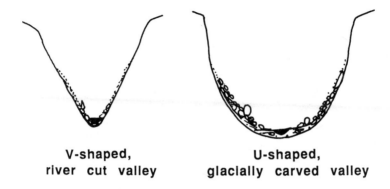

**V-shaped,
river cut valley**   **U-shaped,
glacially carved valley**

U-shaped canyon compared to a V-shaped canyon. SQF

You can walk through these groves, following the Big Thompson River on a leisurely, gently sloping trail. *The Pool* is just over one and a half miles from here.

When you return to the Bear Lake Road, *turn left to reach Deer Ridge Tour*. On your immediate right before making the turn is a cluster of large *Colorado blue spruce*—the Colorado state tree.

In *0.9 miles* from Moraine Park Road, you will have an excellent view of *Mount Ypsilon* straight ahead. This distinctive mountain is framed by the forest, as you descend the north side of the moraine. There are several small turnouts at the base of the hill from which you can walk back to take a photo.

In *1.1+ miles* from Moraine Park Road, you arrive back at the *junction of Bear Lake Road with Deer Ridge Tour*.

Needles and cone of Colorado blue spruce. NPS

Herd of elk running across Moraine Park through snow in April.
Peaks of the Continental Divide on horizon; snow-covered roche
moutonnee described on sidetrip in center of photo. NPS, Potts, 1938

Climb to the alpine tundra through primeval forests on a route used by prehistoric people.

*T*RAIL RIDGE ROAD PROVIDES *many unique discoveries to the careful observer. It takes you to the top of a mountain where you see surrounding peaks at close range. The alpine land enveloping you appears nearly as it did to prehistoric Native Americans who trod across these mountains 11,000 years ago.*

The tundra-carpeted expanses of Trail Ridge must have been a welcome sight to these early travelers who crossed rivers swollen with glacial meltwaters and walked through nearly impenetrable forests below. Their encampment sites and game ambush walls have yielded important archeological information about their way of life.

Since the glaciers melted, many landscape features created by them have been exposed in mountains and valleys viewed from Trail Ridge. At several locations you peer down into deep canyons incised by streams and scoured by glaciers. You also view, almost as a bird does, turquoise lakes cupped in steep-walled cirque basins. Avalanche paths on sheer mountain slopes slice open swaths through subalpine forests. Above the forests and lakes tower gently rolling mountain summits.

TRAIL RIDGE ROAD – EAST

At your feet, dense tufts and cushions of alpine plants only a few inches high shelter each other from the fierce winds and cold temperatures. A plant five inches wide is a true antiquity, growing at the rate of only a sixteenth of an inch per year! These colorful flowering plants form the most luxuriant and extensive alpine carpets found in any alpine region in this nation.

On Trail Ridge, you encounter arctic landscape features rarely found in temperate regions. This undulating, terraced ridge was once an island blown free of snow and surrounded by glaciers. You will see patterns of rocks so regularly arranged they do not seem natural. You will also come upon vast seas of rock containing individual slabs that protrude from the ground like tombstones set oddly askew. These phenomena are products of soil frost activity possible only in an Arctic-Alpine climate.

Trail Ridge is a mountain draped with primeval forests like those that grew on all Colorado's mountains before settlers arrived. Notice how tree types and forms change in response to the climate found at different elevations and exposures along Trail Ridge Road. You, too, will experience extremes of temperature and wind velocity, especially when the sun goes behind a cloud. A brief blizzard is not uncommon in summer, and thunder storms can be a daily occurrence.

Drive Trail Ridge in the morning to see the red orb of the sun rise over the plains. During afternoons, you may revel in witnessing the drama of deafening electrical storms and hail. Remain throughout the day to sample the tundra's many moods and the rosy glow at sunset on distant mountain slopes. Even a drive under a full moon has its special rewards. No matter what time of day you drive Trail Ridge, you will feel that you are on top of the world.

Looking into Forest Canyon from between the tors at Rock Cut along Trail Ridge Road. Stones Peak rises in the center, with peaks surrounding Glacier Gorge on the left. NPS, Alcorn 1972

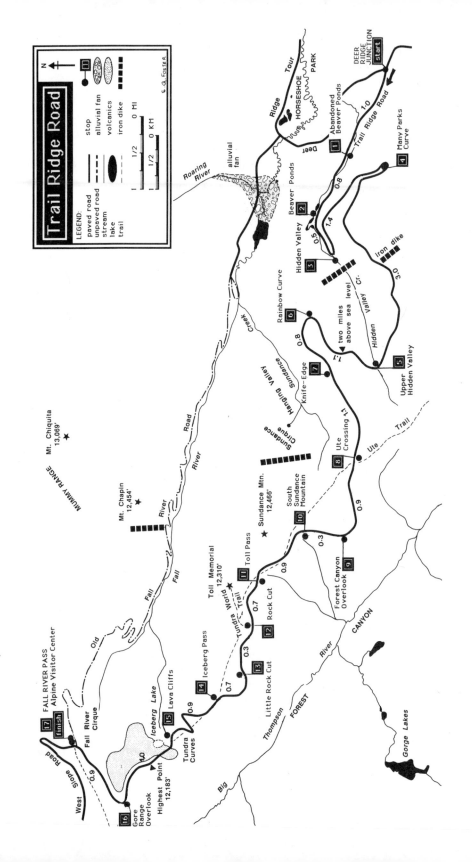

TRAIL RIDGE ROAD

STARTING POINT:	*Deer Ridge Junction on Deer Ridge Tour, (Junction of U.S. 34 and U.S. 36) 4.3+ miles from Park Headquarters*
ENDING POINT:	*Fall River Pass*
DISTANCE:	*17.3 miles*
MAX. ELEVATION:	*12,183 feet (3,713 m)*

Getting Started: *Trail Ridge Road* extends from Deer Ridge Junction on the east side of the Park to the southwestern boundary of the Park north of Grand Lake (38.9 miles). It has the distinction of being the longest continuous paved road (9.6 miles) above 11,000 feet elevation (3,353 m) in the nation. Trail Ridge Road is listed on the National Register of Historic Places.

In 1929 the U.S. Congress appropriated $450,000 to construct Trail Ridge Road. By that fall, C.A. Colt, a veteran road builder from Las Animas, Colorado, was under contract and had 185 men at work constructing "one of the greatest scenic Park highways in the entire U.S." The western section had been open for 12 years as part of the Old Fall River Road. The eastern section was opened in the summer of 1932.

For convenience, we have divided the road at Fall River Pass into two nearly equal segments. We refer to the eastern section as "Trail Ridge Road," and to the western section as "West Slope Road."

To reach the eastern starting point for Trail Ridge Road at Deer Ridge Junction, enter the Park through either Beaver Meadows Entrance on U.S. Highway 36 or through Fall River Entrance on U.S. Highway 34. Drive to Deer Ridge Junction, which is 3.1+ miles from Beaver Meadows Entrance and 4.4 miles from Fall River Entrance.

To reach the western starting place for Trail Ridge Road at Fall River Pass, enter the Park through the Grand Lake

Entrance on U.S. Highway 34 north of Grand Lake. Drive 20.5 miles to Fall River Pass, using the *West Slope Roadside Guide*, page 164.

Visitors traveling the *Old Fall River Road* will arrive at Fall River Pass, where they have three options: (1) continue to Grand Lake on the West Slope Road; (2) return to Estes Park via Trail Ridge Road; (3) drive to Grand Lake and back to Estes Park—covering the full extent of Trail Ridge Road.

Plan to spend at least four hours when you follow this interpretive guide and more if you plan to hike some of the trails. This time does not include the return trip.

No motor fuel or lodging is available between Estes Park and Grand Lake—over 40 miles in distance. Expect your car to use more gasoline than usual at high elevations and on steep grades.

The next campground is at Timber Creek, 29.7 miles west from Deer Ridge Junction. *Food is available* within the Park only at Fall River Pass during the summer.

Be sure you have plenty of warm clothes. Read Precautions 1–4 in on page xvii-xviii about conditions you may encounter above treeline.

DEER RIDGE JUNCTION
8,937' (2,724 m) 〔 ⛺ 🚻
(National Park Service Arrowhead #1)

If you are approaching from Beaver Meadows Entrance, go straight ahead through Deer Ridge Junction onto Trail Ridge Road.

If you are approaching from Fall River Entrance, turn right onto Trail Ridge Road after the stop sign at Deer Ridge Junction.

We have numbered the stops consecutively from *east to west.* Along the way, you will encounter small arrowhead-shaped signs. A pamphlet published by the Rocky Mountain Nature Association contains information about the sites marked by these arrowheads. The locations of the arrowheads are also noted in this roadside guide.

Stop 1 is in 1.0 mile

1 ABANDONED BEAVER PONDS

8,887' (2,709 m)

Park on either side of the road. The small meadow to the left was once the site of an active beaver colony. When their food supplies declined in the early 1950s, the beaver abandoned this spot on Hidden Valley Creek and relocated farther upstream to a site you will see at Stop 2.

Abandoned beaver ponds fill rapidly with silt and debris. Eventually they become lush meadows like this one. The lodges and ponds—even the dams built from logs, twigs, and mud—are now overgrown with Canadian reed grass, sedges, and shrubby cinquefoil. Along the edge of the meadow you can see aspen that were repeatedly cut by the beaver.

You have just "read the landscape" as an ecologist does. Subtle differences in patterns and textures in the natural world are clues to its history. Ecologists describe the processes that create such patterns.

The boulder-strewn ridge on your right is a *south lateral moraine* deposited here about 20,000 years ago by the *Fall River Glacier.* Such recent moraines are composed of a mixture of sand, silt, and rocks of a wide variety of sizes. *Douglas-fir, ponderosa pine, and scattered lodgepole pine* grow on the moraine.

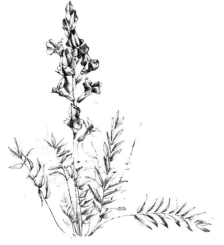

Lambert's locoweed. Ann Zwinger

EASTBOUND VISITORS:

This is the last stop on Trail Ridge Road-East. To reach Estes Park, drive to Deer Ridge Junction, *1.0 miles* ahead, and use *Deer Ridge Tour Roadside Guide*, which describes a road that leads to Estes Park in both directions. The branch that goes straight ahead at Deer Ridge Junction reaches downtown Estes Park in 7.6 miles, compared with the other branch that is 8.9 miles.

If you are transiting through the region, the most direct route is to turn left at Deer Ridge Junction, follow U.S. Highway 34 Bypass past downtown Estes Park to where it joins U.S. Highway 36.

Just to the left of the U.S. Highway 34 and 36 junction is the Estes Park Tourist Information Bureau that is an excellent source of additional information about the region.

Stop 2 is in 0.8 miles

2 | BEAVER PONDS

Pull into the parking area on the right. A nature trail boardwalk accessible to wheelchairs winds through several beaver ponds. This willow wetland was created by *beaver* that moved here in the 1950s from the site you saw downstream. The best times to see these furry engineers in action are shortly after dawn or at dusk.

Beaver create ponds to allow ease of movement and food gathering as well as to protect themselves from preda-

Cross-section of a beaver pond, dams, and lodges. SQF, 1986

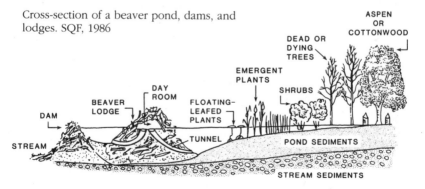

tors. Their lodges—cone-shaped structures made from tree limbs, willow branches, and mud—are impenetrable island fortresses with underwater entrances. Beaver can submerge for 15 minutes at a time. When disturbed, they strike the water with their flat, paddle-like tails, warning each other of impending danger.

Capable of felling trees over three feet in diameter, these large rodents cut *willow* and *aspen* with their chisel-like "buck teeth" (incisors). They eat the bark and underlying fresh wood; the rest of the wood serves as building materials for their dams and lodges. The young devour fresh leaves with great relish.

When the water freezes over in winter, the beaver eat branches stored in the unfrozen mud at the bottom of the pond. Oxygen is available to them in air-bubbles under the ice and through small openings in their lodges.

Beaver hats, once the rage among European gentlemen, made North American beaver trapping a lucrative business between 1750 and 1830. Although fashionable men favored silk hats after 1832, beaver was still used for capes, collars, and trim for several more decades.

Beavers occasionally sun themselves on their lodges. Enos Mills Cabin Collection, permission granted by Enda Mills Kiley from *Beaver World*

120

Once a widely distributed North American animal, the beaver was so decimated (millions of animals trapped in slightly more than 100 years) that the species approached extinction. They are now common once again in the Rocky Mountains, as a result of protection and reintroduction programs started in the early 1900s.

Greenback cutthroat trout were reintroduced in Hidden Valley Creek in 1973 by the National Park Service and the U.S. Fish and Wildlife Service. This trout species, a native to the Colorado Front Range, was on the brink of extinction because of competition, interbreeding with introduced species, and over-fishing, together with destruction of their habitat by human development. Consequently, the greenback was classified as an *endangered species* in 1973.

A small population of greenback cutthroat trout was found in Como Creek south of the Park in 1967. Fish from this population were used to stock Hidden Valley. More recent surveys of Colorado trout streams discovered this fish species surviving in five isolated locations in the state.

State and federal wildlife agencies devised strategies to save the endangered greenback: pure-breeding wild trout were successfully raised in a hatchery; fishing was restricted in their natural habitat to protect the breeding stock; and the greenback cutthroat was reintroduced into sites free of competitors in the Park. Hidden Valley Creek was selected as a reintroduction site because the moraine serves as a barrier to upstream migration of non-native fish.

These strategies were so successful that the species was upgraded to *threatened species* status by 1976. Fishing for greenback trout is allowed here on a catch-and-release basis. If you wish to fish, be sure to check with the National Park Service for current fishing regulations here and elsewhere within the Park.

Mallards and other ducks frequent these ponds; the mallards nest and raise their young here. Between the parking area and the pond you can see Engelmann spruce, subalpine fir, lodgepole pine, and aspen trees.

Stop 3 is in 0.5+ miles

Eastbound: Stop 1 is in 0.8 miles

Greenback cutthroat trout are recognized by their mass of spots near the tail. Lower fish is a brook trout. RMNP collection

Before you reach Stop 3, you will notice more beaver ponds nestled in this small "hidden valley." Watch for aspen stumps cut by the beaver. This area has been colonized since 1957 by the offspring of beaver located downstream; young beavers are driven out by their parents at the tender age of two years. Beaver have a life span of 31 years. You can see the large lateral moraine across the beaver ponds.

3 HIDDEN VALLEY

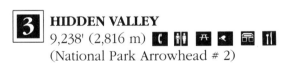

9,238' (2,816 m)
(National Park Arrowhead # 2)

Drive a short distance into the large parking area and park before you reach the first break in the median. If the gate is closed, park outside it without blocking road access. Picnic tables are in the trees beyond the ski lodge, which usually is open only during ski season. Rocky Mountain Nature Association Seminars are held in the lodge during summer and fall months.

From here you have your first good view of *Trail Ridge*—the mountain that rises above you on three sides.

TRAIL RIDGE ROAD

Directly up valley about halfway to the skyline, you can see Trail Ridge Road as it crosses below the upper ski run.

Above the road, treeline is depressed over 1,000 feet, making a V-shaped swath of tundra in the forest. Snow blows over the ridge and accumulates to 12-15 feet deep on these high slopes. The old snowplow on display near the ski lodge once removed deep drifts from Trail Ridge Road in the spring.

To your right across Hidden Valley Creek you can see a rusty-brown rock outcrop 10-12 feet wide rising on a steep diagonal up the slope and disappearing into the trees. This *dike* is composed of blocky, fine-grained, iron-rich, igneous rock—a Precambrian *diabase* or *gabbro*. When molten, it was intruded into cracks in the surrounding rocks.

Named the *Iron Dike* by early miners, this feature is cut and offset by many small faults. The dike extends from west of Boulder, Colorado, to the Wyoming border; it is exposed intermittently along a southeast-northwest trend. You will encounter it twice more along Trail Ridge Road.

Wildflowers bloom abundantly during summer in this area. In September and October, the aspen are resplendent in their colorful fall foliage.

Three *sawmills* operated in this valley around the turn of the century. A mill across the beaver ponds was established by Abner Sprague, a very early settler, to produce

Process of dike and sill formation. SQF

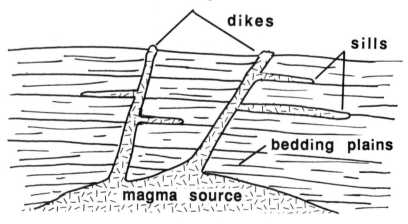

timbers for his hotel in Moraine Park. A second mill, located near the present ski lodge, was called the "Stanley mill" because it was used in 1907 to produce framing lumber for the Stanley Hotel in Estes Park. A third mill functioned in the lower end of the valley for a number of years.

Love ended in flames here on October 31, 1915. The ranger who was posted to watch a burning sawdust pile slipped into town to visit his lady friend. He expected his absence to go unnoticed because everyone was at the Halloween dance. While he was gone, a fire raged up the flanks of Trail Ridge.

Subalpine fir and Engelmann spruce that survived this fire grow above the parking area. For the *next 2.5 miles*, the road passes through forests of aspen and lodgepole pine that have grown since the fire.

When leaving the parking lot, you see Mummy Mountain to your left, its face corrugated with avalanche chutes. From here you will drive up the east flank of Trail Ridge.

Eastbound: Stop 2 is in 0.5 miles

Stop 4 is in 1.4+ miles

 MANY PARKS CURVE
9,620' (2,932 m) 🛖 🚻 ♿
(National Park Arrowhead # 3)

As you approach this area, continue to drive around the sharp curve until you come to a parking lot on your right. The parking area on your left is reserved for downhill, eastbound traffic.

The natural parks seen from this stop are *parques*—a term used by French trappers for large, open, grassy areas nestled among mountains. As you walk down the boardwalk, the park closest to you is Beaver Meadows. Moraine Park is to the right; Estes Park and Marys Lake are in the distance.

Look to your left from the second (lower) alcove on the boardwalk to see the east end of Horseshoe Park. A portion of Hondius Park is visible just beyond it. Interpretive signs are found in each alcove along the boardwalk.

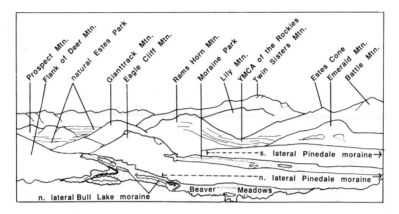

View southeastward from Many Parks Curve toward Beaver Meadows and Moraine Park; this view is best seen from the first (upper) alcove on the boardwalk. SQF

Had you been standing here 12,000 years ago after the last *Great Ice Age glacier* had melted, you would have seen parts of two large, moraine-dammed lakes—one in Moraine Park and one in Horseshoe Park.

Ravens, Clark's nutcrackers, cobalt blue, crested Stellar's jays, and gray jays are year-round residents here and elsewhere in the Park. Chipmunks and golden-mantled ground squirrels race across the rocks in search of hand-outs in summer. PLEASE TO NOT FEED THE WILDLIFE. Research has shown that hand feeding discourages natural foraging instincts and is not nutritionally sufficient. Besides, these little fellows bite an average of one visitor a day, and their fleas carry bubonic plague.

The road has been cut through a rocky knoll where a forest of Douglas-fir trees, large limber pines, and old lodgepole pines grow. These trees survived the 1915 fire. Shrubs of Rocky Mountain maple grow out of the rock crevices. Soft green gentian, yellow sulfur flower, white yarrow and waxflower bloom here in summer.

A forest of lodgepole pine is growing on the slope above the upper parking area. These slender trees established themselves after the 1915 fire, forming a crowded "doghair" stand. This name was used by early settlers because young lodgepole forests conjured up images of giant hair growing on the back of an immense dog.

125

 Gray jay

 Clark's nutcracker

 Golden-mantled ground squirrel

 Western chipmunk

RMNP Collection

TRAIL RIDGE ROAD

Most of the rocks around the overlook are a *metamorphic mica schist*. The banded rocks in the roadcut are mainly gneiss (pronounced 'nice'), some 1.7 billion years old.

Rusty-orange *nitrate lichen* is growing on the mortar of the rock wall along the boardwalk. These lichens—a combination of an alga and a fungus—became established shortly after the wall was built 40 years ago.

Stop 5 is in 3.0 miles

Eastbound: Stop 3 is in 1.4 miles

In *1.0 mile* beyond Many Parks Curve, the road enters a cathedral-like, primeval forest of *Engelmann spruce and subalpine fir* untouched by the 1915 fire. The spruce and fir are growing in shallow gullies; on the rocky, windswept ridges separating the gullies are *limber pine*. Each time the road curves to the right, you will be in spruce and fir forest; each time it curves to the left, you will be driving around a ridge covered with limber pine.

In *1.4 miles* on your left is a roadcut in the *Iron Dike*—identifiable by the dark brown color of its fine-grained rock. This outcrop is sandwiched into light-colored Precambrian granite.

---

5 UPPER HIDDEN VALLEY
10,455' (3,187 m) (no sign)

Pull right into the long narrow parking area before you reach the ski lift. Additional parking is found on the right beyond the creek. This lift carries skiers to the upper slopes of Tombstone Ridge near the headwaters of Hidden Valley Creek. Ten to 15 feet of snow dropped by Pacific storms accumulates here.

Subalpine flowers blooming on these steep unforested slopes in July and August make this area look like a Claude Monet painting. White marsh marigolds and creamy globe flowers emerge as the deep snow recedes in late spring. Sky blue chiming bells, red Indian paintbrush, deep blue delphinium, creamy yellow tall lousewort, and golden arrow-leaved ragwort flower a little later—creating a showy subalpine tall-plant garden.

You are near the upper edge of the *Subalpine life zone*. The large trees with rich, reddish-cinnamon brown bark on the slope above the parking area are *Engelmann spruce*—one of the two dominant trees of this zone. Below the road, you can see the other dominant tree of Subalpine forests—*subalpine fir*—with smooth, silver bark.

These trees grow above 9,500 feet in the well-developed soils of north-facing slopes and sheltered, moist ravines. The floor of this forest is carpeted with miniature blueberry and huckleberry bushes and flowering herbs that thrive in deep shade.

Trees on the slopes below the road were selectively cut during the early 1900s with hand tools and were dragged by horses to sawmills in Lower Hidden Valley. Little evidence of this harvesting is visible today.

On the roadbank grow young trees that sprouted in the mid-1950s.

The large shrubs along the roadside bearing white flower clusters in summer are red-berried elder. In fall they produce many tiny red berries.

In the roadcut just beyond the meadow is a large wedge of boulders extending the full depth of the bank. This is a cross-section of an inactive *stone stripe,* an alpine-type frost feature similar to those you will see on top of Trail Ridge. When the glaciers filled the valleys, this area was in an Arctic-Alpine climate, rather than a Subalpine climate. Since the glaciers melted, the climate has become warmer, allowing the forests to grow higher on the mountainsides. They now nearly obscure these features still so evident on the tundra landscape.

Stop 6 is in 1.1 miles

Eastbound: Stop 4 is in 3.0 miles

The *Iron Dike* is in *1.6 miles.* Eastbound travelers will find more information about it at Stop 3.

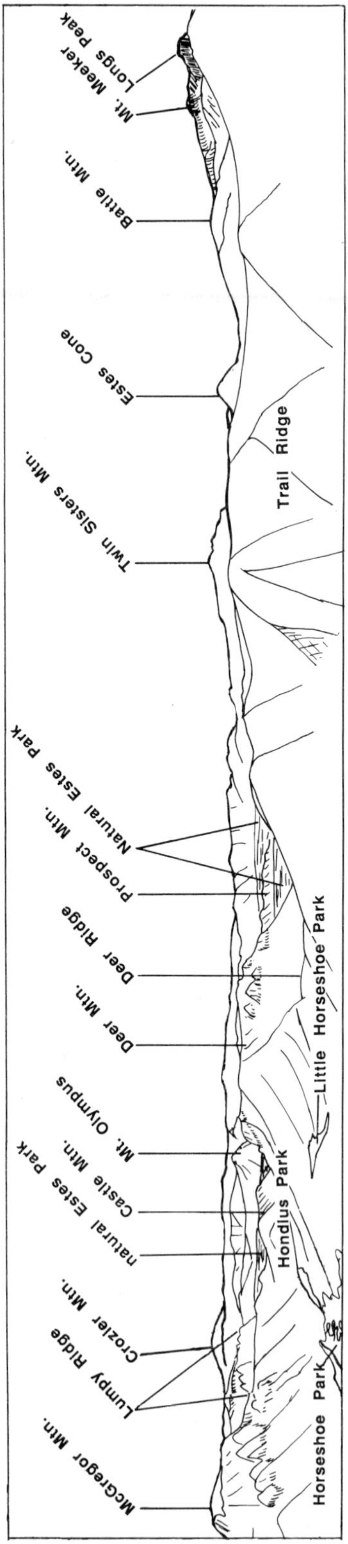

128

From the lower part of the parking area, near the restrooms, you are looking into Upper Hidden Valley. You can clearly see the V where treeline is depressed by the large amount of snow accumulation in winter. Only the summit of Longs Peak is visible over the flank of Trail Ridge. On the slope across the valley are the alternating forests of limber pine and spruce/fir illustrated on page 131. SQF

TRAIL RIDGE ROAD

TWO MILES HIGH
10,560' (3,219 m)

In *0.5 miles,* you will be at two miles in elevation. At this latitude, aspen rarely grow above 10,500 feet elevation. Scrubby, dwarf aspen are at the limit of their range here. Majestic limber pine border the parking lot.

 RAINBOW CURVE
10,829' (3,310 m)
(National Park Arrowhead # 4)

If you stand at this overlook on a summer afternoon, you can almost grasp the rainbows that form after afternoon thunderstorms. To enjoy the vastness of the view, use the illustrated pictorial sketch below to identify points of interest. On a clear day you can see structures on the plains 60 air miles (100 km) from here.

If you can see lightning and hear thunder, stay in your car until the storm passes.

From the center of the rock wall is a birds-eye view of Lower Hidden Valley dotted with beaver ponds. To the left of the ponds is the south lateral moraine left by the Fall River Glacier. This moraine separates Hidden Valley from Horseshoe Park.

Across the road, pinkish Silver Plume *granite* 1.4 billion years old is exposed in the roadcut. This granite is easily quarried because it is *jointed* (cracked) at right angles. Retaining walls along Trail Ridge Road and buildings at Fall River Pass are constructed of this granite and similar stone quarried east of Rock Cut, Stop 12.

Stop 7 is in 0.8 miles

Eastbound: Stop 5 is in 1.1 miles

Just beyond Rainbow Curve on the upper roadbank, you can see Colorado blue columbine and white sky pilot blooming among the boulders in mid-summer.

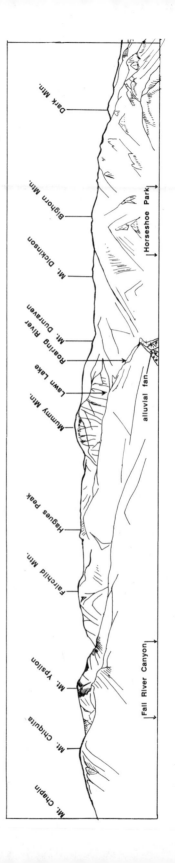

130

From the upper half of the parking area, you can see the Mummy Range, Fall River Canyon, and the upper end of Horseshoe Park, including the recently formed alluvial fan. The Mummy Range on the skyline to the north was thought by William L. Hallett to resemble an Egyptian mummy lying on its back. Hallett was an early resident and mountaineering companion of Frederick H. Chapin, mountain climbing enthusiast from the East Coast. SQF

TRAIL RIDGE ROAD

Alternating limber pine and spires of spruce/fir forests. SQF

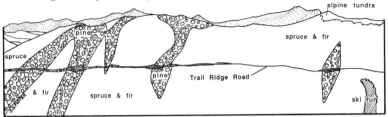

 KNIFE-EDGE
11,060' (3,371 m) (no sign)

Pull into a turnout on the right just beyond the narrow ridge between Hidden Valley and Hanging Valley. This ridgetop, known as the *Knife-Edge*, was not blanketed by the recent glaciers.

The rock amphitheater in the mountainside at the head of the valley is Sundance Cirque. Glaciers quarried rock from the sheer valley wall with the effectiveness of immense biscuit cutters. Sundance Creek now flows from this *cirque* down into a glacially carved *U-shaped valley*.

Notice the large, plate-like slabs of rock along the ridgetop above the road. Water freezing and thawing in bedrock cracks has fractured the granite into *stacks of massive boulders*. Had glaciers swept over this ridge, these loose boulders would have been carried down valley.

A *mature spruce/fir forest* grew in the basin to your right until at least 135 years ago. Fire destroyed most of it, leaving an isolated stand in the upper end of Hanging Valley.

The limber pine and Engelmann spruce trees that grow here are more than twice as old as the lodgepole pine and aspen that you saw in Hidden Valley, 1,500 feet lower in elevation. Because the weather on the Knife-Edge is so severe, the trees before you are short and relatively small in girth; neither aspen nor lodgepole pine can survive here.

Engelmann spruce and limber pine trees became established after the fire only in the shelter of rocks, logs, or surface depressions. Consequently, the first generation of trees following the fire have formed an open, scattered

A twisted tree, photographed by Enos Mills around 1900. Trunks of standing dead trees turn golden-yellow when wet. These tree trunks have been etched and polished by wind-driven sand, gravel, and snow ever since they were burned 135 years ago in a forest fire. Enos Mills Cabin Collection, used by permission of Enda Mills Kiley.

TRAIL RIDGE ROAD

forest. Now that these colonizing trees are well established, younger ones are able to grow in their shelter.

The fire burned both sides of Hanging Valley. *Forest recolonization* has been more rapid on this moist, north-facing slope than on the opposite, south-facing slope. There, solar radiation is so intense in winter that snow melts and evaporates very rapidly. The trees experience extreme drought because their needles lose moisture to strong winds. Since snow-melt cannot penetrate the frozen ground, their roots are also deprived of water.

Willows grow in compact groups at the head of the valley. Ptarmigan—the only alpine bird living year round at this high elevation—seeks shelter in shrubs in winter, feeding on the plants' tender buds.

Thistle, Colorado blue columbine, white American bistort, and narcissus-flowered anemone add colorful accents along the roadside during July and early August.

Stop 8 is in 1.1+ miles

Eastbound: Stop 6 is in 0.8 miles

Three parking areas between here and Ute Crossing enable you to stop to look at the gnarled trees at treelimit.

---

 8 | **UTE CROSSING**
11,440' (3,487 m) (no sign) **Ute Trail**

Turn left into a small pullout on the crest of the ridge. If this pullout is full, there is another one on the left in 0.1 mile. From the first pullout, you can see traces of the Ute Trail leading to the left. The trail continues straight across the road and through the tundra on the right, but it is barely visible there.

Trail Ridge is named for this prehistoric foot route —one of five in the Park that was used from at least 11,000 years ago by Native Americans in their travels back and forth across the Front Range.

These early people constructed low rock walls to channel elk, bighorn sheep, bison, and deer toward hunters

Native American game drive wall. J. Moomaw. Circa 1937, NPS

Arapahos and Oliver Toll's geographic expedition, 1914. Left to right: Shep Husted, Native Americans Gus Griswold, Sherman Sage, and Tom Crispin, interpreter, and Oliver Toll. In front is David Hawkins. The group explored the park area for about two months. The Native Americans shared with Toll their experiences and recollections from their youth growing up in the region. An account of this expedition was published by Oliver Toll in 1962. NPS

waiting in ambush. They also captured eagles on Trail
Ridge for their prized feathers. Artifacts found on Trail
Ridge are catalogued in the Park collections.

You can hike the Ute Trail from here southeast along
Tombstone Ridge down Windy Gap to Beaver Meadows;
you also can follow it northwest from here as far as Lava
Cliffs. It is marked by piles of rocks called "cairns" that
were erected in the late 1800s to mark this route for early
settlers, prospectors, and other adventurers. Most of them
have fallen over in recent years.

Scattered around you are migrating *tree islands,*
dwarfed and sculptured by the wind and snow. Their
isolated growth, surrounded by "seas" of miniature flowering plants, is characteristic of *treelimit.* In this region, environmental conditions and plant communities of both the
Subalpine forest and Alpine tundra life zones interfinger
and blend.

Treelimit—the elevation (or latitude) beyond which
trees cannot grow—averages 11,400' elevation (3,475 m) at
this latitude. The wind has pruned living twigs and needles
from the windward sides of upper branches, leaving
"banners" or "flags" projecting downwind above the main
tree mass. These gnarled trees are also called *krummholz,*
meaning crooked wood in German.

Each large tree island began a thousand or more years
ago as a tree seedling growing in the shelter of a boulder
where there was a small Subalpine environment. Since then
the trees have slowly migrated downwind as their lower
branches have rooted and grown in the plant's shelter.

Wind velocities may exceed 122 miles per hour here in
January. Snow crystals nearly as hard as sand grains pelt
the trees, etching and pitting their needles and twigs.
Wounded foliage dies from moisture loss.

Remains of a migrating tree island are located immediately across the road. It died back at least twice on its
windward side, leaving only a few rooted branches to carry
it yards beyond its point of origin. One such event was in
1977, a drought year in Colorado's 22-year drought cycle.
Its few remaining live branches continued to grow until
1987, when the tree finally died.

"Flagged" tree islands of Engelmann spruce. Bachman 1964 NPS

Beyond the migrating tree island, an outcrop of the
Iron Dike is visible as a long, dark reddish-brown streak
just below and to the left of the high point on Sundance
Ridge. To the left are several large, dark rock outcrops
called *tors*. They are remnants of bedrock protruding above
the deep mantle of soil and rock that covers the top of Trail
Ridge.

Eastbound: Stop 7 is in 1.1+ miles

Stop 9 is in 0.9 miles

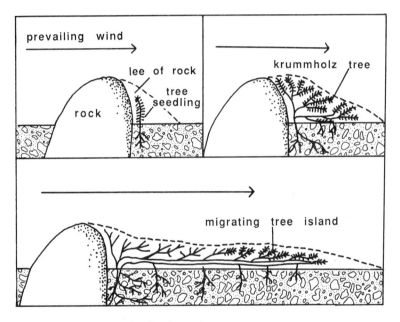

How a migrating tree island is formed. SQF

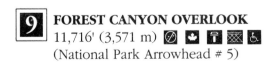

FOREST CANYON OVERLOOK
11,716' (3,571 m) ⊘ 🍁 🚻 ▨ ♿
(National Park Arrowhead # 5)

Pull into the parking area on the left.

Welcome to the alpine tundra! There are few places in
the southern 48 states where you can experience the

138

TRAIL RIDGE ROAD

Aerial view of Trail Ridge from the east in summer. Never Summer Mountains in the distance. R. Foreman

TRAIL RIDGE ROAD

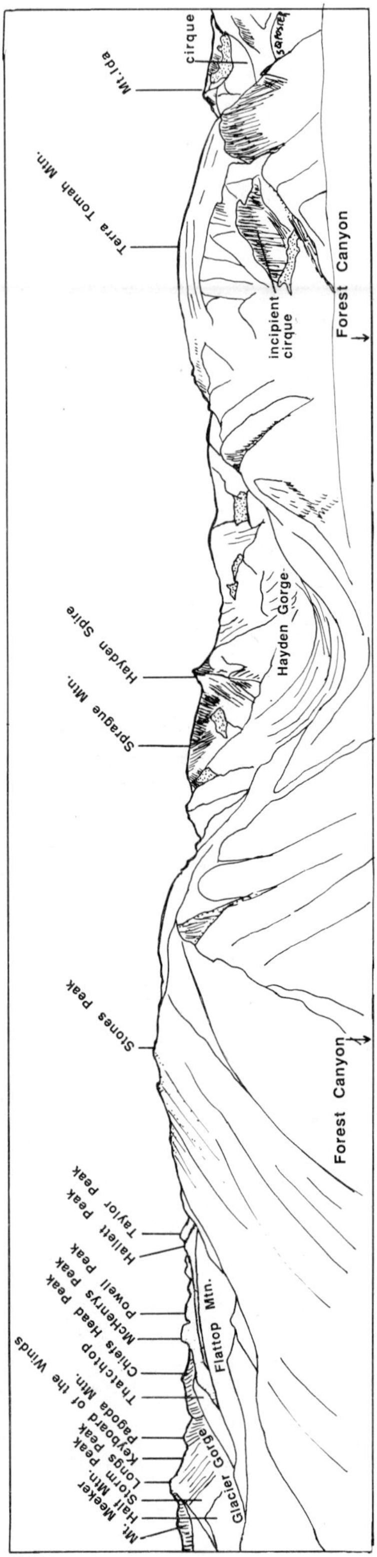

Mt. Ida
cirque
Terra Tomah Mtn.
incipient cirque
Forest Canyon
Hayden Gorge
Hayden Spire
Sprague Mtn.
Stones Peak
Forest Canyon
Taylor Peak
Hallett Peak
Flattop Mtn.
Powell Peak
McHenrys Peak
Chiefs Head Peak
Thatchtop Mtn.
Pagoda Mtn.
Keyboard of the Winds
Longs Peak
Storm Peak
Half Mtn.
Mt. Meeker
Glacier Gorge

Longs Peak and Continental Divide from Forest Canyon Overlook. The bands of light-colored rock in the cirque walls are composed of 1.4 billion-year-old pegmatite intruded into 1.7 billion-year-old metamorphic rocks. SQF

features found in this Arctic-Alpine world. The gently rolling, upland landscape is very similar to northern Alaska, Canada, or Siberia.

The *tundra* is a treeless, harsh, wind-swept area of extreme contrasts and unusual beauty. It is subjected to intense solar radiation and high rates of evaporation. Severe winds often exceed 100 miles per hour and soils frequently freeze and thaw. In winter the winds create deep snow drifts in some places and blow other areas bare of the snow's insulating cover.

By climbing to Trail Ridge, you have left the *Temperate climate* and have entered an *Alpine-Arctic climate.* Winters here are long, summers are short, and winter air temperatures remain below freezing for at least five months each year. In 90 years of monitoring, no air temperatures higher than 63°F (17°C) have been recorded anywhere on the tundra in Colorado.

There are magnificent views into and across Forest Canyon from the overlooks along the short trail. This canyon was cut by the Big Thompson River along a major *fault zone.* Glaciers over the last several hundred thousand years have widened and deepened the valley, while simultaneously carving cirque basins along its rim. Some cirques now hold small alpine lakes.

Along the skyline to the west rise the Never Summer Mountains. They form the western boundary of Rocky Mountain National Park.

The *fellfield community* through which you walk to the overlook lives in one of the most extreme environments on Earth. Fellfields are bouldery, dry, well-drained tundra ecosystems located on high ridgetops. They are *alpine deserts,* because they are swept free of snow and desiccated by perpetual and severe winds. The porous soils here do not retain water, and the plants are robbed of absorbed moisture by evaporation. Plants in fellfields throughout the world have evolved the *cushion life form* to cope with these extreme conditions.

Floral displays on Trail Ridge are at their peak in late June and July. Cushions of pink moss campion, dwarf and alpine clovers; white alpine sandwort; light blue phlox; and

142

A fellfield community in the foreground at Forest Canyon Overlook with Rock Cut in the distance. BEW

Cushion plants: several kinds of alpine plants grow in exceedingly compact masses, hugging the ground where the air is relatively still and warm. Tiny, waxy, or hairy leaves prevent the plants from losing water and heat. Cushion plants have long taproots that penetrate 10 to 20 feet into the earth for water. Flowers bloom on very short stems embedded in the cushions of moss campion, dwarf clover, and alpine sandwort. Ann Zwinger

yellow-green alpine nailwort carpet nearly two-fifths of the ground surface. Scattered in the cushions are wisps of erect plants: brilliant blue chiming bells, yellow alpine avens, and alpine sunflowers. Do not hesitate to get down on your hands and knees at the trail's edge to closely observe and smell these little beauties.

In spite of these difficult growing conditions, a myriad of tiny plants thrive. More than 185 species of flowering plants, in addition to mosses, lichens, algae, and fungi are represented in Trail Ridge tundra. Forty-two percent of these plants live in tundra regions around the Northern Hemisphere. You can find them in Alaska, the Alps, at the North Cape of Norway, and clear across Siberia to Kamchatka, USSR.

Tundra plants, especially the cushion types, cannot survive the impact of human feet. Within three weeks after Forest Canyon Overlook opened, 22 paths were worn into the tundra by sightseers. In immediate response to this unanticipated damage, the National Park Service built the asphalt path and viewpoint.

Snow distribution on Trail Ridge. The slightest depression fills with snow to the general level of the terrain. This produces striking differences of snow depth from near zero to 35 feet. Inset shows how even tiny rocks cause drifts. WW Bryant and CO Harris 1960

Damage to tundra around the parking area has diminished dramatically. More recently, the National Park Service has designated Forest Canyon Overlook and two other heavily used areas on Trail Ridge as *Tundra Protection Zones.* You are asked to stay on established trails in these zones.

Alpine avens—the commonest plant on Trail Ridge. Ann Zwinger

Eastbound: Stop 8 is in 0.9 miles

Stop 10 is in 0.3+ miles

10   SOUTH SUNDANCE MOUNTAIN
(no sign)

Pull into the turnout on the left before the next curve. Above you rises *Sundance Mountain*, 12,466' elevation (3,800 m), the highest point on Trail Ridge. Across the road are large groupings of boulders embedded in the thick turf. Called *patterned ground*, these areas formed during the Great Ice Age when Trail Ridge was nearly surrounded by glaciers. They are features common only to Arctic and Alpine regions.

TRAIL RIDGE ROAD

144

During glacial periods, the global climate was at least two to five degrees colder, and there was considerably more precipitation. Here, above the glaciers, a deep mantle of loose rock, pebbles, sand, and silt built up and froze to great depths. Annually, its surface thawed to a depth of several feet. The rocks were gradually thrust to the surface by repeated seasonal freezing and thawing. This upthrusting results from the expansion of water as it freezes. The resulting movement gradually arranged rocks into a variety of distinctive forms: polygons, circles, stripes, and pavements.

Narcissus-flowered anemone. Ann Zwinger

Eastbound: Stop 9 is in 0.3+ miles

Stop 11 is in 0.9 miles

11 TOLL PASS
(no sign) **Ute Trail**

Pull left into the turnout just beyond a depression through which the road passes. Walk to the outside edge of the pavement. Toll Pass is a truly remarkable place that displays the unique effects an Arctic-Alpine climate has on land forms. Wind and snow are essential to the processes operating here: wind piles snow into low areas, creating drifts up to 35 feet deep. As these drifts melt, water is released into the soil. Freezing and thawing of water over many years creates the unusual features found on Toll Pass.

Down the hill in front of you, a long, narrow *solifluction terrace* extends to the left, under the road and beyond. This terrace may have formed during the Great Ice Age when water-logged soil slowly slumped downhill over a solid layer of permanently frozen ground.

Snowbed plant communities that live on this terrace are snow-covered eight to nine months each year. Snow at least two and a half feet deep acts as an insulating blanket, protecting plants and animals from cold air and high winds.

Native snow buttercups brighten the area with their shiny yellow petals when the snow begins to melt. Later, carpets of clover-leaved rose, stiff bunches of deep green Drummonds rush, and black-headed daisies with white

Fossil patterned ground on Trail Ridge. BEW

Types of patterned ground. Patterned ground features in the Arctic tundra are much larger and more active than they are on Trail Ridge. SQF after Ann Zwinger

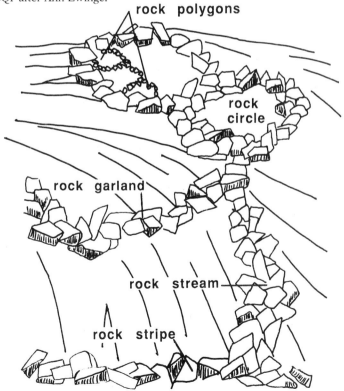

A. SOLIFLUCTION TERRACES

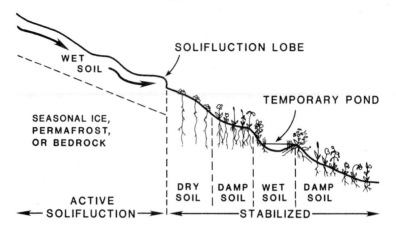

A. *Solifluction terrace*: solifluction means soil flow. Frost-caused expansion and contraction within the thawed ground over permafrost ground triggers slow mass movement of water-saturated soil downhill a few inches per year. This process produces many of the depressions that fill with snow as seen in the illustration. More solifluction terraces and irregular solifluction lobes can be seen on the slope of Sundance Mountain to the east. SQF after Ann Zwinger

B. *Process forming a nivation depression*: over thousands of years, saturated fine materials slowly creep laterally, accumulating in a solifluction terrace on the lower margin of the nivation depression. Flow of both soil and melt water is blocked by ice masses in the rim of the solifluction terrace and in the ground beneath the depression. SQF after Ann Zwinger

B. NIVATION DEPRESSION

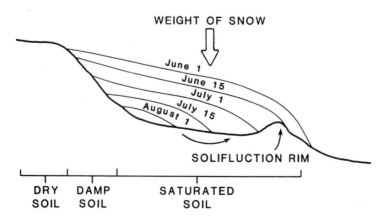

petals bloom in these snowbed sites. They are nurtured by meltwater even after the surrounding tundra has dried and turned to shades of red and gold.

Across the road, you see a hollow called a *nivation depression*. Seldom does snow leave this site before August 1; occasionally it remains until late August. Frost action on the floor of this basin continues to create patterned ground.

The process by which these features are formed is not thoroughly understood. According to one school of thought, fine soil particles become saturated with water and are squeezed out of the area by the weight of the overlying snow. This is analogous to the depression formed by fingers squeezing a tube of toothpaste. A recent amplification of this explanation has the fine material flowing from the depression almost the way water flows downhill.

Look beyond and a little to the right of the nivation depression where the ground is lumpy with *frost hummocks and frost boils*. Frost hummocks are a trademark of arctic landscapes, blanketing vast areas and making ground travel by any means very difficult.

Distinct communities of alpine plants and animals, including some of Colorado's rarest plants, live in these wet areas. Plants common to this habitat include: pink Rocky Mountain lousewort, and queens crown; white marsh marigold; and dark brown Rocky Mountain sedge.

Water pipits nest in holes in frost hummocks and under large rocks. You may see these sleek, light brown birds snatching insects off the snow or swooping about in undulating flight. Tiny *meadow voles* (cousins of lemmings) in velvety dark brown coats scoot quietly from hole to hole.

Stop 12 is in 0.7 miles

Eastbound: Stop 10 is in 0.9 miles

Between here and the next stop, you will drive through *Rock Cut*—the only place above treeline where blasting was necessary in the construction on Trail Ridge Road.

Active patterned ground on floor of nivation
depression at Toll Pass. R. Contor, 8/1962
NPS

12 ROCK CUT

12,110' (3,691 m) 🚫 🚻 🍁 🧺 🗑️

(National Park Arrowhead #6) ♿

Roger P. Toll, Park
Superintendent from
1921 to 1929. NPS

Awe-inspiring views to the south and west await you at this
stop. Morning is the best time for photos of the Continental
Divide with its glacially carved cirques and lakes.

The *Tundra World Trail* starts at the lower end of the
sidewalk. Signs along this one-half mile trail identify plants,
animals, and unusual Arctic-Alpine landscape features.
These include patterned ground and *felsenmeer*—a dramatic sea of rocks created by frost action in the ground. The
trail ends atop a large *tor.* A plaque mounted there
commemorates *Roger Toll,* third superintendent of the Park.
The plaque also indicates the names and locations of
mountains seen from the tor.

Roger Toll first envisioned the very novel idea of building Trail Ridge Road. Toll responded to the goal of the
founder and first Director of the National Park Service,
Stephen T. Mather, who wanted a major scenic road
constructed in each national park. A native Coloradan and

avid mountain climber, Toll realized how awe-inspiring mountains are when seen from their tops than from their bases.

Boulders of pink granite that formed 1.4 billion years ago lie in patterned ground adjacent to the parking area. The granite has broken into massive blocks, because of the large crystals in its structure.

Rock outcrops at Rock Cut are composed of gray *schist* and marbled *gneiss* 1.7 billion years old. Large *dikes* and *sills* of younger, white pegmatite contrast sharply with the schists and gneisses. These outcrops have weathered into *tors*.

From early July into August, the tundra around the rock patterns is festooned with tiny alpine blossoms, looking like a royal tapestry set with colorful jewels. Getting down on your hands and knees will help you see the amazing intricacy and diversity of these miniature plants.

This slope is blown free of snow all winter. Several plants grow here specifically because it is snow-free. More kinds of plants grow in this kind of plant community than in any other alpine community in the Rockies. Dominant among them is *superturf sedge*, covering three-quarters of this community. Its protein-rich leaves provide elk, bighorn sheep, deer, pika, and marmots with abundant nourishment.

Rocky Mountain sedge forms exceedingly tough, resilient carpets over frost hummocks, insulating ice beneath. When frost thrusts the hummock up into the wind, the sedge weakens and dies—allowing the hummock surface to erode.
Ann Zwinger

Cross-section of a frost hummock and the hummock/boil cycle. Each hummock is created by an ice mass that forms in the thawing layer on top of frozen ground. As ice masses grow, hummocks are pushed up so far that their insulating vegetation begins to die and erode. This causes the ice to melt and the hummock to collapse two or more feet into a flat patch of mud and gravel. These patches become churned by frost—appearing to "boil" over a period of years. Ann Zwinger

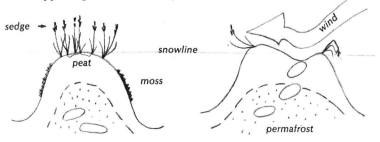

sedge →
peat
snowline
moss
wind
permafrost

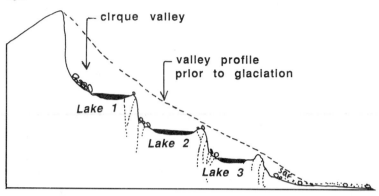

cirque valley

valley profile
prior to glaciation

Lake 1

Lake 2

Lake 3

Cirques, and lakes within them, are formed by glaciers. SQF after Longwell, et al. 1939

The fenced *study plot* next to the parking area was established by the National Park Service in 1959 after the tundra had received 25 years of human foot traffic. Its recovery was monitored by Dr. Bettie Willard for 30 years as of 1988. During that time, no new sedge plants have established themselves; some have died; none of the existing ones have expanded. The study suggests that it will take a minimum of 500 years for this trampled tundra

Construction of Trail Ridge Road at Rock Cut. The debris from blasting was caught on canvas and carted away to be used in road fill. This preserved some of the pristine appearance of this area. NPS

community to regain its former cover, vigor, and species composition.

Tundra World Trail passes through a *Tundra Protection Zone* established as a result of this research. Thank you for staying on trails in compliance with Park regulations. You may follow the Ute Trail both east and west from its junction with the Tundra World Trail at the top of this slope.

Eight kinds of *birds* nest above treelimit on Trail Ridge: ptarmigan, water pipit, rosy finch, horned lark, white-crowned sparrow, raven, swallow, and prairie falcon. Frequent summer and fall visitors are the grey, black, and white Clark's nutcracker, grey jay, and red-tailed hawk. In late summer and fall, sparrow hawks and northern harriers fly up from the plains.

Along the Tundra World Trail in early morning and late evening, you may encounter *white-tailed ptarmigan* within their summer breeding range. Ptarmigan lay their eggs on the open tundra in the shelter of rocks. They winter near treelimit in willow thickets.

Superturf sedge—a slow-growing, grass-like sedge in dense tough clumps, with straight, hair-like leaves. Deep, fine humus soil beneath the sedge develops at an estimated rate of one inch each thousand years. The sedge grows only where there is four or more inches of this black soil. In some places on Trail Ridge the soil is 13 inches deep. Ann Zwinger

Felsenmeer in granite seen from Tundra World Trail east of Rock Cut. BEW 1962

Bouncing and flouncing along the rock wall next to the parking area are *yellow-bellied marmots,* or rockchucks, that hibernate most of the year. Hamster-sized *pikas,* or rock rabbits (incorrectly called conies), may be heard squeaking elusively, as they scurry busily back and forth from rock patterns to tundra with their mouths ladened with plant clippings. Their haying activities reach a frenzy as winter approaches. These compact balls of fur have round ears, short legs, and no tail—all adaptations for conserving body heat in a cold climate.

Marmot, pika, pocket gopher, and meadow voles comprise the *mammals* that live in the tundra throughout the year. Other mammals periodically come to the ridge to feed, including coyote, weasel, fox, bighorn sheep, elk, deer, bear, and mountain lion. Many invertebrates, including grasshoppers, butterflies, bees, ants, flies, and mites live on the tundra year round.

Eastbound: Stop 11 is in 0.7 miles

Stop 13 is in 0.3 miles

 LITTLE ROCK CUT
(no sign)

Turn right into a long, narrow pullout past the curve and next to a rail fence. Beyond the fence is a *nivation depression* similar to the one at Toll Pass. Notice its steep back slope and flat floor formed by movement of the plastic soil out of the depression over thousands of years.

When this depression is free of snow, you can see its floor paved with *patterned ground.* The process that forms patterned ground is no longer active in this nivation depression. Frost has thrust up many *monument rocks* —the large slabs of schist standing on end. The schist fractures into thin, flat plates in contrast to block-forming granite.

Eastbound: Stop 12 is in 0.3 miles
Stop 14 is in 0.7+ miles

153

Ptarmigan (the "p" is silent)—a member of the grouse family—blends well with the lichen-covered rocks. In winter, their feathers are totally white. Perry Conway, 1989

All summer, pika diligently, even frantically, cut and dry tundra plants, and pile them in haystacks under large rocks. Pika live in colonies and are active all winter, surviving on their cured hay. NPS

View east of Ute Trail, crossing Iceberg Pass. Jon Raese, 1979

ICEBERG PASS
11,827' (3,605 m) (no sign) **Ute Trail**

Pull into either turnout. This stop offers excellent views of the Mummy Range and the Continental Divide. You may also see alpine flowers and permafrost features from the *Ute Trail*. This ancient Native American route goes both west and east from the turnouts. Please follow the trail in single file, so as not to disturb the tundra. This trail was called *taienbaa* by the Utes and Arapahos—meaning "Child's Trail." The origin of this name is not clearly understood.

From late June into August, all colors of the rainbow are captured here in alpine flower gardens. Particularly showy are large yellow alpine sunflowers—Rydbergia or old-man-of-the-mountain. They bow their flower heads to the east in response to the prevailing westerly winds. Rydbergia plants bloom only once, then die. Pink moss campion and alpine clover hug the ground, and blue sky pilot, green-leaved chiming bell, yellow alpine avens, and white American bistort are erect and sway in the wind.

Alpine sunflowers, sky pilot, and alpine clover at Tundra Curves. Ann Zwinger

The largest population of *pocket gophers* on Trail Ridge lives at Iceberg Pass. From Ute Trail, look for mounds of dirt and patches of gravel among tundra plants. Gophers tunnel under the ground, searching for edible roots to satisfy their appetites. While digging, they clear dirt from their tunnels and toss it out. The resulting piles of dirt smother tiny tundra plants.

While being blanketed by dirt is one of the most destructive things that can happen to tundra plants, this loose soil makes a perfect environment for *gopher gardens*. Tall, short-lived, and rapidly growing plants, such as sky pilot, kings crown, and alpine avens, thrive because of this disturbance. Plants in gopher gardens produce showy colors during the tundra's summer bloom.

Stop 15 is in 0.9 miles

Eastbound: Stop 13 is in 0.7+ miles

West of Iceberg Pass, Trail Ridge Road climbs in two sweeping switchbacks known as *Tundra Curves*. The soil in this area is deep and has few rocks. Its plant cover is highly diverse. Watch for two long solifluction terraces stretching the length of Lower Tundra Curve.

Proof that superturf sedge cannot tolerate snow cover was discovered on the lee side of the road embankment on the lower curve. After this bank was built in 1931, snow accumulated on top of a large stand of this sedge and killed it. Today, a sharp line between dead and living sedge marks the extent of the late-lying snowdrift.

The burrowing activities of gophers destroy tiny tundra plants, but create conditions for lush tall plant growth. SQF after BEW 1979

Fresh gopher mound.	Mound deflated nearly flat.	Gravel mulch and new gopher garden.

156

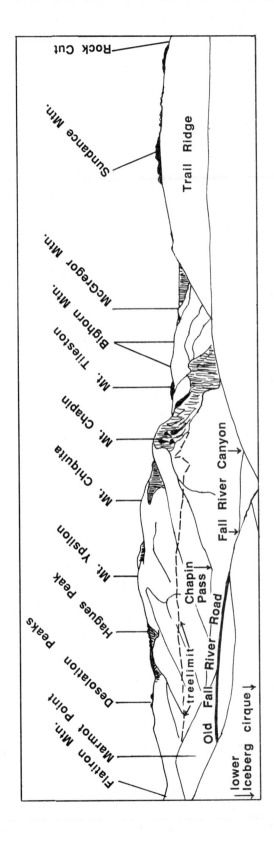

Mummy Range
from Trail Ridge
near Lava Cliffs.
SQF

TRAIL RIDGE ROAD

15 LAVA CLIFFS
12,085' (3,684 m) ⊘
Ute Trail crosses the road here, but is closed for restoration of the tundra
(National Park Arrowhead # 7)

Turn into the parking area and walk to the rock wall. From this location, you are looking down into a large bowl-shaped amphitheatre that is a *glacial cirque*. Several glaciers have quarried rock out of this cirque, steepening Lava Cliffs.

This site used to be called "Iceberg Lake Overlook." Recently the name was changed because the small lake in the cirque basin has shrunk almost to obscurity. It is likely that the ice within the uppermost, very recent moraine is thawing, and gently "pulling the plug" on the lake.

Lava Cliffs are composed of 28 million year old *volcanic welded ash flow tuff*. This material flowed from a volcano in the Never Summer Mountains about 12 miles west-southwest. These eruptions produced hot, fine-grained, gas-filled materials that accumulated in a valley here. This volcanic tuff flowed rapidly and buoyantly from west of Kawuneeche Valley on the west side of the Park across Specimen Mountain, Milner Pass, and Cache la Poudre Valley to as far east as this part of Trail Ridge.

When the ash flow stopped moving, its heat welded the ash into rock. The point of contact between the volcanic tuff and much older granitic and metamorphic rocks is marked by a change in color and texture seen in the far wall of Lava Cliffs Cirque.

Ravens, rosy finches, swallows, and prairie falcons nest in the protected hollows of the cliffs. This habitat provides them with warming morning sun and protection from wind.

Stop 16 is in 1.0 mile

Eastbound: Stop 14 is in 0.9 miles; read about Tundra Curves in the box.

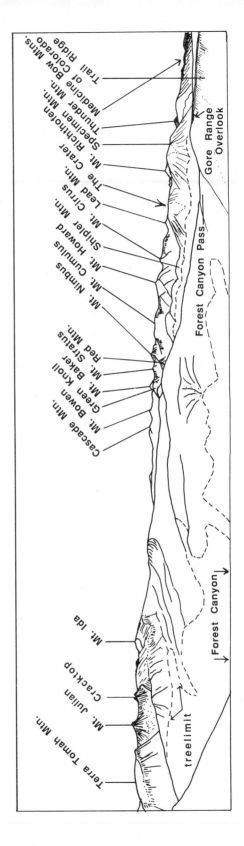

The labels on the illustration, from top to bottom:

Trail Ridge
Medicine Bow Mtns.
of Colorado
Specimen Mtn.
Thunder Mtn.
Mt. Richthofen
The Crater
Lead Mtn.
Mt. Cirrus
Shipler Mtn.
Mt. Howard
Mt. Cumulus
Mt. Nimbus
Red Mtn.
Mt. Stratus
Mt. Baker
Green Knoll
Mt. Bowen
Cascade Mtn.

Gore Range Overlook
Forest Canyon Pass
Forest Canyon
Forest Canyon
treelimit
Mt. Ida
Cracktop
Mt. Julian
Terra Tomah Mtn.

Never Summer Mountains
and Specimen Mountain
from the highest point on
Trail Ridge Road. SQF

TRAIL RIDGE ROAD

In the next *0.1 miles* from Lava Cliffs (*0.9 miles* from Stop 16), watch for *stone garlands* wreathing the hill just above and below the road. These are an unusual type of patterned ground.

In *0.1+ miles* from Lava Cliffs (at *0.8+ miles* from Stop 16), *volcanic rock meets metamorphic rock.* For *0.3+ additional miles* (at *0.7+ miles* from Stop 16), you drive beside lavender to gray-brown ash flow tuff that looks very different from the other rocks you have been seeing along Trail Ridge. Within this distance, you traverse the *Highest Point of Trail Ridge Road*—12,183' elevation (3,713 m) above sea level.

At *0.5 miles* from Stop 15 (*0.4 miles* from Stop 16), you leave the ash flow and enter a region where rocks in the roadcuts are colored shades of yellow, white, rust, and orange. They are fine-grained, crumbly, and clay-like. These rocks are metamorphic schists and gneisses that were chemically and physically changed by the heat and gases in the ash flow that once was hundreds of feet deep in this area.

 GORE RANGE OVERLOOK
12,020' (3,664 m)
Ute Trail crosses the road here, but is closed for restoration of the tundra
(no sign)

Turn left into the parking area. The Gore Range is 75 miles south of this overlook (121 km).

The *Continental Divide* runs along the high peaks to the left. It is the watershed division between the Atlantic and Pacific oceans. In front of and below you, the Divide dips to Forest Canyon Pass, the head of Forest Canyon. Then the Divide goes even lower to Milner Pass, crossed by West Slope Road.

This end of Trail Ridge receives the full force of westerly winds. On any given day, the temperature on Trail Ridge is 15 to 20 Fahrenheit degrees cooler than at the Park

Snow removal from Trail Ridge Road in spring. C.O. Harris NPS, 1960

entrances. The reason for this difference is that air temperatures drop three to five degrees Fahrenheit for every 1,000-foot rise in elevation (304.8 m).

Gore Range Overlook is a *monitoring site* for atmospheric visibility. Air quality is impaired by natural factors, such as forest fires and high humidity. It is also influenced by human-caused urban and industrial pollution that is carried great distances by winds. By monitoring air in remote areas such as this, we are better able to determine the extent and effects of regional and global pollution.

From the left (east) end of the parking area, you see the form of the valley that was on Trail Ridge before the ash flow filled it. The valley is outlined by the margin of the dark ash flow tuff in the steep mountain wall above and below the road.

Eastbound: Stop 15 is in 1.0 miles at Lava Cliffs. The first feature of interest in transit is in *0.5 miles.*

Stop 17 is in 0.9 miles

TRAIL RIDGE ROAD

The drive from Grand Lake to Estes Park was high adventure in cars that were notoriously unreliable. Autos were open to the elements and everyone wore dusters to protect their clothing. Prudent drivers brought extra gasoline and tires, anticipating the long climb and rough roads ahead. NPS, 1923

17 FALL RIVER PASS
ALPINE VISITOR CENTER

11,798' (3,596 m)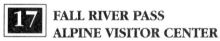
(National Park Arrowhead # 8)

Fall River Pass has been a favorite stop since 1920 when the *Old Fall River Road* opened. It was the first road over the Continental Divide in northern Colorado. Old Fall River Road originates today in Horseshoe Park and terminates here. This road and the buildings associated with the pass have been nominated for the National Register of Historic Places.

Alpine Visitor Center has exhibits about alpine tundra, a viewing window overlooking Fall River Cirque, and a book and map sales counter. Park Naturalists are on duty to answer questions. *Fall River Pass Store* has a lunch counter and souvenir gift shop.

Be sure to walk to the stone wall between the buildings to look down into *Fall River Cirque.* You may see elk grazing on the cirque meadows.

The cirque's nearly vertical wall and amphitheatre-like form are characteristic of cirque basins. Snow accumulates to great depths just beyond the wall along the rim of the cirque each winter. This basin was the birthplace of several glaciers that quarried rock from the basin during the last several hundred thousand years.

Freezing and thawing of water pries rocks from the cirque face and they are pulled away by the glacial ice, leaving a nearly vertical cirque headwall. Along the floor of the cirque, the glacier froze to bedrock in winter and melted along its base in summer. As it flowed down valley in summer, the stress pulled out loosened pieces of bedrock. These rocks became frozen into the base of the glacier and chattered along the valley floor—gouging and chipping pieces of bedrock away.

As a consequence of the area's heavy use by visitors, the tundra has been severely damaged and even eliminated in some places. To prevent further deterioration, Fall River Pass has been declared a *Tundra Protection Zone*. You are asked not to walk off the trails onto the tundra.

Across the road, west from the parking area, a faint swath cuts through the tundra to the skyline. This scar is all that remains of Old Fall River Road from here to Milner Pass. A hiking trail to Forest Canyon Pass and Milner Pass now follows this route.

163

In 1935 the roadbed was removed and the original topography restored by the hand labor of the Civilian Conservation Corps. During the intervening years, alpine plants have slowly reclaimed the area by natural processes.

Whether traveling east or west, you should *set your trip odometers to 0.0,* or write down mileage, when leaving the parking area from the righthand exit as you face the road. This is the starting point for the *West Slope Roadside Guide* that terminates at Kawuneeche Visitor Center near Grand Lake.

This is also the starting point for *visitors bound east* toward Estes Park, who will use the *Trail Ridge Roadside Guide.* Suggestions for using roadside guides in reverse direction are found in the section on how to use the guides.

Eastbound: Stop 16 is in 0.9 miles

Fall River Pass Ranger Station. This building is an excellent example of classic National Park Service Rustic Architecture. NPS, 1932

Visit a land of contrasts and tranquility near the headwaters of the mighty Colorado River.

*T*HE WEST SLOPE ROAD *bridges two worlds—the Alpine tundra on Fall River Pass and the Subalpine Kawuneeche Valley. To experience both worlds in one day is exhilarating.*

The tundra world changes character quickly: one minute a place of bone-chilling wind and the next, sleep-inducing sunshine. The world up this high may telescope, yielding views at once of massive mountain ranges and minute alpine plants. This rolling, alpine landscape interfingers with precipitous cliffs at lower elevations where tall coniferous forests announce the Subalpine life zone.

As you descend into Kawuneeche Valley, you maneuver hairpin curves cut into glacially bevelled, contorted, and marbled Precambrian bedrock. These curves, when unpaved, elicited near-rollercoaster excitement from drivers and passengers alike in the 1930s. On the valley floor, you may be soothed by sounds of the meandering Colorado River and serenaded in summer by choruses of frogs and fluttering aspen leaves.

Prehistoric Native Americans lived with this land and its moods for

TRAIL RIDGE ROAD –
WEST SLOPE

thousands of years. They crossed the mountains frequently, trekking back and forth from western parklands to the eastern plains. Along the way, they harvested nature's bounty—the game, herbs, berries, and seeds— giving thanks to the Great Spirit for their provisions. When the necessary chores were done, they had time to enjoy games, story-telling, songs, dancing, and crafts.

The lush valleys and abundant water here at the source of the Colorado River attracted settlers to farm and ranch. Winter storms blanketed the surrounding mountains with deep snows that filled streams to overflowing in spring and lingered into late summer. Grand Lake, Colorado's largest natural lake, captivated the imagination of many a pioneer.

The West Slope has something for everyone. Visitors can relax in the same beauty and solitude that attracted early settlers like the Holzwarths, the Harbison sisters, and Squeaky Bob Wheeler. Fishermen will relish the exhilaration of catching trout in crystal clear lakes and streams. Enticing trails, less traveled than those on the East Slope, present many options, including hiking, birdwatching, exploring, admiring wildflowers, and photographing superlative Rocky Mountain scenery.

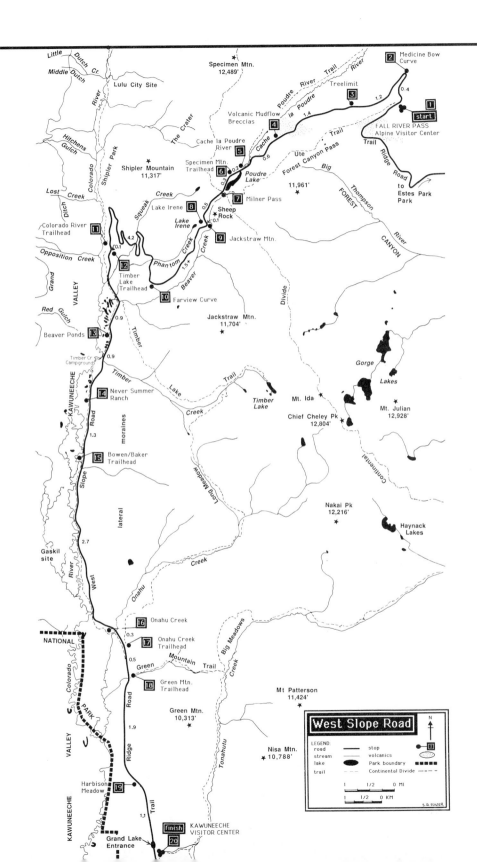

TRAIL RIDGE ROAD— WEST SLOPE

STARTING POINT: *Westbound—Fall River Pass—Alpine Visitor Center*
Eastbound—Kawuneeche Visitor Center just south of the Grand Lake Entrance to Rocky Mountain National Park

ENDING POINT: *Westbound—Kawuneeche Visitor Center*
Eastbound—Fall River Pass—Alpine Visitor Center

DISTANCE: *20.8 miles*

Getting Started: This is a guide to the western half of Trail Ridge Road, covering the section from Fall River Pass to Kawuneeche Visitor Center. To start West Slope Road, set your odometer to 0.0 at the exit from the Fall River Pass Parking Area and turn right. You will encounter several signs along the road shaped like arrowheads and numbered consecutively. These mark points of interest described in the *National Park Trail Ridge Road Guide.*

 **FALL RIVER PASS
ALPINE VISITOR CENTER**
11,796' (3,595 m)   🚲 🅲 🚻 ❓ 🚶 🍴 🛒
(National Park Arrowhead # 8)

Fall River Pass was a transmountain route used by prehistoric Native Americans for thousands of years. Four such routes existed within the Park, and several more outside the Park crossed the Front Range. In laying out the alignment for both Fall River Road and Trail Ridge Road, contemporary surveyors followed where others had gone long before. Trail Ridge Road is listed on the National Register of Historic Places.

Construction of the first road between Grand Lake and Estes Park was an eight-year project. The Grand Lake-Fall River Pass section was surveyed in 1912 by Frank Huntington; construction was started in 1913. A dirt road was completed to Milner Pass in 1918, and the section over Fall River Pass down Fall River Canyon to Estes Park opened in 1920. This easternmost section is called "Old Fall River Road" today. It is still unpaved and is open only in the summer months to traffic bound uphill from Endovalley in Upper Horseshoe Park.

Stop 2 is in 0. 4 miles

 MEDICINE BOW CURVE
11, 640' (3,548 m) (no sign)
(National Park Arrowhead #9)

Park in the turnout on the outside of this sharp curve. Names of mountain peaks and ranges are given on the pictorial sketch. Be sure to look over the rock wall to see the Cache la Poudre Valley below. It has a U-shape typical

Old car in snow on west side of Fall River Pass. NPS

Never Summer Mountains through Medicine Bow Mountains of Colorado at Medicine Bow Curve. SQF

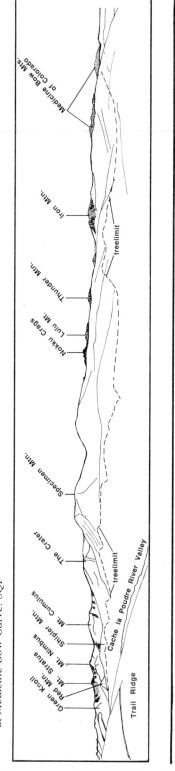

From Medicine Bow Mountains to Mt. Ypsilon. SQF

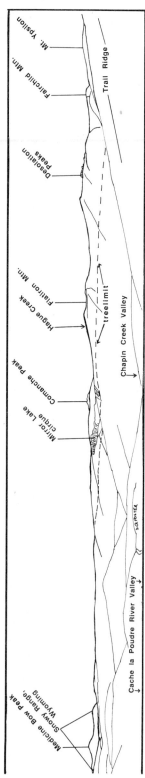

of valleys scoured by glaciers. Envision the valley filled with glacial ice during the last glacial period up to the present limit of trees. You are looking into the northern reaches of the National Park and into the Snowy Range of Wyoming, which is 75 air miles away (125 km).

Used by Native Americans in their ceremonies, a "medicine bow" was made of a curved piece of wood festooned at one end with bow strings. A lance point was sometimes attached to the other end, depending upon tribal custom. Medicine bows were carried by war parties to insure good fortune.

Herds of *elk* are often seen grazing in the meadows at treelimit on the northern flank of Specimen Mountain across the valley. In the quiet of fall evenings, their bugle-calls create a remarkable symphony as they echo across the valley. An evergreen forest extends along the Cache la Poudre Valley from treelimit to its floor. Willows, shrubs, grasses, and wildflowers flourish in the rich, moist soil along the valley floor, completely excluding any trees.

Stop 3 is in 1.2 miles

Eastbound: Stop 1 is in 0.4 miles. From Fall River Pass, you can either continue to Estes Park on Trail Ridge Road-East or return to Grand Lake.

Between here and Milner Pass, you will descend to treelimit through the Alpine life zone. Many alpine plants and low-growing willows surround patches of Engelmann spruce *krummholz*. Forests of krummholz here are pruned into bizarre forms by fierce westerly winds. Unlike treelimit areas on Trail Ridge where prevailing winds push migrating tree islands downhill, these trees migrate slowly uphill in battalion-like patterns called *ribbon forests*.

---

3 | TREELIMIT
11,263' (3,433 m) (no sign)

Stop in a small pulloff on the right. The elevation of tree-limit along this ridge varies as a function of wind direction, wind speed, snow depth, and slope angle. Engelmann spruce trees that grow straight, tall, and close together at lower elevations are gnarled, short, and widely spaced here. They struggle for survival in this Arctic-Alpine climate.

The lowest branches of trees below the road are "layered"—rooted and growing out beyond the tips of higher branches. Layering is characteristic of Engelmann spruce trees established in open areas where deep snows press the lowermost branches against the soil.

The land surface above and below the road is decidedly uneven. These alternating ridges and hollows contrast with the smooth tundra slope you just passed. Two processes probably produced this terrain: bedrock slumping along rock fractures and eroding of soft rocks sandwiched between harder ones.

Vegetation is more lush here than on the East Slope. This is because the prevailing climate on the West Slope is

Mudflow breccia in road cut. This material was erupted about 26-28 million years ago. W. Alcorn 1972. NPS

characterized by much less wind, more precipitation, and deep snow accumulation. Trees growing below treelimit on this side of the Continental Divide appear more vigorous; they are larger and more widely separated than trees on the East Slope. There is also more dense undergrowth on the forest floor.

White marsh marigolds and creamy globeflowers dot openings among the trees when the snow melts in June and early July. Elk graze in these dells in early morning and evening. They are often seen resting there in midday.

Blooming in the swales and along the edges of the road in late July and August are blue sky pilot and chiming bells; yellow alpine avens and black-tipped groundsel; white American bistort; burgundy kings crown; and off-white Rocky Mountain thistle.

Stop 4 is in 1.4 miles

Eastbound: Stop 2 is in 1.2 miles
Watch for feature en route.

Marsh marigold.
Ann Zwinger

EASTBOUND VISITORS:

Welcome to the Alpine Tundra. This is the fascinating "land above the trees," the Arctic of temperate latitudes, where freeze/thaw processes have created rock patterns on surfaces untouched by glaciers. The tiny plants that hug the ground in dense mats have adapted to the extreme cold, drying winds, and a short growing season.

---

4 **VOLCANIC MUDFLOW BRECCIAS**
(no sign)

A small parking area on the right is opposite a roadcut exposing volcanic *mudflow breccias.* These unconsolidated materials flowed off volcanic cones some 28 million years ago in the vicinity of the present Never Summer Mountains along the west boundary of the Park. This mudflow breccia extends south nearly to Poudre Lake. It is one of the youngest rocks in the Park.

Recent geological investigations have discovered that *Specimen Mountain,* 12,489' elevation (3,807 m), across the valley is composed of layer upon layer of these breccias and several other types of volcanic rocks. They formed from materials that erupted from vents in a row of volcanos that once paralleled the east side of the Never Summer Range. These volcanos have long been extinct.

Eastbound: Stop 3 is in 1.4 miles
Watch for feature en route.

Stop 5 is in 0.6+ miles

 ### CACHE LA POUDRE RIVER
(no sign)

A turnout is on the right. The Cache la Poudre River was named by a party of early French trappers who, having buried their gunpowder along its banks, returned to recover their "cache of powder." Its headwaters are Poudre Lake, coming into view on your left. The grass-covered hump you see at the lake outlet is an abandoned and over-grown beaver dam.

Eastbound: Stop 4 is in 0.6 miles

Stop 6 is in 0.2 miles

 ### SPECIMEN MOUNTAIN TRAILHEAD
(no sign)

This once-popular trail to the summit of Specimen Mountain is now closed to protect bighorn sheep summer range. Lambs are born on rocky outcrops and steep south-facing slopes during June. By mid-July, when the lambs have grown large enough to fend for themselves, you may hike to the rim of The Crater, an excellent place to watch the animals.

The flocks feed on the open tundra during the summer months, retreating into rocky areas when disturbed. Natural salt licks in The Crater provide them with essential minerals. They migrate in the late fall to winter range in the Never Summer Range.

Bighorn ram and two young rams. Bill Border 1982 RMNP Collection

WEST SLOPE ROAD

The wet meadow across the road is resplendent in mid-summer with white marsh marigolds and American bistort; blue tall chiming bells; fuschia subalpine paint-brush; little red elephants; yellow arrow-leaved groundsel; and dark-headed sedges and Parrys rush. These plants manage to grow for several months each year with their roots in ice-cold, saturated soils.

Dandelion, the European immigrant that is best known and least liked as a lawn weed, colorfully edges the parking area. Dandelions were probably introduced here by air-born seeds held aloft by their silky parachutes.

Eastbound: Stop 5 is in 0.2 miles

Stop 7 is in 0.3 miles

7 MILNER PASS and the CONTINENTAL DIVIDE
10,758' (3,279 m)
(National Park Arrowhead #10)

Park on the left and walk to the upper end of the parking area to enjoy a view of the lake. Milner Pass was named for T. J. Milner, an engineer who designed a railroad to run from Denver through Fort Collins to the Continental Divide via the Cache la Poudre Canyon around the turn of the century.

You are now standing on the *Continental Divide.* Precipitation falling here flows either to the Atlantic or to the Pacific Ocean. Unlikely as it seems, Milner Pass, 1,425 feet below the high point on Trail Ridge Road, gives rise to tributaries of both the mighty Mississippi and Colorado rivers. Water in the Cache la Poudre River flows northeast into the Platte River, a tributary of the Missouri River. After the Missouri enters the Mississippi River, the water empties into the Atlantic Ocean.

The low, tree-covered hill next to the parking area is a moraine left by a Pinedale-age glacier. Just on the other side of this moraine, water flows into Beaver Creek and starts its long journey to the Colorado River and thence to the Pacific Ocean.

The largest expanse of glacial ice within the Park filled this valley during the Great Ice Age. It flowed northeast down the Cache la Poudre Valley, as well as southwest down Beaver Creek Valley, joining the Colorado River Glacier. In addition, this glacier spilled east over both Fall River and Forest Canyon passes. A low peninsula nearly divides Poudre Lake in half. This curious land feature is a small moraine left by the last retreating glacier.

A hiking trail beginning at the upper end of the parking area skirts the moraine and the shore of Poudre Lake. It generally follows the route of the original Fall River Road to Forest Canyon Pass and continues north to Fall River Pass. Early Native Americans called this route the

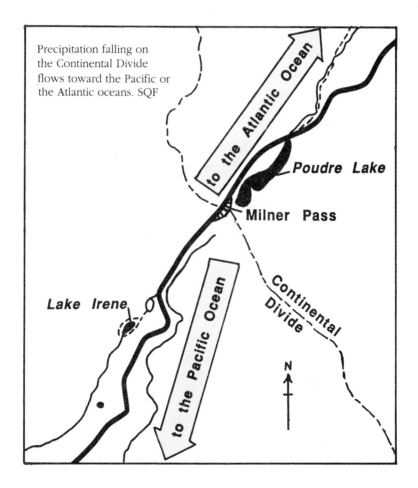

Precipitation falling on the Continental Divide flows toward the Pacific or the Atlantic oceans. SQF

to the Atlantic Ocean

Poudre Lake

Milner Pass

Lake Irene

to the Pacific Ocean

Continental Divide

N

"Dogs Trail," because they used dogs to haul their belongings along it.

Two rock monoliths stand on the far side of the lake above the trail. These outcrops are composed of highly resistant, light-colored pegmatite that was intruded into older metamorphic rocks 1. 4 billion years ago; erosion has stripped away the older rocks.

Stop 8 is in 0.5 miles

Eastbound: Stop 6 is in 0.3 miles

As you descend from Milner Pass, you will see *Sheep Rock* on your left. Its dramatic slate-gray face rises sharply toward the sky.

---

8 LAKE IRENE
Ute Trail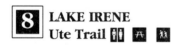

Turn right and drive into the parking loop. *Lake Irene* is a small moraine-dammed lake located down valley from the picnic area. The Ute Trail, encountered several times on Trail Ridge, follows the shore of Lake Irene. This trail also leads up valley to Milner Pass, Stop 7.

"Squeaky Bob" Wheeler, who ran a dude ranch in the Kawuneeche Valley, led many outings to this delightful site where he had homesteaded decades earlier. It is rumored that he named the lake for a young lady from the East who stayed at his ranch one summer.

Looking back across the road, you can see *Sheep Rock*—the smooth, slate-gray bedrock mass jutting up from the valley. A portion of the Milner Pass Glacier flowed over this knob, rounding its right side and quarrying and shearing off its left side. Outcrops like this were named *roche moutonnees* by a Swiss gentleman in 1787. He saw in them a resemblance to the curly wigs smoothed with mutton tallow that were fashionable at that time.

Tundra plants on Sheep Rock's ledges are blown clear of snow. They provide winter forage for bighorn sheep; the ledges also serve as promontories from which predators can be seen.

You are surrounded by a Subalpine forest of Engel-mann spruce, subalpine fir, and lodgepole pine untouched by forest fire for many centuries. The carpet of blueberry bushes on the forest floor turns a beautiful shade of red in the fall.

A mess hall next to the parking area is the sole survivor of a group of buildings constructed in the late 1920s to house road crews. This building is a fine example of the National Park Service Rustic Architecture developed to blend buildings with their surroundings. A residence, bunkhouse, and stable were removed in 1960 to restore the area's natural beauty.

Eastbound: Stop 7 is in 0.5 miles

Stop 9 is in 0.1 miles

Visitors on horseback at Lake Irene in 1891. Before completion of an auto-mobile road between Grand Lake and Estes Park, many visitors rode across Trail Ridge past Lake Irene on horseback. They were preceded by Native Americans who used this route for thousands of years. The hillsides still show the effects of the fire of 1871. NPS

9 JACKSTRAW MOUNTAIN

(no sign)

Turn left into a small parking area on the outside of the next right curve. From the picnic table on the edge of Beaver Creek gorge, you view *Jackstraw Mountain*, 11,704' elevation (3,567 m) to your right across the valley. If this pullout is full, there is another view of Jackstraw Mountain on the left in one half mile.

The upper slopes of Jackstraw Mountain are rounded and hummocky. They result from large slumps of loosened bedrock and glacial debris. Trees scattered across the mountain were burned by forest fire in 1871. The helter-skelter positions of these trees reminded Park Superintendent Roger Toll of the child's game of pick-up-sticks or jackstraws.

Loss of trees changed environmental conditions on the mountain slopes. Arctic-Alpine climate extended several hundred feet down into an area that had a Temperate-Subalpine climate before the fire. Consequently, alpine tundra plants now grow below treelimit in a region once covered by a subalpine forest similar to the one you saw at Lake Irene.

Rate of reforestation is very slow at this elevation. Trees become established only in the protection of rocks and logs. As the first pioneer trees grow, they project an environment downwind in which other young trees can begin to grow, eventually crowding out the tundra plants.

Trees burned more than 100 years ago have yet to fully decompose because of the dry, cold climate at this elevation. Charred logs and stumps still remain between here and Kawuneeche Valley.

Forest fires burned throughout the West in 1871. Clarence King, a geologist with the U. S. Geological Survey, complained in his journals of skies so obscured with smoke that surveying had to be halted. A similar dense haze was created by smoke blown southeast from forest fires in Yellowstone National Park during the summer of 1988.

Stop 10 is in 1.5+ miles

Eastbound: Stop 8 is in 0.1 miles

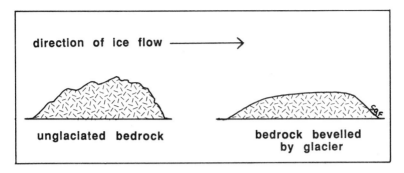

Glaciers smoothed bedrock surfaces as they moved over them. SQF

You traverse a wall of the steep, narrow valley of Beaver Creek between here and Farview Curve. Rounded boulders, cobbles, and pebbles are perched on top of flat, beveled schist in many roadcuts. They were left behind by the most recent Great Ice Age glacier.

 FARVIEW CURVE
10,120' (3,085 m) (no sign)
(National Park Arrowhead #11)

Turn left into the overlook parking area. A spectacular view of the *Never Summer Mountains* and *Kawuneeche Valley* awaits you. The best time for photos is in the morning.

The Never Summer Mountains, called *Ni-chebe-chii*—Never No Summer—by the Arapaho Indians, accumulate deep drifts of snow that melt slowly in the brief summer season. Mt. Stratus, Mt. Nimbus, and Mt. Cumulus, high along the Continental Divide, are true to their names on summer afternoons when clouds form around them.

The basins you see below these peaks are *cirques*. These amphitheatres were scooped out by glaciers that flowed down from the mountain crests. Glaciers in neighboring valleys almost met at ridgetops as they quarried headward, or upslope, toward each other. Their proximity produced carved ridges called "aretes" and pyramid-shaped peaks called "horns."

182

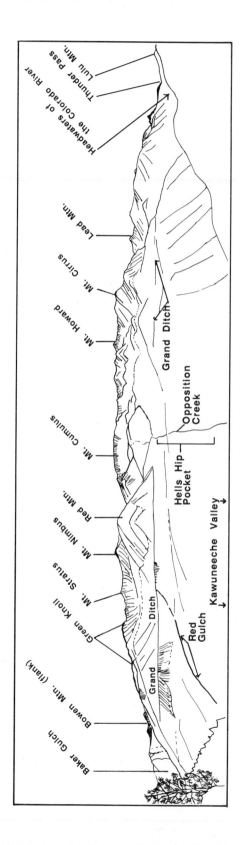

The Never Summer
Mountains from Farview
Curve. SQF

WEST SLOPE ROAD

This mountain range has the most complex geology of any region in the Park. The southern quarter is old Precambrian metamorphic rocks; an *igneous stock* forms the core of the northern three-fourths of the range. This stock was intruded into a segment of the earth's crust that was thrust from east to west during the Laramide mountain-building period 70 to 60 million years ago. Later uplifting arched the overthrust producing the discrete mountain range.

As a consequence of the overthrust and subsequent erosion, some of the younger rocks in the Park form a thin crust on the summits of Mt. Cumulus, directly across from you, and Nokku Crags on the northern end of the range. These rocks are 100 million year old Pierre shale that was baked and folded by volcanic activity. They contain seashells, the only fossils known within the Park. This side of the Never Summers became part of Rocky Mountain National Park by act of Congress in 1930.

The flat, broad valley below you is *Kawuneeche Valley.* Early settlers called it "North Fork Valley" for the stream that meanders lazily across its floor. It is the North Fork of what was then known as the Grand River. The Colorado Geographic Board decided in 1915 to rename the valley "Kawuneeche," the Arapaho word for "coyote."

Kawuneeche Valley was created by water and ice erosion along a major fault zone. The valley has been widened and its walls steepened by several glaciers over the past several hundred thousand years.

The *Colorado River* originates at the head of this valley to the right, just out of sight. It is the same river that has created the Grand Canyon over millions of years. Initially it was called "colorado" for its silty red water by Spanish explorers in the sixteenth century. Not knowing of the Spanish name, the American explorer, John C. Fremont, called it the "Grand River." Other early explorers referred to it as the "Blue River." The U. S. Congress settled the confusion when it officially adopted the name "Colorado River" in 1921.

At least three times during the past million years, the *Colorado River Glacier,* fed by smaller glaciers from both the Never Summer Mountains and the Milner Pass area,

The original Fall River Road on this valley wall was constructed by hand and horse labor. This was a particularly unstable section that required shoring up the slope with rock walls. NPS 1918

created a large ice sheet penetrated only by the high mountain peaks. It covered La Poudre Pass at the head of Kawuneeche Valley and extended south through Shadow Mountain Lake, nearly 20 miles downstream.

Although densely forested with lodgepole pine, you can see portions of two lateral moraines of the Colorado River Glacier lying against the far side of the valley. These moraines are ill defined, compared to free-standing ones found in Horseshoe and Moraine parks. In certain lighting, their undulating surfaces are visible below Grand Ditch, the horizontal cut on the opposite valley wall. The moraines were deposited by the valley's two most recent Great Ice Age glaciers.

The *Grand Ditch* is an aqueduct that diverts water from West Slope streams to farms, ranches, and towns on the eastern plains. It is one of the earliest transmountain diversions in Colorado. Following construction of a railroad between Denver and Cheyenne in 1870, farmers on the eastern plains could ship agricultural products elsewhere in the nation. This increased market soon caused depletion of available water on the East Slope. Then, farmers and communities began to explore how to divert water from the wetter West Slope.

Construction of the Grand Ditch was a monumental undertaking. This made the Ditch a prime candidate for inclusion on the National Register of Historic Places as an Historic District. The district also includes Specimen Ditch and Camp 2, both out-of-sight upstream.

Oriental and Swedish laborers worked with picks, shovels, wheelbarrows, black powder, and teams of horse-drawn scrapers. They lived in crude camps thrown together along the route. With primitive equipment and wearing inadequate clothing, they shoveled tons of snow each spring to open the ditch.

The first segment of the Grand Ditch was constructed in 1890 and went into operation immediately. Over the next five decades, the Ditch was gradually extended south to intercept 15 streams flowing from the Never Summer Mountains. With the use of machinery during the final year of its construction, the last segment of the 16.2 mile system was completed in 1936.

Currently, Grand Ditch delivers an average of 20,000 acre feet of West Slope water annually to the Water Supply

Workers digging the Grand Ditch by hand with the help of horses, circa 1900. NPS

and Storage Company in Fort Collins. One acre foot of water is adequate to meet the needs of of a family of four for one year.

The slopes below the ditch are still raw and unvegetated, despite the passage of almost a hundred years. Debris removed from the eight-to-ten foot wide trough during construction and each spring since has been tossed down the mountainside. This unstable material makes soil development and revegetation very difficult. Since 1969, the National Park Service and the ditch company have been working together to prevent environmentally unsound practices, such as this.

Today virtually every West Slope stream is tapped by transmountain water diversions to support growing municipalities and to irrigate farms on the eastern plains. A complicated network of pipes, ditches, reservoirs, and tunnels has sprung up. Transmountain diversions over the past 50 years have so reduced Colorado River flow that salinity levels downstream exceed allowable standards. As West Slope communities have grown and flourished, opposition to such diversions has increased.

Colorado, along with the majority of her sister states west of the 100th Meridian, uses the Prior Appropriation Doctrine to allocate and settle water claims. In contrast, eastern states adhere to the Riparian Doctrine. Adopted in Colorado in 1875 to augment East Slope water, Prior Appropriation is based on the notion that rights are established when water is diverted to any point where it can be put to beneficial use. The doctrine allows the transfer of water from one natural drainage basin to another, sometimes hundreds of miles from its source. In some instances, this method can have major ecological ramifications.

Stop 11 is in 4.2 miles, at Colorado River Trailhead

Eastbound: Stop 9 is in 1.5 miles
Watch for features en route.

Points of interest in the *next 4.2 miles* are not identified by signs or parking areas. You can locate them by noting their distances from Farview Curve.

For the first 0.3 miles (Eastbound visitors: *between 3.9 and 4.2 miles from Colorado River Trailhead*), notice the road-cuts displaying a variety of rock types. They contain very old metamorphic rocks intruded by much younger granitic rocks, both of which have been highly altered by volcanic activity. They hint at the geological complexity of the Kawuneeche Valley and the Never Summer Mountains.

Several large Engelmann spruce—the tall evergreen trees with cinnamon-colored bark—survived the 1871 fire. They are scattered through the forest between here and the valley floor.

At 0.6 miles from Farview Curve (3.6 miles from Colorado River Trailhead), the road cuts through a *lateral moraine left by the Colorado River Glacier.* The moraine has recently been sprayed with hydromulch, a mixture of water, seed, fertilizer, and mulch to stabilize and revegetate the soil.

At 0.9+ miles from Farview Curve (3.1+ miles from Colorado River Trailhead), you cross Squeak Creek on the first of five switchbacks. These sharp curves provided a thrill to passengers and were a major challenge to drivers negotiating the original dirt road in the 1920s.

Squeak Creek was named for Bob Wheeler, an early dude rancher on the Colorado River. His falsetto voice earned him the nickname "Squeaky Bob."

Steeply dipping, layered schists exposed by the road construction underwent extensive tilting and faulting during the regional overthrusting of rocks that formed the Never Summer Mountains.

At 1.2+ miles below Farview Curve (2.9+ miles from Colorado River Trailhead), *box gabions* are arranged in steps above the road. First used in the mountains of Europe, these rock-filled wire baskets stabilize loose material on mountain slopes. Plants will eventually cover the gabions as soil and seed are blown or washed into them.

Rock walls along the road were constructed during the Great Depression in the 1930s by the Civilian Conservation Corps (CCC).

Rocks from quarries at Rainbow Curve and near Rock Cut on Trail Ridge were used in their construction.

Camp 3 on the Grand Ditch. John C. Preston, 1931, NPS

In 3.9 miles from Farview Curve (0.3 miles from Colorado River Trailhead), you may wish to pull off on the right shoulder of the road to inspect the yellow-brown, crumbly clay that fills a *fault zone*. Schist was sheared, broken, and ground up by movement along this fault. Percolation of water through the broken rock altered it into an iron-rich clay.

COLORADO RIVER TRAILHEAD
9,010' (2,746 m)

Make a sharp right into a parking area below the road. This is a lovely place to enjoy the valley's vistas and wildflower gardens. Three different trails originating here lead to regions rich in both natural beauty and human history.

The *Valley Trail* winds down the Kawuneeche Valley to the Never Summer Ranch. The *Colorado River Trail* leads up the valley past the site of Squeaky Bob Wheeler's hotel and on to Lulu City and La Poudre Pass. The third trail, *Red Mountain Trail,* leads across the Colorado River, up Opposition Creek and Hells Hip Pocket to the Grand Ditch.

Serious hikers can reach beautiful cirques in the Never Summer Mountains via this trail.

The large pyramid-shaped peak silhouetted against the sky across the valley is *Red Mountain,* 11,605' elevation (3,537 m). It is thought to be the most likely source of the volcanic rocks you saw on Trail Ridge and at Stop 4 in this roadside guide.

On the lower flanks of Red Mountain is a tree-covered, flat-topped ridge. This is a group of *lateral moraines* deposited by the Colorado River Glacier. To the right of Red Mountain, an area covered with boulders that is likely a much more recent *rock glacier.*

A large, tree-covered *roche moutonnee,* similar in origin to Sheep Rock at Milner Pass, can be seen up valley from the Colorado River Trailhead. Its steep, glacially gouged side faces you. Roche moutonnees occur frequently along the floor of the Kawuneeche Valley.

A dude ranch known as *Camp Wheeler, Squeaky Bob's Place,* and *Hotel de Hardscrabble* was located up the valley one-half mile. Started in 1908, it was an instant success, providing the only accommodations between Horseshoe

Squeaky Bob Wheeler with his dog, Jack, in front of his cookhouse where he prepared trout and wild strawberry shortcake for his guests. NPS

Inn on the east side of the Park and Grand Lake. Squeaky Bob Wheeler was a popular host and memorable personality, as well as an outstanding cook. Guests enjoyed his tent cabins from which they could hear the Colorado River and singing birds. Few knew that Bob had three ancestors on the Mayflower.

Wheeler sold his property in 1926 to Lester Scott who renovated and renamed it Phantom Valley Ranch. This name came to Scott as he rode down the valley one evening from Lulu City. He sensed the presence of phantoms from the past: Native Americans who discovered the valley's plenty, trappers and miners who tried to tap its wealth, and land surveyors and laborers who engineered access to its rich resources.

The site of *Lulu City* is three miles up valley beyond Camp Wheeler. The future for mining there seemed bright in 1876, following discovery of silver and gold in formations somewhat like those in productive mines of Leadville, Colorado.

William B. Baker and Benjamin Franklin Burnett of Fort Collins organized the Middle Fork and Grand River Mineral and Land Improvement Company. They proceeded

Miners and prospectors camping near Lulu City, circa 1882 to 1887. F. E. Baker, from the Kaufman Collection, NPS

to lay out their "city" in 1880 to accommodate the expected influx of miners. Burnett's beautiful daughter, Lulu, was the mining camp's namesake.

By summer's end in 1880, the town included a post office, hotel, real estate agency, butcher shop, blacksmith shop, and numerous cabins. But a flurry of prospecting activity produced little ore, and Lulu City was ultimately abandoned in 1885. Only a few logs remain marking the location of this once thriving community in the North Fork Mining District. The Lulu City site is on the National Register of Historic Places.

Names given the mines and their environs were at once colorful and descriptive. One name in the Lead Mountain Mining District, Hells Hip Pocket, was especially imaginative. Reputedly named by Bob Wheeler, who served in the Rough Riders during the Spanish-American War, it refers to a very rugged, precipitous area along Opposition Creek. This creek was named for a large, immovable boulder that for many years defied efforts to extend Grand Ditch.

Dutch Creek and Dutchtown were named for eight German ("Deutsch") miners who were encouraged to leave Lulu City after a barroom brawl. They moved farther up the mountain to settle near the yet-to-be-staked claims of a man named Hitchings, the namesake of Hitchens Gulch.

Stop 12 is in less than 0.1 miles

EASTBOUND VISITORS:

As you leave the valley of the Colorado River and ascend the steep slopes to Trail Ridge, the summits of the *Never Summer Mountains* emerge above their densely forested base. This wild and mysterious range looms against the skyline in a most intriguing fashion. You will see the Never Summers especially well from Farview Curve, Stop 10.

Points of interest in the *next 4.2 miles* between Colorado River Trailhead and Farview Curve are not identified by signs or parking areas. You may find them by noting their distances from Colorado River Trailhead. Commentary is located at the end of Stop 10. You will need to read these descriptions in *reverse order* as you climb to Farview Curve.

12 TIMBER LAKE TRAILHEAD

Upon leaving the Colorado River Trailhead, turn right on the main road and take the first left. Timber Lake Trail leads high into the Park's wilderness near the Continental Divide.

The lodgepole pine forest near the picnic area has grown since the 1871 forest fire. Lodgepole pine are fast-growing trees that sprout in full sunlight on newly disturbed mineral soils. In time, small Engelmann spruce and subalpine fir, growing in the shade of the pines, will tower over and replace the lodgepole forest.

Aspens with gray scars extending three to six feet up their trunks grow on both sides of the trail. Hungry elk nibble aspen bark when other food sources are scarce in winter.

Stop 13 is in 0.9 miles at Beaver Ponds

Eastbound: Stop 11 is in less than 0.1 miles

Fireweed is named for its capacity to grow in areas that were recently disturbed by fires and other causes. Ann Zwinger

One resident of these wetlands, the Rocky Mountain wood frog, is so limited in distribution that it is listed as threatened by the federal government under the Threatened and Endangered Species Act of 1974. G. A. Hammerson/DOW

WEST SLOPE ROAD

In *0. 3 miles*, you cross Beaver Creek; within *0. 1+ mile*, the Beaver Creek Picnic Area is on your right, overlooking beaver ponds.

EASTBOUND VISITORS:

Straight ahead, you glimpse Lulu Mountain, a rusty-rose, tundra-carpeted pyramid. Several other neighboring peaks at the head of Kawuneeche Valley are just out of sight. They form the northern anchor of the Never Summer Range.

BEAVER PONDS

Turn right into the parking area. The picnic site is located on a *glacial outwash terrace* formed as braided waters, flowing from beneath the melting glacier, that redistributed glacial debris into this flat. Walk to the fence beyond the picnic tables to view beaver ponds and wetlands.

The Colorado River repeatedly has wandered back and forth across the floor of Kawuneeche Valley since the last Great Ice Age glacier retreated about 13, 000 years ago. The river is now located on the far side of the valley where you

River otter are returning to Kawuneeche Valley waters, thanks to restrictions on trapping them. Ana Dronkert/DOW

can see a stand of dead spruce trees. The trees died when their roots were flooded by water dammed by beaver.

A series of beaver dams created a string of ponds along the valley floor. The dams are now overgrown with willows, sedges, and a few spruce trees.

Ponds and wetlands throughout the Kawuneeche Valley provide valuable food and habitat for wildlife. Mallards and other ducks nest here in spring and early summer, raising broods of ducklings. Blackbirds, warblers, and sparrows call raucously as they compete for prospective mates. All of this activity is accompanied by the steady drone of croaking frogs.

The well being of the sleek and playful *river otter* is also dependent on the preservation of wetlands. It too is a threatened species that was once distributed throughout much of North America. Its numbers dwindled when its valuable pelts made trapping a lucrative business. Also, human land development has reduced its habitat.

About 40 river otters have been reintroduced to the Kawuneeche Valley and to the East Inlet of Grand Lake

Phantom Valley Trading Post, a part of the Phantom Valley Ranch owned by Lester Scott, was located in the meadow beyond the upper end of the parking area. In 1959, the federal government acquired it and removed the buildings in 1960. Rostel, 1941 NPS

since 1978. Their movements and activities are monitored by biologists with the aid of implanted transmitters.

Wetlands act as giant sponges retaining flood water, removing sediments and pollutants. They gradually release clean water downstream. In recognition of their ecological importance and their rapid rate of destruction, Congress passed legislation protecting wetlands in 1972.

Stop 14 is in 0.9+ miles at the Never Summer Ranch

Eastbound: Stop 12 is in 0.9 miles
Watch for feature en route

From here to Grand Lake (over 10 miles), the road parallels and cuts through low hills of unsorted glacial debris ranging in size from fine clay particles to boulders. These hills are portions of *lateral moraines* left by the Colorado River Glacier as it melted.

Occasionally, the road also cuts through bedrock knobs. These are *roche moutonnees* rounded by the Colorado River Glacier.

You pass *Timber Creek Campground* in *0.5+ miles (0.4 miles* north of Never Summer Ranch). In addition to camp-sites, it has a telephone, restrooms, and picnic tables. Evening campfire programs are held here during the summer.

EASTBOUND VISITORS:

This is the only campground before you reach those on the eastern side of the National Park. There are 35 winding miles of road between here and Estes Park. Even without stopping along the way, plan on a one and a half hour drive due to the 35 mile per hour speed limit, steep grades, numerous curves in the road, and slow traffic.

Directly ahead and up valley on the skyline is *Lulu Moun-tain*, 12,228' elevation (3,727 m). Across the valley to the left on the skyline are Mt. Stratus 12,520' elevation (3,816 m) and Mt. Nimbus 12,706' elevation (3,873 m); to the right of them is Mt. Cumulus 12,725' elevation (3,879 m).

Never Summer Ranch, one of the early dude ranches in the valley, became very well-known in the 1920s. John Holzwarth's son, Johnny, built and operated the ranch. In the early 1970s, he sold the property to The Nature Conservancy which acted as liaison with the National Park Service to acquire the land. Hellbush, 1959 Insert of Johnny, Jr. age 20. NPS

14 NEVER SUMMER RANCH
8,884' (2,708 m) 🚻 🥾 ♿ ❓ 🍁
(National Park Arrowhead # 12)

Turn right into the parking area. A half-mile path, accessible to wheelchairs, leads to the *Holzwarth Homestead*, an early working ranch that is listed on the National Register of Historic Places. Although John Holzwarth, Sr. , claimed this homestead in 1883, he and his family did not ranch this large spread until 1916. In the interim he ran a successful saloon in Denver that was eventually closed by Prohibition. The Holzwarths soon discovered, as many homesteaders did, that housing tourists and feeding them wild game and fish was an excellent way to earn money. The ranch was sold to the federal government in the early 1970s.

The trail crosses the Colorado River and winds through an extensive wet meadow that was cut for highly nutritious hay by the Holzwarths. The meadow blooms in mid-summer with many wildflowers of the Upper Montane zone. Tours of the Holzwarth home and one original tourist cabin are conducted during the summer months.

Johnny Holzwarth was an avid hunter in his youth; later, he became an equally avid conservationist. Soon after Rocky Mountain National Park was established, Johnny would often encounter Fred McLaren, the first Park ranger on the West Slope, in the Grand Lake Post Office. They were very cordial, but Fred frequently picked bits of elk and deer hair from Johnny's coat—evidence of his poaching activities in the National Park. Years later, after Johnny no longer hunted inside the Park, he jokingly admitted, "Old Fred finally got to me and I quit poaching!"

Overnight horseback trips for dude ranch guests were a special attraction of the Never Summer Ranch. Groups would occasionally ride over 40 miles across the Continental Divide to Central City. They attended the opera and stayed at the Teller House, famous for its "face on the barroom floor."

Johnny readily told all who would listen that the bottles and cans he had buried in the backcountry of the Park were "burping up on him" 30 years later. Today, all backcountry travelers are required to carry out their trash.

A long vertical strip of aspen on the slope across the meadow contrasts sharply with the dark evergreen forest. The aspen replaced lodgepole pines that were washed out by a break in the Grand Ditch.

Stop 15 is in 1.3 miles

Eastbound: Stop 13 is in 0.9+ miles.
Watch for features en route.

The meadows of Kawuneeche Valley turn an unusual salmon pink when fall approaches. Aspen and narrow-leaved cottonwood leaves provide bright accents in the evergreen forest. During October evenings, bull elk enter their fall mating period called the *rut*. During this time, they bugle frequently to defend their territory against other challenging bulls. You have the opportunity to witness this autumn drama in evenings anywhere along the Kawuneeche Valley.

15 TRAILHEAD for BOWEN and BAKER GULCHES

Turn right into the parking area. The road that crosses the bridge is a trailhead for hiking routes into Bowen and Baker gulches in the Never Summer Mountains. The upper end of the *Grand Ditch* is visible as it wraps around the flank of Mt. Baker, 12,397' elevation (3,797 m), across the valley. This mountain is named for John R. Baker, a trapper and miner credited with being the first 19th century explorer to climb it. He staked a mining claim on its upper slopes in 1875.

Walk out onto the bridge where you can see *meanders* in the Colorado River. On nearly level valley floors, these river bends become so tightly curved that the river eventually cuts across them, taking the shortest route downstream. Abandoned meanders form crescent-shaped *oxbow lakes* that gradually fill with sediments and wetland plants.

Oxbow ponds are home to many bird and wildlife species. Pools and gravel bars offer a variety of stream habitats for aquatic insects and the predatious trout. The Colorado River cutthroat is native to these waters. As you continue down valley, you will see numerous oxbows, where the Colorado River once flowed, and may flow again someday.

Stop 16 is in 2.7 miles at Onahu Creek

Eastbound: Stop 14 is in 1.3 miles.
Watch for features en route.

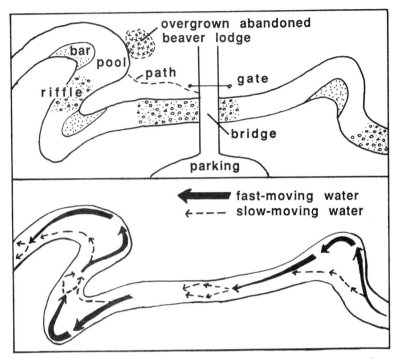

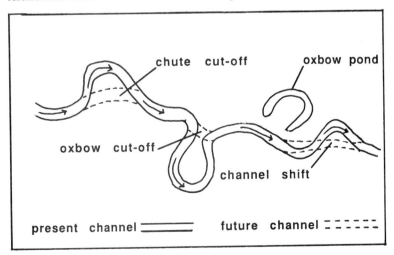

Streams undercut the outer bank of meanders, eventually causing them to erode. The collapsed material is transported downstream and deposited on the inside of the next bend. SQF

Abandoned stream meanders create oxbow ponds. SQF

EASTBOUND VISITORS:

The two pyramid-shaped peaks across the meadow up valley are Bowen Mountain, 12,524' elevation (3,817 m), on the right and Ruby Mountain, 12,008' elevation (3,660 m), on the left. These peaks are in the Never Summer Mountains, but they are outside Rocky Mountain National Park.

In the late 1800s, Jim Bourn staked a claim to the Wolverine Mine on the south flank of Bowen Mountain, his namesake. Someone in the County Clerk's office misread his handwriting—a mistake that lives on today.

WESTBOUND VISITORS:

From here to Stop 18, the Colorado River meanders close to the road. How different it is here than when you see it in the Colorado Plateau country to the southwest. One hundred and fifty years ago, this reach of the river carried an average of 20,000 acre feet of water more per year than it does today. The flow reduction resulted from diversion of water into the Grand Ditch.

In *2.0+ miles* beyond Bowen/Baker Gulch parking area, a dirt road on the right leads to the *Trail Creek Ranch* and other privately owned land, as well as to a section of Arapaho National Forest.

A small mining community, *Gaskil,* was established in 1880 directly across the valley. Named for the manager of the Wolverine Mine—Captain L. D. C. Gaskill (correctly spelled with two l's)—the community was the headquarters for the major mine in the North Fork District.

Wintergreen and pinedrops are characteristic of shady forests with moderate moisture. Ann Zwinger

 ONAHU CREEK
(no sign)

Pull right into the turnout before crossing Onahu Creek. Known initially as Fish Creek, this small stream was renamed Onahu Creek by the Colorado Geographic Board in 1914. An Arapaho word meaning "warms himself," Onahu was the name given to an Indian pony who stood close to the campfire on cold evenings—a behavior very atypical for horses.

Straight and tall, lodgepole pine, like those across the road, once served as supporting poles for Native American tipis. Today their trunks are used as rails for National Park Service fences.

Low bushes of buffalo berry and blueberries cover much of the forest floor, together with a variety of wild-flowers. These forests are more lush than they are on the East Slope. The lodgepole community is the most common forest on the West Slope of the Park, because they replaced

Car crossing Onahu Creek. Before roads were paved, driving was high adventure. Service stations were few and far between, and cars also had more frequent engine or tire trouble. 1910 NPS

Dense stands of slender lodgepole pines like the ones you see across the road captured the imagination of early settlers. Perhaps reminiscent of the hair on Paul Bunyan's giant dog Blue's back, the pioneers called these forests "doghair stands." Joe Arnold, N.P.S. Horace Albright fellow, 1988.

trees burned by West Slope fire in 1871. Before the fire, Engelmann spruce and subalpine fir grew here.

Lodgepole pines downstream are dying because their roots have been suffocated by water from a recently constructed beaver dam.

Eastbound: Stop 15 is in 2.7 miles; the first feature in transit is in *0.7 miles.*

Stop 17 is in 0.3 miles

17 ONAHU CREEK TRAILHEAD

Turn left into the parking area. The *Onahu Creek Trail* leads to Long Meadows, where it connects with the Timber Creek Trail. A wetland dominated by willows, shrubby cinquefoil, Canadian reedgrass, and sedges is located to the left of the trail.

An old path, just beyond the parking area, branches right from the Onahu Creek Trail and enters the mature lodgepole pine forest. In early summer, you may find unusual, fragile red columbines blooming on the forest floor. Pink twinflowers and pipsissawa, and white one-sided pyrola grow here. Rotting tree stumps are covered with mosses, as well as pixie-cup and dog-tongue lichens.

Eastbound: Stop 16 is in 0.3 miles.

Stop 18 is in 0.5 miles

18 GREEN MOUNTAIN TRAILHEAD

Turn left into the parking area. Green Mountain Trail joins the *Tonahutu Creek Trail* at Big Meadows, a pleasant 1.8 mile hike from here. The trail passes through lovely forests and around glacial ponds surrounded by wildflowers during the summer months. This trail was once a wagon road to ranches in Big Meadows.

The mixed *evergreen forest* of lodgepole pine, Engelmann spruce, and subalpine fir is intersected by a swath of aspen, river birch, and alder growing along the creek.

Homesteader Henry Schnoor's original cabin at Green Mountain Ranch, built in 1898. He built the bay window in anticipation of the geraniums his fiancee, Kitty Harbison, would plant there. Schnoor's homestead cabin was incorporated into the two-story lodge of Green Mountain Ranch. NPS

Several large Engelmann spruce with rusty-red bark stand near the parking area. Woodpeckers and sapsuckers in search of insects have riddled the trunks of both spruce and aspen in this area.

The West Slope's cool and moist climate permits Subalpine zone species to grow at lower elevations than they do on the East Slope. For example, Engelmann spruce here grows down to 8,700' elevation (2,652 m); on the East Slope, it is rarely found below 9,500' elevation (2,743 m).

Green Mountain Ranch, located just down valley from here, once was a very popular dude ranch. Homesteaded in 1888, the ranch spanned many successful decades before it was sold to the federal government in 1972.

Eastbound: Stop 17 is in 0.5+ miles

Stop 19 is in 1.9 miles

19 HARBISON MEADOW
8,680' (2,646 m) (no sign)

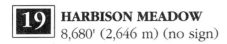

Turn into a parking area on the right at a wide curve in the road. The peaks in the distance are the *Vasquez Mountains*, west of Winter Park. *Elk* are seen here in the early morning and at dusk. This is an excellent place to hear bull elk bugle during their rutting season in late September and October. Sagebrush, shrubby cinquefoil, green gentian, and willows mix with the dense grasses and sedges in this wetland meadow.

The meadow was part of the *Harbison Homesteads*—the first homesteads on the West Slope of the Park. Two sisters, Annie and Kitty Harbison, filed on this land in May 1895. The wild grasses provided valuable feed for their dairy cows, both as green fodder in summer and dry hay in winter.

Each young woman built a cabin on her own land, conforming with the provisions of the Homestead Act; they were only 30 feet apart. Within a few years, they added a large house for their parents and brother Robert. Early

The Harbison sisters, their family, and the two Schnoor girls on their homestead in 1908. By this time, Annie and Kitty were taking in tourists. NPS

Rob Harbison's sled used for delivering milk around Grand Lake in 1907. Rob helped his sisters in running the dairy on their homestead, which was located due west of Kawuneeche Visitor Center. NPS

settlers all said that, "the Harbison girls worked just like men."

Stop 20 is in 1.1 miles

Eastbound: Stop 18 is in 1.9 miles

The west entrance to Rocky Mountain National Park, *Grand Lake Entrance*, is in *0.7+ miles.*

20 | KAWUNEECHE VISITOR CENTER
8,720' (2,658 m) 🚻 🚻 ❓ 🥾

Park naturalists stationed at the *Kawuneeche Visitor Center* can answer your questions about the Park. A new exhibit room and auditorium were added in 1989, funded by private donations. You can also purchase maps and books on a variety of topics. A schedule of Park interpretive activities and back country camping permits are available inside.

Scattered through the lodgepole and aspen forest that surrounds the building are large *glacial boulders* sitting on small uneven recessional moraines. They were left by the melting Colorado River Glacier 14,000 years ago.

You may reach the *Tonahutu Trail* by taking the *Tonahutu Spur Trail* from the visitor center. Tonahutu is an Arapaho Indian word meaning "Big Meadows, " referring to the grassy mountain park encountered along this trail. Tonahutu Trail follows a Native American migration route from Grand Lake into some of the Park's most scenic back country along the Continental Divide.

The *Harbison Ditch*, constructed by Harry Harbison in 1894-5, flows through the parking area and carries water from Tonahutu Creek to Columbine Lake. A merchant in Grand Lake, Harbison was a step-brother of the Harbison sisters whose homestead cabins were directly across the road from here on the edge of Harbison Meadow.

VISITORS TRAVELING EAST to FALL RIVER PASS and ESTES PARK:

In the next 15 miles you will travel along the headwaters of the mighty Colorado River that created the world-famed Grand Canyon. You are close to some of the most remote and beautiful sections of Rocky Mountain National Park, which can be reached only by trails. Despite its rugged character, this terrain has been explored and inhabited by humans for over 11, 000 years.

Set your trip odometer to 0. 0 (or record your mileage) as you leave the parking lot. See page xv for specific instructions about using a roadside guide in reverse.

NO MOTOR FUEL OR LODGING IS AVAILABLE along the 48 miles of winding, high elevation road between here and Estes Park, two hours driving non-stop. *Food* is available only at Fall River Pass during the day in summer and early fall. Timber Lake Campground is the *only camping facility* on this side of the Park.

You will find numbered signs shaped like arrowheads. They mark points of interest identified in the National Park Trail Ridge Road Guide pamphlet.

Eastbound: Stop 19 is in 1.1 miles at Harbison Meadow.

---

*Enjoy an authentic western
community nestled beside
Colorado's largest natural lake.*

*Y*OU EXPERIENCE GRAND LAKE
*and other interesting facets of
Rocky Mountain National Park's
western edge as you drive this loop.
Grand Lake village was once a frontier town—the business and social
center for homesteaders and neighboring mining communities along
Kawuneeche Valley. Its colorful and
occasionally violent past can be
brought to life by visiting the Kaufman Museum and strolling the
boardwalks of Grand Lake village.*

*The lake basin was scooped out by
three major glaciers during the Great
Ice Age. Massive glacial moraines
line Grand Lake's shores and
impound its waters. These rivers of
ice also carved long, U-shaped valleys
known as "inlets." Vast and pristine
back country along these tributaries
was traveled by Native Americans
during the past 11,000 years; it
awaits your exploration today.*

*East Slope water users, living in the
rain shadow of these mountains,
have often eyed West Slope water
resources with envy. Construction of
the transcontinental railroad and a
spur line to Denver allowed farmers
on the eastern plains to export their
agricultural products by the 1870s.*

GRAND LAKE LOOP

Soon, their need to irrigate crops surpassed the water resources available. They diverted water across the Continental Divide for the first time in 1890, when the Grand River Ditch opened.

Today, a complex network of ditches, pumping stations, reservoirs, and tunnels transfer water from the headwaters of the Colorado River into rivers on the East Slope. Shadow Mountain Lake and Grand Lake, both natural in origin, have been adroitly linked into a recent water development project.

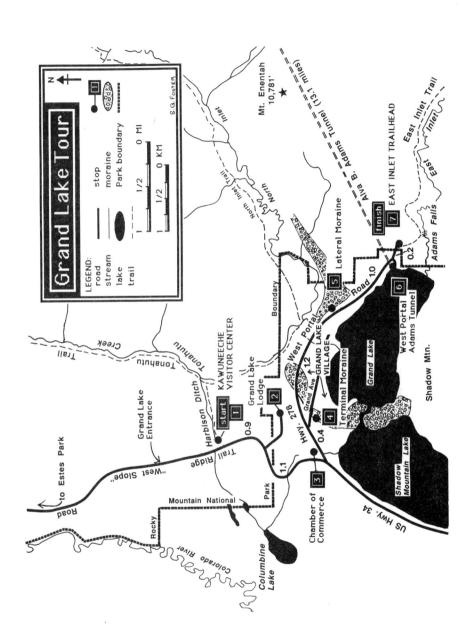

GRAND LAKE LOOP

STARTING POINT: *Kawuneeche Visitor Center just south of the Grand Lake Entrance to Rocky Mountain National Park*

ENDING POINT: *Kawuneeche Visitor Center*

DISTANCE: *9.4 miles roundtrip*

Getting Started: This short drive skirts the southwestern margin of Rocky Mountain National Park, as well as Grand Lake village, one of the oldest West Slope communities.

 KAWUNEECHE VISITOR CENTER
8,720' (2,658 m)

Park naturalists stationed at the newly enlarged *Kawuneeche Visitor Center* can answer your questions about the Park. Maps and books on a variety of topics are available here, as well as a schedule of National Park interpretive activities. Back country camping permits, necessary for overnight stays in remote areas, are issued in the office.

Set your trip odometer as you exit the parking area, then turn left onto U.S. Highway 34, a continuation of the West Slope Road.

Stop 2 is in 0.9 miles at Grand Lake Lodge

> Between the visitor center and the park boundary, *0.8 miles,* and just beyond the turnoff to Grand Lake Lodge, you drive through a series of low hills. They are boulder-strewn recessional moraines of the most recent Colorado River Glacier. A few ponds occur where water is trapped between some of the moraines.

2 GRAND LAKE LODGE
8,630' (2,630 m)

Turn left in *0.5+ miles* and follow the road marked *"Grand Lake Lodge"* to the parking area. (The lodge is closed in winter.) Walk down the path to where it curves to the right. From this vantage point, you gain a sweeping view of the Grand Lake area, including the village of Grand Lake and Shadow Mountain Lake.

Grand Lake, 8,367' elevation (2,671 m), is the largest natural lake in Colorado—nearly one and a half miles long and over two-thirds of a mile wide. It was rumored to be bottomless by early settlers, who had not measured its true depth of about 200 feet.

The lake retains one of the early names for the Colorado River, once known as the "Grand River." Native Americans called it "Spirit Lake" or "Holy Lake," in keeping with their belief that a supernatural buffalo lived in its depths. The Lake was also thought by Ute Indians to be haunted by the ghosts seen in the misty vapors rising from it on a cold morning. These spirits may have belonged to

Stagecoach between Grand Lake and Granby is shown on a postcard mailed on June 18, 1907. NPS

GRAND LAKE LOOP

Grand Lake from site of Grand Lake Lodge, showing (right to left) Shadow Mountain, Mt. Wescott, and Mt. Craig. BEW

Ute women and their children, who had drowned when rafting out on the waters to escape a band of enemy Cheyenne and Arapaho Indians.

Across the lake, you see a large, glacially carved, U-shaped valley. This valley and the river flowing through it have been called *East Inlet* since the area's first settlement. The mouth of *North Inlet* can be seen to the left much nearer to you.

The Grand Lake basin was scooped out of bedrock by glaciers and dammed by glacial moraines. Several glaciers flowed down East and North inlets from the Continental Divide during the past million years. The most recent glaciers are estimated to have melted by 13,000 years ago.

Grand Lake Lodge is typical of architectural style associated with growth of the National Park System in the early part of this century. Built in 1920 by A. D. Lewis with encouragement from both the Park superintendent, Clarence Way, and the first director of the National Park Service, Stephen T. Mather, the lodge was within the Park boundary until 1962. At that time, in keeping with the policy of removing nearly all human structures from the Park, the boundary was moved to exclude Grand Lake Lodge.

Reset your trip odometer before returning to U.S. Highway 34. When you reach the highway, turn left to continue this sidetrip. As you approach the highway, you will pass a quiet lily pond containing water held by a depression in the moraine.

Stop 3 is in 1.1 miles

 GRAND LAKE CHAMBER OF COMMERCE

Turn left into the parking area at the *Grand Lake Chamber of Commerce,* just before you reach *Colorado Highway 278.* The Chamber of Commerce is an excellent source of information about accommodations and activities in the greater Grand Lake area.

Grand Lake village retains many historic buildings and boardwalks from its early days as a western frontier community. For those interested in delving into this

Grand Lake with sailboats and East Inlet and Mt. Craig beyond. Taken in the 1870s by William Henry Jackson, pioneer western photographer. NPS

community's fascinating history, detour from this tour at Stop 4 to visit the Kaufman House. This early hotel has been converted into an historic museum. It is located near the lake on Pitkin Street, one block from Grand Avenue.

With your back to the highway, you can survey the Grand Lake area from a new perspective. Beyond the village and the lake, in the middle of East Inlet, rises a barren, dome-shaped mountain with craggy cliffs called *Mt. Craig,* 12,007' elevation (3,660 m). It is named for William Bayard Craig, a relative of Colorado's Governor John Routt and pastor of Central Christian Church in Denver. Craig owned property here.

Flanking East Inlet on the left is a massive, forested ridge with a large cliff on the right side bordering East Inlet. This summit is *Mt. Cairns,* 10,880' elevation (3,316 m), named after James Cairns, a Canadian who established the first general store in Grand Lake village in 1881. To the left a higher summit along this ridge above treeline is named *Mt. Enentah,* 10,781' elevation (3,286 m). The full name is *Enetah-Notaiyah,* translates as "man-mountain." The barren

Troublesome Formation and associated glacial debris. This formation is volcanic and accumulated in lake sediments. SQF from NPS photo

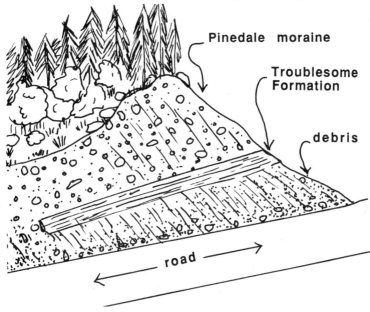

Pinedale moraine

Troublesome Formation

debris

road

summit fringed with trees reminded the Arapahos of a bald man's head.

Across U.S. Highway 34 is a large road cut in light-colored, crumbly rock. The bottom three-fourths of this exposure is composed of the *Troublesome Formation*— sediments deposited in Middle Park 40 to 30 million years ago. These sediments were overlain 28 to 26 million years ago by volcanic materials, which in turn were capped with a thin layer of glacial outwash deposited about 13,000 years ago. The Troublesome Formation is exposed in several other road cuts between here and Granby.

Stop 4 is in 0.4+ miles at Terminal Moraine

> Turn left from the Chamber of Commerce parking area onto Colorado Highway 278. After you have turned, look for a large valley straight ahead beyond Grand Lake village. This is *North Inlet*. Notice how the lower left flanks of Mt. Enentah, cut away by glaciers, drop nearly vertically into this valley.
>
> In *0.3 miles* bear right at a junction onto Grand Avenue, the main street of *Grand Lake village*. There is no sign indicating its name.

 TERMINAL MORAINE of EAST INLET GLACIER (no sign)

Soon after you turn onto Grand Avenue, pull over on either side of the road beyond the buildings. Ahead of you, the road has been cut through a large, steep hill that is a *terminal moraine.*

As the recent East and North Inlet glaciers slowed and melted near their composite snout 20,000 and more years ago, rocks, sand, and silt rolled off and piled up, forming this large mound of glacial till. By 13,000 years ago, when the glaciers had receded into the high mountains, the moraine created Grand Lake by impounding East and North Inlet creeks.

The moraine is composed of rock fragments quarried from bedrock along East and North inlets and Tonahutu Creek. Some of it has come from as far away as the Conti-

Cairns General Store that was on Grand Avenue in 1896. NPS

Saloon on Grand Avenue, Grand Lake, circa 1890 NPS

nental Divide, over eight air miles from here. The unsorted mixture of huge boulders, smaller rocks, and finely powdered materials is typical of moraines. Its full extent can be seen on the Grand Lake Guide map.

Notice that the fine materials are grayish white, a sign of recently deposited material. Soils on older moraines are weathered yellowish-brown to brownish-orange by rusting (oxidation) of iron.

Stop 5 is in 1.2 miles at North Inlet Lateral Moraine

Drive less than *0.1 mile* back the way you came and turn right onto the first side street. It dead ends within a block on *West Portal Road,* where you will turn right again.

West Portal Road skirts the north edge of Grand Lake village and then parallels the north shore of Grand Lake. Between here and the crossing of North Inlet, West Portal Road cuts through several glacially rounded bedrock hillocks, called *roche moutonnees.*

In *0.7+ miles* from Stop 4, a dirt road turns left and climbs very steeply to the *Tonahutu Creek and North Inlet Trail-heads, 0.3 miles* from West Portal Road. The intersection is marked by a conspicuous sign for Shadowcliff Lodge.

These trails penetrate the heart of the Park's wild and majestic high country. The *Tonahutu Creek Trail* follows a route called the "Big Trail." It was used for thousands of years by Native Americans who crossed Flattop Mountain and descended the East Slope near Bierstadt Lake over 18 hiking miles away. The Big Trail goes north through Big Meadows, past Haynack Lakes tucked into a cirque, and climbs onto the Divide's high, rolling, tundra-covered surface, known as Bighorn Flats.

North Inlet Trail connects with Tonahutu Creek Trail on Flattop Mountain. Recognizing that North Inlet provided a shorter route between Moraine Park and Grand Lake, pioneer explorer and East Slope resident, Abner Sprague enticed his brother Fred and surveyor Franklin Huntington into blazing a trail through it in 1901. A decade later, Huntington surveyed the route for Old Fall River Road.

You cross *North Inlet* creek in *1.0 mile* from Stop 4. At this point, Tonahutu Creek has already joined it.

NORTH INLET LATERAL MORAINE
(no sign)

Pull over onto the right shoulder next to another big hill. West Portal Road is cut through a sizeable *lateral moraine* deposited by the most recent North Inlet glacier. Similar to the terminal moraine you examined at Stop 3, this ridge is composed of a mixture of fine particles and immense boulders. Some of these boulders were transported nearly seven miles from the peaks of the Continental Divide.

Stop 6 is in 1.0+ miles

In *0.5 miles,* you catch glimpses of *Shadow Mountain,* 10,155' elevation (3,095 m), across Grand Lake. This ridge was so designated by the Colorado Board of Geographic Names because of the shadow it casts on the lake surface. This decision settled a dispute among local residents over five other names commonly used for the mountain.

From Stop 5 to the upper end of the Lake, the road traverses several moraines and glaciated bedrock outcrops. Above the road, you can see a few large ponderosa pine and Douglas-fir trees growing on the moraines. The presence of these trees indicates that you are now in the Upper Montane life zone.

If you have just driven across the National Park, you are seeing these trees for the first time since you left Many Parks Curve on Trail Ridge's east slope. Ponderosa pine is quite rare on the West Slope of the Colorado Rockies. It was logged for timbers during the state's settlement period and has not grown back.

 WEST PORTAL of the ADAMS TUNNEL
(no sign)

Follow the paved road to the parking area on the shore of Grand Lake. This place was buried by hundreds of feet of glacial ice. Straight across the Lake is a low hill with cabins on its right flank. This is the glacier's terminal moraine, part of which you saw at Stop 3. This moraine impounds the the waters of Grand Lake.

221

At the base of the slope behind you is the *West Portal of the Alva B. Adams Tunnel.* This 13.1 mile aqueduct carries West Slope waters under Otis Peak on the Continental Divide to Lake Estes. It is stored there for agricultural and urban uses on Colorado's eastern plains.

U.S. Senator Alva B. Adams introduced landmark legislation in 1937 creating the extensive Colorado Big Thompson Water Diversion Project. Water from the Colorado River began to flow through the Adams Tunnel in 1947. Tunnel cutting was done from both east and west ends at once; the two sections met with only one inch difference.

Visitors are welcome at the Lake Granby Pumping Station located south of Grand Lake near U.S. Highway 34. They may also tour the Lake Estes Power Plant during the summer season.

Stop 7 is in 0.2+ miles

7 EAST INLET TRAILHEAD
8,395' (2,559 m)

A gravel road turns right from the pavement just as you leave the Adams Tunnel area; it leads to the *East Inlet Trail-*

Pinedale-age lateral moraine deposited by North Inlet glacier. West Portal Road has been cut through the moraine. W. Alcorn 1972, NPS

West Slope features of the Colorado Big Thompson Water Project. SQF
1. Willow Creek pumping station
2. Granby pumping station
3. West portal of Adams Tunnel on Grand Lake
4. East portal of Adams Tunnel

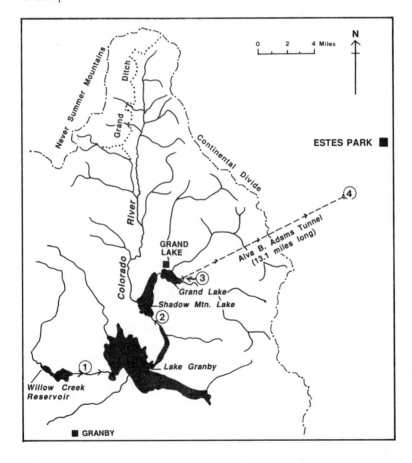

GRAND LAKE LOOP

223

head. From this short circle road, you glimpse the beauty of East Inlet's immense U-shaped glacial valley with its many cliffs and wetlands. The righthand valley wall rises to *Mt. Wescott,* 10,421' elevation (3,176 m)—named for "Judge" Joseph Wescott, the first permanent resident of the area.

Born in Nova Scotia, Wescott came to Colorado in 1859. His frail health led him to the Middle Park region and Hot Sulphur Springs down river from Grand Lake. He moved to the west shore of Grand Lake in 1867 and lived in a cabin abandoned by a fur trapper. In the summer of 1868, he hosted the Powell-Byers party before they made the first ascent of Longs Peak.

East Inlet Trail leads to a string of glacial lakes in exceptionally remote and beautiful wilderness. The trail also follows one of four Native American routes in the National Park, climbing to the Continental Divide, crossing Boulder-Grand Pass, and descending into Wild Basin on the East Slope of Rocky Mountain National Park.

A delightful half-mile walk on East Inlet Trail brings you to *Adams Falls,* named for Jay E. Adams, who came to Grand Lake from Texas in 1886. Adams built a small summer cabin on a rock near the southeast shore that was accessible only by boat.

A memorable event in the history of these mountains got under way here in early August 1868. Major John Wesley Powell and William N. Byers departed with five of Powell's geology students on the *first successful climb of Longs Peak* made by white people.

This party followed the Native American route up East Inlet and over Boulder-Grand Pass into Wild Basin, from which they ascended the south flank of the Longs Peak massif, reaching the summit on August 23. Powell and his companions collected data on weather and some geographic features along the way. Today both a lake and a mountain located west of Longs Peak bear Powell's name in commemoration of this and other feats.

This accomplishment was only a hint of things to come for Civil War veteran John Powell, who soon was to launch the first voyage down the Green and Colorado rivers and

Mule deer doe and two fawns. Mule deer are often seen in early morning and evening along roads in Rocky Mountain National Park. B. Border, RMNP Collection

GRAND LAKE LOOP

John Wesley Powell.
From *Exploration of the
Colorado River*, by J.W.
Powell, 1895. Dover
Books.

through the Grand Canyon. Powell later was appointed as
the first director of the U. S. Geological Survey.

William N. Byers, owner and editor of Denver's *Rocky
Mountain News*, described the expedition in his newspaper.
He and three companions had tried to scale Longs Peak
from the East Slope near Estes Park in 1864 but were only
able to reach the summit of neighboring Mt. Meeker. Byers
Peak in the Vasquez Mountains memorializes the man for
his contributions to Colorado's mountaineering history.

From here, you return to U.S. Highway 34 by West
Portal Road. Highway 34 skirts Shadow Mountain Lake and
Lake Granby, both known for their trout and kokanee
salmon fishing. The route cuts through low, rounded hills,
some of which are moraines of two stages of the Colorado
River Glacier. Others are uplifted sections of the Troublesome Formation seen at Stop 3. U.S. Highway 34 terminates
at U.S. Highway 40 just west of the town of Granby.

Track a glacier to its source, up a rugged canyon and through pristine forests along a road surveyed by early highway engineers.

*C*OLORADO RIGHTFULLY *claims more miles of high mountain roads than any other state. The first high road in Rocky Mountain National Park, Old Fall River Road, was built primarily so that visitors could enjoy the scenery from Fall River Pass. Native Americans had followed the same route up Fall River Canyon for thousands of years.*

The term "motor nature trail" appropriately describes this one-way road. You can mosey along in your car as you might stroll along a trail, stopping whenever you wish to photograph scenery, or listen to birds and wind in the trees. The road places you in intimate contact with forests, wildlife, streams, and a glaciated canyon. You can track an extinct glacier from near its terminus in Horseshoe Park to its source on the cirque headwall at Fall River Pass. And you may marvel at the vision of those who surveyed and constructed this route through the mountains.

Fall River Road begins near an alluvial fan born during a flood on July 15, 1982. The road parallels a fault zone that constructs Fall River

OLD FALL RIVER ROAD

into deep, narrow channels wherever the rock has cracked at right angles. The stream's roaring cascades contribute to the wildness of the canyon.

As you ascend, mountain spires tower above you. Their jagged unglaciated surfaces are sculpted by blasting winds and chisels of frost. Steep mountain slopes are furrowed by snow avalanches—one of the most powerful tools shaping landscapes above the reach of glaciers. You will see pathways bulldozed through forests by these massive snowslides.

High in the canyon, the road winds through a spruce-fir forest extraordinary for its age and vigor. It has grown since the last Great Ice Age glacier melted some 12,000 years ago. Emerging from the forest at tree-limit, you will gaze directly into Fall River Cirque.

This amphitheatre-like basin is where Fall River glaciers formed and into which they retreated as they melted. Magnificent elk may be seen grazing among flowers on grassy slopes. White-crowned sparrows may be singing from atop dwarfed spruce trees silhouetted against a brilliant blue sky. The road makes its final ascent diagonally across the cirque headwall onto Fall River Pass at the west end of Trail Ridge.

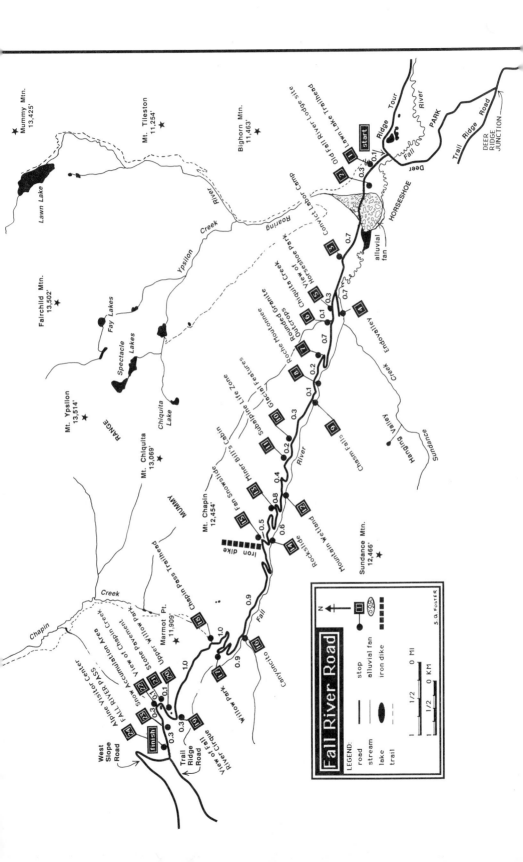

OLD FALL RIVER ROAD

STARTING POINT:	*Junction, Deer Ridge Road with Fall River Road*
ENDING POINT:	*Fall River Pass on Trail Ridge Road*
DISTANCE:	*10.9 miles*
MAXIMUM ELEVATION:	*11,796' (3,595 m)*

Getting Started: The road is two-laned and paved only to *Endovalley*. From that point on, it is *one-way up only and unpaved*.

This upper section of road has been nominated recently as an Historic Transportation District on the National Register of Historic Places.

Following Trail Ridge Road's opening in 1932, Fall River Road received little use. It was closed in 1953 by a massive rockslide. In 1968 Fall River Road was cleared and reopened as the present Motor Nature Trail.

This road follows a route used by Native Americans for thousands of years as they came to the mountains in search of game and cooler temperatures. The Arapaho Indians called it the "Dog's Trail," because dogs were used to drag travois over it.

Stop 1 is in 0.1 miles

1 LAWN LAKE TRAILHEAD
8,520' (2,597 m)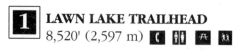

Pull into the parking area on the right. A six-mile trail leads to Lawn Lake, 10,987' elevation (3,349 m), one of the largest lakes in the park. The gently-rolling meadow just down valley of the parking area is the site where Rocky Mountain National Park was dedicated on September 4, 1915.

Every autumn, bull elk congregate in Horseshoe Park, bugling to both attract females and to repel competing males. They are best observed in early morning and evening. Please stay at the edge of the road, keeping a respectful distance from these animals.

Stop 2 is in 0.3 miles

 SITE of OLD FALL RIVER LODGE (no sign) **Stock loading ramp**

Turn left into a small paved parking area. Where this turnout is today stood *Fall River Lodge,* known originally as "March's Place." It was built in 1913 by D. J. March and his wife Minnie, who homesteaded 160 acres west of here in 1907. In 1909 they bought another 160 acres, including this land. March drove the first automobile into Upper Horseshoe Park in 1912, fording Roaring River where the new alluvial fan is today.

D. J. March suddenly passed on in 1917, but his wife continued to operate the lodge, eventually assisted by Sam Service, an Estes Park merchant whom she married. The lodge was purchased and removed by the National Park Service in 1959 in keeping with the Congressional mandate to restore land within the Park to its natural form and function. Large, mature ponderosa pines, a tree species typical for this elevation, still grow on the site.

Stop 3 is in 0.7 miles at Convict Labor Camp

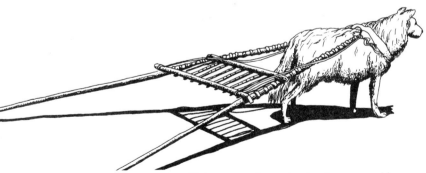

A Native American travois. This means of carrying loads was used by Native Americans on the Dogs' Trail through Fall River Canyon. After C.P. May 1971 *The Early Indians* by Ken Bernstein.

In *0.1 miles* from Stop 2, you reach the *Eastern Alluvial Fan Trailhead.* A nature trail crosses the alluvial fan created by the 1982 Lawn Lake Flood. The flood is described at Stop 10 in the *Deer Ridge Tour Guide.*

The *Western Alluvial Fan Parking Area* is *0.3 miles* from Stop 2. From here, you can take the alluvial fan nature trail. You can walk to the new lake created on Fall River by debris deposited across its channel by the 1982 flood.

A lovely stand of mature ponderosa pines and Douglas-fir borders the parking area. Here, the bark on both these species is a rich cinnamon color. Trees this mature are rare in Colorado today because most were logged in the late 1800s.

In *0.5 miles* beyond Stop 2, the road passes through a small grove of *balsam poplar.* These rough-barked trees with arrow-shaped, aromatic leaves are common in Wyoming, Montana, Canada, and Alaska, but are seldom found in Colorado. Balsam poplar grows this far south only in cool, moist locations.

3 CONVICT LABOR CAMP
National Park Service Signpost # 1

Park on the left. This is the first point of interest described in the booklet, *Old Fall River Road,* sold at visitor centers and in a dispenser at the entrance to Endovalley, *0.7 miles* ahead. This and other sites interpreted in that booklet are identified by the consecutively numbered sign posts located along Fall River Road.

Balsam poplar leaf. NPS

State convicts were housed during 1913 and 1914 in a camp on the slope across the road. These men labored with only hand tools to build the first three miles of Fall River Road up to Chasm Falls. Collapsed log walls of a few cabins can still be found.

During the period of the road's construction between 1913 and 1920, editorials in the *Estes Park Trail* convey excitement about its significance to the community: "It is of prime importance that the Continental Road (as Old Fall River Road was first called) through Estes Park should be built with the least possible delay." By mid-summer, 1913, came predictions of the road's near completion: "There are only 14 miles remaining to be built in order to connect the east and the west on a six percent grade and all below timberline."

In spite of such optimism, it was a false hope that the route could be completed in only two summer seasons. Few people understood the difficulty of the terrain and the complexity of this construction project carried out mainly by hand labor. The indomitable spirit of park superintendents Charles R. Trowbridge and L. Claude Way and the road's surveyor, Franklin I. Huntington, saw the eight-year long task through to completion in 1920.

Scarred by the nibbling teeth of hungry deer and elk, aspen in this area are charcoal gray on their lower trunks. Aspen bark provides these animals with winter meals when grasses and shrubs are buried by deep snows.

The aspen grove is being invaded by Engelmann spruce and Douglas-fir that are now large enough to compete with aspen for light and water. The spruce and fir will tower above this forest within a few decades.

Stop 4 is in 0.7 miles

Old Fall River Road under construction. 1925 NPS

OLD FALL RIVER ROAD

Aspen groves harbor many flowering herbs in summer. Joe Arnold, Albright Fellow, NPS

Between here and Endovalley, large clumps of Rocky Mountain maple grow on both sides of the road. These tall shrubs, with gray branches and red winter twigs, have leaves decorated with fuschia red galls—tiny, fuzzy knobs encapsulating eriophyd mite eggs.

The wetlands along the valley floor were created by beaver dams on Fall River. These dams, engineered by the crafty rodents to maintain protective water levels around their lodges, also maintain water levels vital to wetland plants and other animals. Early settler, Horace Ferguson, tells of catching 184 trout in these ponds in only a few hours one afternoon.

4 ENDOVALLEY
8,588' (2,618 m)

Turn left into *Endovalley*. Originally, this land was bought from the Marches in 1926 to provide a crude campground for travelers over Old Fall River Road. Its name was coined from "end-of-the-valley." Large surfaces of bedrock smoothed by the glaciers are scattered through the area.

Notice the Engelmann spruce and subalpine fir trees growing along Fall River. They survive here, fully 1,000 feet below their usual elevation, because of the cold air that moves down Fall River Canyon from the high mountains at night. Such frigid drafts are common in canyons that originate on high mountain ridges.

Fall River supports a population of brook trout. Watch here for a slate gray bird, the *American dipper,* feeding from the rocks in the river. Dippers dive into small rapids in search of aquatic insects on the river bottom. Known also as "water ouzels," they have a beautiful and distinctive song, especially audible as they fly up and down stream just above the water.

To take the Motor Nature Trail up Fall River Canyon, turn left as you exit Endovalley. Turn right to return to Deer Ridge Tour. Above here, Fall River Road is unpaved and for uphill traffic only. Because of this, THERE IS NO TURNING BACK BEYOND THIS POINT. The use of lower gears, even for vehicles with automatic transmissions, is recommended. There are numerous turnouts where you can stop to enjoy the scenery.

American dipper
Ken Bernstein

Stop 5 is in 0.3 miles

 VIEW OF HORSESHOE PARK
National Park Service Signpost # 2

Horseshoe Park down valley and the flood-caused lake are best seen from the outside of the curve. The outcrops are strewn in many places with loose debris dropped by the glaciers.

The dip in the ridge line across the valley marks the lower end of *Hanging Valley*. Sundance Creek, which arises in a cirque on the eastern end of Trail Ridge, emerges from Hanging Valley and joins Fall River.

Many Douglas-fir trees in this area have been killed by the Western spruce bud worm, a native insect that infests trees in forests throughout the Rocky Mountains.

Stop 6 is in 0.1 miles

Mayfly larva.
Ann Zwinger

 CHIQUITA CREEK
National Park Service Signpost # 3

Chiquita Creek probably was named for "Chipeta," a character in an early 1900s novel about the Ute Indians. The creek rises between Mount Chapin and Mount Chiquita in the Mummy Range to your right.

A small shrub called *ninebark,* with round, crinkled-edged leaves, grows next to the bridge. It bears flat-topped clusters of small white flowers in midsummer. *Waxflower* shrubs grow from cracks in rocks along the road. Other plants growing here among the rocks and on the forest floor are pink wild roses, lilac Fremont's geranium, red-orange paintbrush, and yellow cinquefoil and stonecrop.

Stop 7 is in 0.7 miles at Rounded Granite Outcrops

A relative of the hydrangea, the early summer flowers of waxflower are waxy, creamy white, and slightly fragrant. Its leaves turn apricot to rose colored in the fall. NPS

In *0.3 miles,* watch carefully for a particularly interesting feature, a *glacial pothole,* at the National Park Service Sign-post # 4, next to the road on the right. This unusually fine example of a glacial pothole, about six feet in diameter, is located in the granite bedrock.

ROUNDED GRANITE OUTCROPS
(no sign)

At the second switchback beyond the pothole, pull over on the outside of the curve to inspect the granite outcrops, rounded and deeply grooved by several glaciers. This rock does not display the glass-like glacial polish seen on granite in Yosemite National Park. Glacial polish has been erased from these rocks by more rapid weathering caused by frequent Rocky Mountain summer showers.

These outcrops, the pothole you just saw, and the rock at Chasm Falls are 1.4 billion-year-old Silver Plume granite, once overlain with even older metamorphic rocks. The granite was exposed after water and ice stripped away the metamorphic rocks, a process taking tens of millions of years.

Lichens grow in profusion on rock outcrops. These slow-growing plants have become established since the last

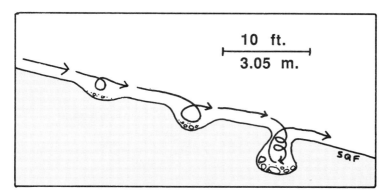

Meltwater, dropping down through the glacial ice, swirled pebbles and cobbles around in a depression. Gradually, it scoured out this deep, round basin, a glacial pothole. SQF

glacier melted from this valley some 13,000 years ago. They play an important part in weathering rocks and in subsequent soil formation. Lichens secrete a weak acid that helps to dissolve the cement between tiny mineral grains. The lichens themselves, together with the mineral particles, form a thin layer of rudimentary soil in cracks and on rock surfaces.

Several trees and shrubs grow in pockets where soil has collected. Growing roots and freezing water ultimately pry the rocks apart.

Lichens.
Ann Zwinger

Stop 8 is in 0.2 miles at a roche moutonnee

In *0.1 miles, Mt. Chapin,* 12,454' elevation (3,796 m), the rounded mountain on the skyline, comes into view at National Park Service Signpost # 6. It is composed of dark, banded metamorphic rock; its jagged crags become even more conspicuous as you proceed up the valley. They have been furrowed by the action of snow avalanches and by freezing and thawing water.

Mt. Chapin was named for Fredrick Hastings Chapin of Hartford, Connecticut, who first came to the Estes Park area in 1886 to climb with members in the Appalachian Mountain Club; William Hallett was their guide. Chapin wrote a popular book published in 1888 called *Mountaineering in Colorado: the Peaks about Estes Park* after several climbing trips in the region.

---

8 ROCHE MOUTONNEE
(no sign)

The tree-covered hill in the middle of Fall River Canyon is a large bedrock knob, rounded and sculptured by glaciers. Features like it were named *roche moutonnees* by H.B. de Saussure, who observed them in the Swiss Alps in 1787. They reminded him of men's glistening wigs plastered down with mutton grease. You will have another view of this sheep rock just beyond Chasm Falls, the next stop.

Ground or common juniper.
Ann Zwinger

Stop 9 is in 0.1 miles

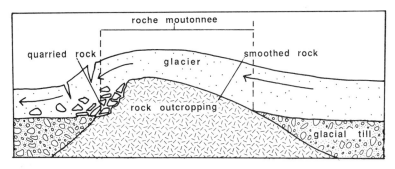

Literally translated from the French, *roche moutonnee* means "fleecy rock," but "sheep rock" is in more common usage. SQF

CHASM FALLS
9,060' (2,761 m)
National Park Service Signpost # 7

The *Chasm Falls* parking area is on your left. A paved path leads several hundred feet down a steep canyon wall to the falls. You will find the best lighting for photographing the falls in the morning.

Fall River drops about 25 feet into a glacial pothole containing pebbles and boulders that continue to swirl, deepening the glacial mill. The entire length of Fall River Canyon follows an ancient fault zone. The step-like cliffs, over which Chasm Falls plunge, formed in the granite where bedrock joints intersect each other at right angles.

Originally called "Upper Horseshoe Falls," the name was changed to Chasm Falls in 1913 by D.J. March to make a distinction between this falls and Horseshoe Falls on Roaring River. Horseshoe Falls were obliterated by the Lawn Lake flood.

Stop 10 is in 0.3 miles

> You are about to drive through a *mixed forest* of aspen, Douglas-fir, ponderosa pine, lodgepole pine, Engelmann spruce, and subalpine fir. The high diversity of tree species is made possible by overlapping environmental conditions characteristic of both the Upper Montane and the Subalpine zones.

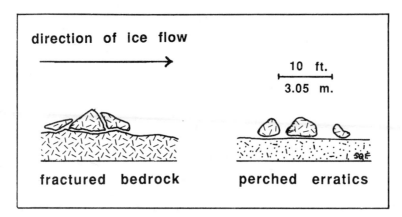

direction of ice flow

10 ft.
3.05 m.

fractured bedrock   perched erratics

Perched erratics often are of a different rock type than that on which they are sitting. They may be transported long distances by glaciers. SQF

10 | GLACIAL FEATURES
National Park Service Signpost # 8

Pull off on the left side of the road opposite a steep granite outcrop. Notice grooves in the rock that run parallel to the length of the valley. They indicate the direction that the ice was flowing. Several pits and gouges still remain on the rock surface.

A *perched erratic*—the large rounded boulder sitting on top of the outcrop—was transported several miles down valley and deposited here by the last Great Ice Age glacier.

The crags on Mt. Chapin loom on the skyline.

Stop 11 is in 0.2 miles

11 | SUBALPINE LIFE ZONE
9,305' (2,836 m)
National Park Service Signpost # 9

As you gain elevation, you enter the *Subalpine life zone* where Engelmann spruce and subalpine fir are common. Lodgepole pine and aspen are evident as well. These two tree species "heal" disturbed areas in both the Subalpine and the Upper Montane zones.

Clumps of mountain alders grow along the road edges. They are characteristic of moist areas in the mountains. They are much less common in the Colorado Rockies than

Mountain alder leaves and catkins. Ann Zwinger

in other western mountains. Native Americans used powdered alder bark to make a red dye.

You may discover wildflower gardens blooming here in July and August. In open places, you probably will find yellow golden banner, arnica, and wallflowers; blue penstemon and short chiming bells; white cow parsnip, elderberry, yarrow, pussytoes, and composite daisies; pink wild roses; fuschia Lamberts locoweed, and fireweed; and lilac whiplash daisies. In wet areas beside the roadbed, you might encounter fuschia shooting stars in early summer. On the forest floor blue Jacobs ladder blooms. Coralroot may display its brown stalk of flowers; it has no green leaves and feeds on decaying plants.

This is also a good area for *birdwatching*. Hermit thrushes, dark-eyed juncos, mountain chickadees, pine siskins, and ruby-crowned kinglets are abundant in Subalpine forests. Dusky grouse may appear suddenly and quietly beside the road. Chickaree squirrels, chipmunks, and golden-mantled ground squirrels are common mammals.

Shooting star.
Ann Zwinger

Stop 12 is in 0.4 miles

12 MOUNTAIN WETLAND
(no sign)

A space large enough to accommodate only two cars is on the left. Beyond some aspen and spruce trees is a small *wetland*. It was once a pond trapped between heaps of glacial moraine. During the last 13,000 years, it filled with silt and plant debris to form *peat*. Boggy areas like this are known as *sedge fen wetlands*.

Stop 13 is in 0.8 miles at Miner Bill's Cabin

For the *next 2.0 miles*, a narrow band of *young lodgepole pine* is growing on soil disturbed by road construction. Lodgepoles thrive in full sunlight on mineral soils laid bare by fire or other disturbances: they literally "heal" these areas. In contrast, Engelmann spruce and subalpine fir require shade and stable, organic soil.

242

As you continue *0.6 miles* from Stop 12, you will encounter trees toppled in the winter of 1985-86 by a *snow avalanche.* They lie in a scrambled mass to the right of the road. Snow accumulating on the steep slopes of Mount Chapin eventually becomes so heavy that it slides down the mountain without warning, destroying much in its path. Avalanches pose a great threat to backcountry skiers.

13 SITE of "MINER BILL'S" CABIN
National Park Service Signpost # 10

Bill Currance settled here around 1908, before the National Park was established. He worked several extensive, but unproductive, mining claims in the area. His cabin once stood in the small clearing to the right of the road. "Miner Bill" delighted in watching the early morning sunlight play on Sundance Mountain across the valley. He is said to have named the mountain.

Currance lived undisturbed until Fall River Road reached this site in 1919. He left the area in 1928 to live in a dwelling loaned to him by F. O. Stanley.

Stop 14 is in 0.6 miles

"Miner Bill" Currance's cabin and barn in Fall River Canyon. Humberger 1940 NPS

The bedrock outcrops from here to Fall River Pass are metamorphic schists and gneisses. Thin patches of glacial debris cover the outcrops.

In *0.4 miles,* the road crosses the path of a *recent snow avalanche.* During the winter of 1985-86, a huge snowslide roared down the side of Mt. Chapin, cutting a swath through this mature spruce-fir forest. Large trees were broken into pieces like twigs by the slide's enormous power. Looking from here up the the avalanche chute, you can see where the slide crossed Fall River Road.

The size of downed aspen, spruce, and lodgepole pine trees indicates that this slide was inactive for many years prior to 1985-86. Aspen and lodgepole require 75 years to reach full size; spruce take much longer.

Raspberry, gooseberry, Fremont's geranium, thistle, cow parsnip, and paintbrush grow in the avalanche path.

LANDSLIDE
National Park Service Signpost # 11

A large landslide is perched like a terrace on the slope of Sundance Mountain across the valley. This mass of material slipped downslope at some time since the last glacier

Landslide across Fall River Canyon. SQF

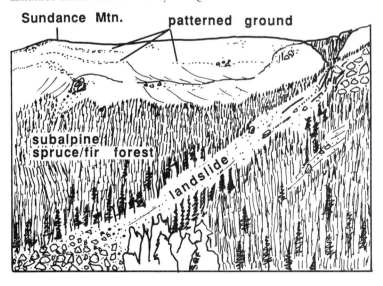

receded. The downhill side of it has slumped recently, exposing light-colored material that contrasts with the dark, weathered, and lichen-covered debris on either side of it.

Rock streams and *solifluction terraces*—two features limited to high alpine and arctic areas—are visible in the tundra above treelimit on Sundance Mountain.

Stop 15 is in 0.5 miles

Within *0.1 miles, box gabions* form terraces above the road at National Park Service Signpost # 12. Avalanches and rock-slides from Mt. Chapin have damaged the road periodically, burying it under 30 or more feet of snow in spring. A section of the road was washed out in 1953 by a heavy rain-storm, and again in 1970 by a landslide.

The box gabions are heavy wire mesh baskets filled with rocks. When tied together, they effectively support unstable slopes. Plants grow in soil that accumulates in the gabions, and eventually obscure them.

In *0.3 miles* from Stop 14. Deer Mountain, Fall River Canyon, and Horseshoe Park come into view at National Park Service Signpost # 13.

 FAN SNOWSLIDE
10,240' (3,121 m)
National Park Service Signpost # 14

You may find enough space to park on this sharp hairpin curve. Before cars were equipped with fuel pumps, gasoline was gravity-fed to engines. Consequently, some cars had to *back up* steep grades to keep fuel flowing to the engine.

Fan Snowslide is visible below the outer edge of the curve and slightly to the right. You have crossed this snowslide twice in your ascent. Snowslides funnel into this avalanche chute from a steep gulley on Mt. Chapin and transport large rocks and broken trees down the mountain. Avalanches have sculpted the face of Mt. Chapin above you.

Old car on hairpin turn at Fan Snowslide. Autos and busses in the 1920s could not negotiate these sharp curves without forward and backward "see-sawing." Needless to say, some riders, especially those in back seats, were disconcerted to find themselves hanging out over thin air. NPS

OLD FALL RIVER ROAD

The light-colored outcrops around the parking area were intruded into older, dark-colored schists and gneisses nearly 1.7 billion years ago.

Stop 16 is in 0.9 miles at Canyoncito

Geology enthusiasts will recognize a *diabase dike* about 100 feet up the road on the right. It is one in an *en echelon* series of dikes that surfaces at several places in the park. These geological features are known collectively as the "Iron Dike."

The dark rock in the dike contains iron minerals that oxidize wherever they are exposed, giving their surface a rusty appearance. Miner Bill Currance dug a shaft into the dike in search of gold. Unfortunately for Currance and many other prospectors, this part of the Front Range contains almost no precious metals.

Just beyond the Iron Dike and above the road, a statuesque limber pine tree grows out of the rock. It has survived the stresses of wind and drought for several hundred years.

In *0.1+ miles* from Stop 15, just a short distance beyond the Iron Dike, you cross the narrow path of *Old Faithful Snowslide*. Named for its predictable and tumultuous assault on the road, this avalanche chute continues to challenge road crews. Between May 5 and June 5, 1926, it buried the road six times; in June 1929, it ran daily for 13 consecutive days between two and three each afternoon.

Snowslides greatly complicated life for Park superintendents when Fall River Road was the only route to Grand Lake. They were under great pressure from bus tour operators to open Fall River Road by mid-June at the latest. Consequently, they welcomed the goal of National Park Service Director Stephen Mather to find an alternative route by 1926. Trail Ridge was selected and the new road was open in 1932, just three years after construction began.

As you drive from here to Willow Park (Stop 17), you will see patches of sand and rounded pebbles perched on bedrock. This debris was left by a Fall River Glacier as it retreated up valley 13,000 to 14,000 years ago. Glacial ice was nearly 1,500 feet deep here. It deposited most of its load of rocks and boulders along the margins of Horseshoe Park six miles down valley.

In *0.3+ miles* at National Park Service Signpost # 15, snow *avalanche paths* are visible across the valley on the slopes of Sundance Mountain.

More potholes, smaller in diameter than the one you saw in the granite down valley, are found in metamorphic rock along the right side of the road.

In *0.5 miles* from Stop 15, *glacial polish* on gneiss and schist bedrock surfaces is visible for several hundred feet beyond the National Park Service Signpost # 16. Nestled in cracks and on ledges are clumps of alumroot displaying round, serrated leaves that turn a lovely shade in the autumn.

Car in fresh snow slide at Old Faithful Avalanche Track, May 15, 1926. F. T. Francis NPS

OLD FALL RIVER ROAD

16 CANYONCITO

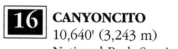

10,640' (3,243 m)
National Park Service Signpost # 17

Park your car in the area just before the signpost. You can walk back to see Canyoncito (Spanish for little canyon). Fall River has followed right-angle *joints* in the rock to form both the photogenic little waterfall and the abrupt turn in the river channel.

Stop 17 is in 0.9 miles at Willow Park

Just up the road from Canyoncito, the valley widens and several beautiful Subalpine meadows come into view. These meadows may have been lakes, dammed by recessional moraines of recent glaciers. Sediment and decaying plants gradually filled their basins, creating lush wetlands.

Subalpine willows grow along the stream. Meadows adorned with wildflowers and a very fine, mature Subalpine forest are found on better-drained soils. Immature spruce and fir are queued up along roadsides.

In *0.8 miles, Fall River Pass* appears on the horizon at National Park Service Signpost # 18. You can also see the *Alpine Visitor Center* and the *Fall River Store.* The second rise to the right of the buildings is *Marmot Point,* 11,909' elevation (3,630 m).

---

17 WILLOW PARK

10,710' (3,264 m)
National Park Service Signpost # 19

From the edge of the meadow, you can survey an immense bowl up valley. This is *Fall River Cirque,* the source of the glacier.

The side road leads to a patrol cabin and stable built in 1924 to house road crews. The cabin was also used by skiers when the sport was popular in Fall River Cirque.

Stop 18 is in 1.0 mile at Chapin Pass Trailhead

For the next mile, the road passes through an excellent example of a *mature Engelmann spruce-subalpine fir forest.* Treat yourself to a walk to savor its calm and grandeur. Notice individual trees and the wide range of their sizes.

Mixed-aged stands of trees are at a *dynamic equilibrium.* As the older trees die, younger ones of the same species replace them. If you were to return in a thousand years, this forest would probably look much the same as it does today, barring fire, major climate change, or some other disturbance.

Forests like this one are *very rare* except in national parks, where they are protected from logging. Not only do these forests give visitors immeasurable pleasure, they are valuable subjects of scientific research and important reserves of natural genetic diversity.

Blueberries carpet this forest floor. Their leaves change to a deep red in late summer. Wildflowers blooming on the Subalpine slopes display glorious colors: yellow black-tipped groundsel with greyish leaves; crimson paintbrush; white pearly everlasting, mountain figwort, yarrow, and thistle; fuschia fireweed; and blue harebells. These are but a few of the many species that flower in mid-summer. At lower elevations, many of these plants flower earlier.

Mountain chickadees, ruby-crowned kinglets, and pine siskins are common birds in Subalpine forests.

18 CHAPIN PASS TRAILHEAD
11,020' (3,359 m)
National Park Service Signpost # 20

Chapin Pass Trail ascends the divide between Chapin Creek and Fall River, from which it parallels Chapin Creek north to the Cache la Poudre River. Glacial ice poured over this pass from the north several times during the last half million years, destined to join the Fall River Glacier.

During early negotiations about the construction of Old Fall River Road, one route considered was over Chapin Pass, down Cache la Poudre River, and east into Fort Collins. This option would have created a scenic loop within Larimer County. In anticipation of this route, road crews cleared timber beyond this pass in 1917 and 1918. It was not until the spring of 1919 that the State decided to go the "Highline Route" over Fall River Pass.

In 1962 Dr. Bettie Willard examined trees in this area. She found the 45-year-old new growth trees averaged only eight inches in diameter and 20 to 25 feet in height. Her observations demonstrated that a spruce-fir forest grows much more slowly at this elevation than was previously believed. This was a two- to four-fold increase over previous estimates of the time spruce and fir trees take to reach marketable size at this elevation.

Stop 19 is in 1.0 mile at Fall River Cirque

In *0.1 miles* from Stop 18, at National Park Service Signpost # 21, *Fall River Pass* and the *Alpine Visitor Center* appear once again. Deep snow drifts that accumulate here just below treelimit prevent the development of a dense forest.

In *0.6 miles* from Stop 18, just before National Park Service Signpost # 22, *rock stripes* are on the hillside above the road. They are composed of masses of loose rocks that have crept slowly downhill with the help of freezing and thawing water in the soil. Such features are characteristic of the Arctic-Alpine environment that awaits you just up the road.

Pikas and marmots are common small mammals at high elevations. They sun themselves on rocks and squeal or whistle, if they spot you. Pikas busily harvest grass and herbs all summer for winter food. Marmots, in contrast, eat nearly constantly during summer to produce a thick layer of fat that will sustain them through nine months of hibernation. Despite their plump appearance, they frolic over the rocks with their tails swinging in circles.

In *0.7 mile* from Stop 18, you reach National Park Service Signpost # 22. The dense and luxuriant Subalpine spruce-fir forest thins into wind-battered clusters of low trees. You are now entering the *treelimit region.*

Marmot. Bill Border 1982 RMNP Collection

OLD FALL RIVER ROAD

Treelimit area. Wind and snow cause Engelmann spruce to change form and to migrate across the landscape. NPS

19 FALL RIVER CIRQUE
National Park Service Signpost # 23

Below the Alpine Visitor Center, you have a full view of *Fall River Cirque,* the basin where several glaciers formed during the past million years.

A *glacial cirque* is quarried into its amphitheatre-like shape by moving ice masses that periodically occupy it. The steep face of the cirque headwall plunges to a valley floor planed flat by glaciers. Many cirques in the Park contain crystal-clear lakes held in basins scooped out by ice. Water is pumped from the cirque floor to facilities on Fall River Pass.

Down the valley, Willow Park is flanked on the right by Trail Ridge and on the left by Mt. Chapin. Rock outcrops along the Tundra World Trail on *Trail Ridge* are visible on the skyline. Elk grazing in the wetlands during summer months have created game trails on the slopes above Willow Park.

Stop 20 is in 0.3 miles

20 UPPER WILLOW PARK
11,560' (3,523 m)
National Park Service Signpost # 24

At this elevation, you have reached the uppermost growth limit for trees in these mountains. *Treelimit,* as this region is called, visually marks the boundary between the Subalpine and Alpine life zones.

Just below treelimit, trees are stunted and gnarled by their battle to survive in a very harsh climate. These *krummholz trees,* as they are called (meaning 'crooked wood'), grow either in elongated ribbons or in isolated islands. You are surrounded by tree islands. Ribbon forests can be seen at treelimit across the valley.

Tree islands gradually migrate across the tundra as their windward branches die and leeward branches root in the shelter of the growing tree. Engelmann spruce have adapted best to these environmental extremes; subalpine fir and lodgepole pine rarely survive in treelimit areas.

OLD FALL RIVER ROAD

Visible below you is a small pond just inside the curve on Fall River Road. It is gradually being filled by an *alpine wetland*. These wetlands are speckled with floral colors in July and early August when burgundy kings crown, white marsh marigolds and American bistort, and pink queens crown and alpine lousewort bloom. A solifluction terrace damming the pond is rimmed with bog birch and willows. The terrace formed as soil slowly oozed down the hill during a colder climatic period.

Stop 21 is in 0.1 mile

 STONE PAVEMENT

Pull off on the right just before the curve. Welcome to the land of *alpine tundra,* a place where dwarfed cushion plants, grasses, sedges, and Arctic willow grow. The tundra may appear at first to be a stark and forbidding place. Actually, it displays many plants and animals that have extraordinary adaptations for survival in these severe arctic-alpine conditions.

The shallow basin on your right may be filled with water in early summer. When it is empty, you can see that its floor is tiled with flat rocks. The stones were arranged into a *stone pavement* by pressure in the soil produced by freezing and thawing of water. From the Alpine Visitor Center, you will look down on a patch of stone pavement on the floor of Fall River Cirque, where Koenigia grows.

Stop 22 is in 0.1 miles

 VIEW OF CHAPIN CREEK VALLEY
National Park Service Signpost # 25

Below the road on the right you have a view into *Chapin Creek Valley* and the Mummy Range. The valley's broad, glacially created U-shape is clearly displayed from this vantage point. Visualize it filled up to tree line with glacial ice, as it was during the most recent major glaciation.

Chapin Creek is separated from Fall River by this small divide. It is a tributary to the Cache la Poudre River.

OLD FALL RIVER ROAD

Elk may be grazing in the meadows below, especially in the summer and fall months. You may be lucky enough to hear them bugling in the early morning or late evening during their fall rut. Elk trails are laced throughout the meadows.

Stop 23 is in 0.3 miles

> The road passes through outcrops of light-colored *pegmatite*, a mineral that was injected into metamorphic rocks hundreds of millions of years ago.

SNOW ACCUMULATION AREA
National Park Service Signpost # 26

Deep snowdrifts on this portion of Fall River Road melt late in the spring. Winds moving briskly across Fall River Pass eddy as they blow over the crest of the cirque, losing their momentum and dropping their burdens of snow on the top of the steep cirque face. Drifts rimming Fall River Cirque usually linger all summer.

It was in this area that road crews worked the hardest to clear the road each season by the June 20 opening date. During the first few years, workers removed drifts up to 25 feet deep with picks and shovels, assisted by horses pulling large snow scoops.

By the mid-1920s road crews were assisted by horse-drawn wagons and a steam shovel. Early rotary snowplows were not powerful enough to cut through the frozen, compacted snow. TNT and dynamite put in place the previous fall were occasionally employed to break up the snow in the spring. Today the National Park Service lets the sun do the job, a cost-effective application of solar energy.

Stop 24 is in 0.3 miles

Queens crown (opposite page) and Koenigia. Ann Zwinger

OLD FALL RIVER ROAD

Clearing snow was made more difficult when the men had dug so deep that they could not throw the snow out over the top of the drift. June 18, 1924 NPS

 FALL RIVER PASS

11,796' (3,595 m) 🚫 🅲 🚻 🍴 🚌 🚶

National Park Service Signpost # 27

The *Alpine Visitor Center* is open from mid-June through mid-September. There are several exhibits about the Alpine Tundra life zone located inside. Books and maps about the Park are available for purchase. You also will find food and gifts at the *Fall River Pass Store.*

The road you have just driven and the buildings at the Pass have been nominated to the National Register of Historic Places.

To continue on to Grand Lake, turn right at the lower exit of the parking area and follow the *West Slope Roadside Guide.*

To cross Trail Ridge to Estes Park, turn left at the lower exit and follow the *Trail Ridge Roadside Guide.*

Official opening of the road in the 1920s constituted dragging seven buses filled with tourists through the slush in the corridor sliced into the snowdrift. June 25, 1926 Fred P. Clatworthy NPS

Tour Enos Mills's country in the shadow of Longs Peak and Mt. Meeker—stopping often to listen for singing birds and cascading brooks.

PEAK-TO-PEAK HIGHWAY offers superb views of the highest mountains in Rocky Mountain National Park: Longs Peak, Mt. Meeker, and Mt. Lady Washington. From this route, you see the east face of Long Peak with its 1,000-foot sheer wall called the Diamond. This mountain massif has beckoned climbers to scale its heights for more than a century.

You will encounter sweeping vistas of natural Estes Park, the mountain grassland after which the community was named. They may fascinate you, as they did Joel Estes and his family, as well as explorer-geologist John Wesley Powell, surveyor Ferdinand Hayden, eastern climbers Anna Dickinson and Frederick Chapin, and inventor Freelan O. Stanley.

The Park's East Slope is rich in history from the 1800s. You will meet Elkanah Lamb, a minister who homesteaded in Tahosa Valley; William L. Hallett, a mountain climber and mining engineer; Windham Thomas Wyndham-Quin, fourth Earl of Dunraven, who laid claim to most of the vast lands and

PEAK-TO-PEAK HIGHWAY

*wildlife resources of Estes Park;
Alexander MacGregor, who operated
one of the earliest cattle ranches; and
Ruth Ashton Nelson, pioneer botanist
in the Park.*

*At the heart of this region's history
is naturalist and writer Enos A. Mills.
A deep, driving admiration of nature
gave rise to his successful efforts to
promote the establishment of Rocky
Mountain National Park. Revel with
him at the wonder of Longs Peak and
Tahosa Valley, the land that shaped
his conservationist philosophy.*

*Peak-to-Peak Highway passes
through areas shaped by glaciers, the
earliest dating back perhaps a
million years. The topography
combines high mountain ridges,
U-shaped river valleys, and fault
zones. Forests of ponderosa and
lodgepole pine cloak the mountain
slopes.*

*In Wild Basin, you can walk along
the tumbling cascades of North St.
Vrain Creek, observing evidences of
glaciers long gone. Several jewel-like
lakes may lure you even higher via
hiking trails.*

*The Peak-to-Peak Roadside Guide
terminates at the end of the spur
road into Wild Basin, but the
highway continues south to Idaho
Springs on Interstate 70 near the base
of 14,260-foot Mt. Evans. The mining
towns of Allenspark, Ward, Neder-
land, Black Hawk, and Central City
along the way are among the corner-*

stones of nineteenth century Colorado history. A side trip expands your views and knowledge of Estes Park Valley, passing through its northern section, where Alexander Quinter MacGregor staked out his homestead at the base of Lumpy Ridge in 1872. Along with his contemporaries—Joel Estes, the Earl of Dunraven, Abner Sprague, and Horace Ferguson—MacGregor grazed cattle on vast grasslands populated by large herds of deer, elk, and bighorn sheep.

You can explore the Stanley Hotel, built by inventor Freelan Stanley, a brilliant man who regained good health following his move to live in the clean, dry mountain air of Estes Park. Stanley's vision and generosity gave important impetus and guidance to development of the Estes Park community. Also included in the side trip is the Estes Park Area Museum.

This side trip skirts the base of Lumpy Ridge, where you gain expansive vistas of the high mountain backdrop of Estes Park across flower-strewn meadows closer at hand. One understands why this area fascinated early botanist Ruth Ashton Nelson, who rode across the valley frequently to her homestead behind Eagle Rock. The side trip terminates at the brink of Devils Gulch, which is on the margin of the region affected by the 1976 Big Thompson flash flood.

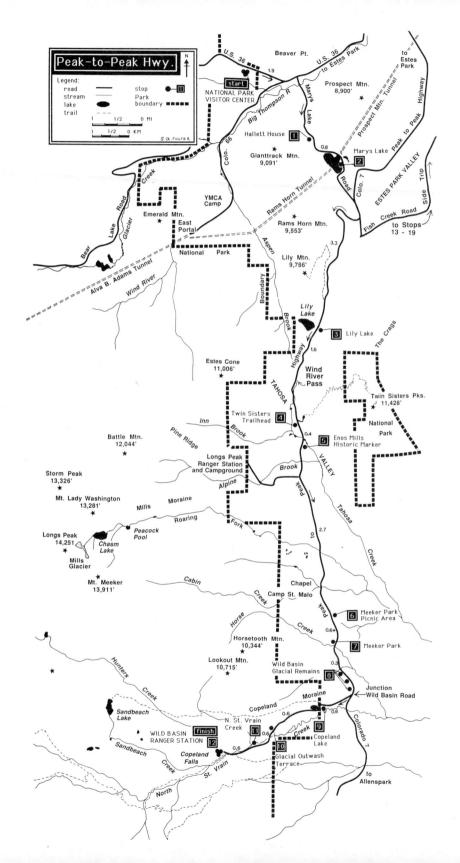

PEAK-TO-PEAK HIGHWAY

STARTING POINT: *Rocky Mountain National Park Headquarters, on US Highway 36*

ENDING POINT: *Wild Basin Ranger Station, off of Peak-to-Peak Highway, Colorado #7*

DISTANCE: *15.7 miles plus a 10.7 mile side trip*

Getting Started: Beginning at *Park Headquarters,* turn right from the parking lot onto U.S. Highway 36 and set your trip odometer to 0.0 as you leave.

Stop 1 is in 1.9+ miles at Hallett House

For an interesting side trip offering views of Longs Peak and the Big Thompson River, turn right in *0.7 miles* onto *Colorado 66.* This *6.9-mile*-long route follows the river to the YMCA of the Rockies Conference Center. It passes the Estes Park Campground and ends at *Emerald Pool,* the East Portal of the Alva B. Adams Tunnel. This 13.1-mile tunnel under the Continental Divide carries water that is diverted from the Colorado River.

In *0.9+ miles* from Park headquarters, turn right at the signal light onto *Marys Lake Road.* From here on, you will be traveling the first road completed between the plains and the National Park. It crosses the Big Thompson River and passes between Gianttrack Mountain on your right and Prospect Mountain on your left. The tramway seen on Prospect Mountain is accessible from downtown Estes Park. The nearly 360 degree view from the top of the tramway is spectacular.

HALLETT HOUSE
(no sign)

Pull into a small turnout on the right just before the drive-way to a Victorian-style frame house that is just below the road.

This small building was built in 1881 by William L. Hallett as a summer home. Hallett, his wife, and six children spent their summers here at Edgemont, as the place was then called. It is one of the oldest structures in Estes Park. *Estes Echoes* reported on September 9, 1881 that ". . . another of those social gatherings for which Mr. Hallett's residence has become noted. . ." was held, complete with speeches, poetry readings, refreshments, and fireworks.

A mining engineer from Springfield, Massachusetts, Hallett first came to Estes Park to climb mountains in 1878. The next year, he and his bride returned to spend their honeymoon traveling by horseback from Estes Park to Grand Lake with Abner Sprague as guide.

Hallett became acquainted with Frederick H. Chapin, another avid climber from the East. In time, both men named a mountain peak in the other's honor. They char-

Hallett and his family in front of Edgemont in 1883. NPS, DFA collection

265

tered the Rocky Mountain Club, the first mountaineering club in Colorado, in 1896, along with 18 other men from Denver.

Hallett began cattle ranching with two partners and 1,200 cattle in North Park in 1879. He expanded his activities that year into Wyoming's Powder River Basin, building one of the largest cattle domains in the region. In 1890 Hallett moved his ranching business to near Loveland, returning to Estes Park in summers to graze his cattle. He eventually returned to mining engineering, managing the Leadville Smelter. Hallett lived to be 90 years old.

Horace W. Ferguson and his family homesteaded this area in 1875 in outright defiance of the British Earl of Dunraven, who acquired this and other large parcels of land in Estes Park under special provisions for foreigners in the Homestead Act.

Stop 2 is in 0.8 miles

Looking west across the meadow at Ferguson's Ranch. Soon after arriving, the Fergusons built the Highlands Hotel and several tent cabins at the base of Gianttrack Mountain. Ferguson used lumber from a sawmill near Bear Lake Road. F.H. Chapin, 1888 NPS Horace Ferguson, founder of Highlands Hotel, by Charles Reed, owner of Brinwood Lodge. NPS

2 | MARYS LAKE
8,046' (2,452 m) (no sign)

After crossing the first dam near the campground, turn right into a parking area that overlooks Marys Lake. It was named in 1861 for Mary I. Fleming Estes, the daughter-in-law of Joel Estes—after whom Estes Park was named. Sections of the *Continental Divide, the Mummy Range, and parts of Lumpy Ridge* are visible along the skyline to the north.

Marys Lake is set in an open, mature ponderosa pine forest, scattered with bitterbrush and wax currant shrubs. The early settlers in the region counted 20 tepee rings in the meadow near the lake, all with openings facing east. These remains of Arapaho use are now all under Marys Lake. Across the lake on the north-facing slopes of Rams Horn Mountain is a dense stand of Douglas-fir, a tree species common in the middle elevations of Colorado's mountains.

Rounded outcrops of Precambrian metamorphic and granitic rocks jut up from the meadows. Some of these outcrops are dome-shaped, indicating a very cohesive rock. Other outcrops are blocky, because of the perpendicular joint planes created during their early formation over one billion years ago.

Some of the water in Marys Lake arises from the Colorado River on the West Slope of the Park. It is collected in Lake Granby, Shadow Mountain Reservoir, and Grand Lake before it is transported to the East Slope through the Alva B. Adams Tunnel. First released from its 13.1 mile underground journey into Emerald Pool at the base of Emerald Mountain west of here, the water then passes through the Rams Horn Siphon and rushes down a *penstock* into Marys Lake.

The cement structure you see on the far side of the lake is the Marys Lake Hydroelectric Power Plant with a generating capacity of 8,100 kilowatts. From Marys Lake the water is routed to the Estes Park Power Plant through another tunnel, this one under Prospect Mountain. See Stop

6 in *Grand Lake Loop Roadside Guide* for more information on the Colorado Big Thompson Project.

The *Colorado Big Thompson Water Project,* which includes the tunnel and reservoir complex shown above, was completed in 1947 by the U.S. Bureau of Reclamation using public funds. Its purpose is to augment water supplies for eastern plains agriculture and municipalities. When the project was first proposed in the 1930s, supporters of Rocky Mountain National Park feared that facilities for it would damage the land's wilderness character. Park officials and their supporters continued to express concern at Congressional hearings and throughout the planning and construction period. Consequently, the project was completed with a minimum of environmental effects on the National Park.

Stop 3 is in 3.3 miles at Lily Lake

Drive on around Marys Lake. A very large dome called *Sheep Rock* comes into sight. It was a destination of hunting parties in the late 1800s. Milton Estes, a son of Joel, recalled: "When we saw a flock of (bighorn) sheep within a mile or two of Sheep Rock, we (set) a trained dog . . . upon them . . . and the sheep would strike straight for Sheep Rock (where) we would get the whole flock."

Continue to the junction with Colorado Highway 7, known as the *Peak-to-Peak Highway, 0.7 miles* from Stop 2. Turn right. In *0.3 miles* the *Fish Creek Road* veers sharply left from a wide bend in Peak-to-Peak Highway. This is a side trip suggested for your return trip from Wild Basin.

Between the curve and Stop 3, you will climb more than 750 feet in elevation along the flank of *Lily Mountain.* The road cuts through striking knobs of 1.4 billion-year-old granite and even older gneiss and schist. You drive through an Upper Montane zone forest composed of Douglas-fir and ponderosa pine, with scattered aspen trees.

In *2.1 miles* at the *Lily Mountain Trailhead* is a small turnout on the right side of the highway. The hike to the top of Lily Mountain will reward you with views in all directions.

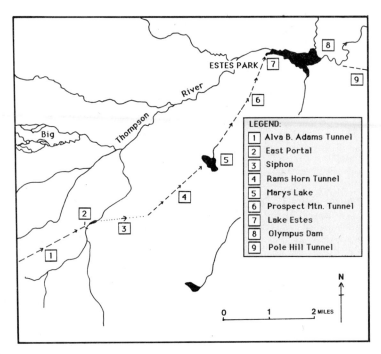

The Big Thompson Project is the largest water project in Colorado. It diverts water from Grand Lake on the West Slope to Lake Estes. SQF

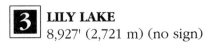

3 LILY LAKE
8,927' (2,721 m) (no sign)

Turn left into the parking area for Baldpate Estates. Lily Lake is across the road in a small meadow. It was probably named by the Gardiner party of the Hayden Survey who camped in Estes Park Valley in the summer of 1873. Pioneer photographer William Henry Jackson and early Rocky Mountain botanist John M. Coulter were in this exploration team.

Isabella Bird, an English lady who traveled by horseback throughout the Colorado Rockies in 1873, admired the lily gardens floating on the lake surface. She wrote that it was ". . . fittingly called Lake of the Lilies." Visitors today can only imagine its former beauty, as lilies have been absent since the water level was raised years ago. Enos Mills, another one of the lake's admirers, reported that he regularly saw beaver, bighorn sheep, and wolves here.

Marys Lake in 1900s, showing original road to Estes Park. Enos Mills knew of Indian tipi rings along its southern shore before the water level was raised. NPS

Walk to the lower end of the parking lot to look down into *Fish Creek Valley*, a section of Estes Park Valley. Once the winter range for thousands of elk, deer, bighorn sheep, antelope, and bison, the open meadows are rapidly being filled with subdivisions. It was called "The Circle," *tah-kah-aanon*, by Arapaho people who frequented it for hundreds of years. To your right and above you, *The Crags's* sheer outcrops of metamorphic rock on the flank of Twin Sisters Peaks reach skyward.

The road joining the highway from the east leads to *Baldpate Inn*, famous for its collection of keys acquired around the world. The collection started with a key given the owner, Gordon Mace, by presidential candidate Clarence Darrow. Built in classic rustic Elizabethan style, the inn's name comes from the mystery novel, *The Seven Keys to Baldpate*, written by Earl Durr Biggers. Also the author of the Charlie Chan series, Biggers visited Estes Park after publishing the novel and commented that this was the real Baldpate Inn (Biggers's was pure fiction).

Elkanah Lamb and his first house at the site of the present Wind River Ranch. Farmer, lay minister, and barrelmaker, Lamb laid claim to this land in 1873 and soon built the toll road up Fish Creek. Lamb shortly discovered that it was more profitable to accommodate early visitors than it was to farm at this high elevation. Lamb also became a highly capable climbing guide, often joking that he "had trouble guiding people to heaven, but they gladly paid him dollars to be taken part way" (up Longs Peak). 1885 Enos Mills Cabin Collection; by permission of Enda Mills Kiley.

Lily Lake and a beaver lodge with the Mummy Range beyond. Enos Mills Cabin Collection; by permission of Enda Mills Kiley.

The road to Baldpate is a remnant of the toll road connecting Estes Park with Wild Basin built in 1876 by Reverend Elkanah Lamb (more about Elkanah at Stop 4). From here south to Wild Basin, Peak-to-Peak Highway follows closely the route of Lamb's Toll Road.

Stop 4 is in 1.6+ miles at Twin Sisters Trailhead

As you travel south from Lily Lake across Wind River Pass, you drive through a dense forest of short lodgepole pine. This type of forest composed of crowded pines of uniform age is called a "doghair" stand, because it resembles the dense hair on a giant dog.

In *0.8 miles* from Stop 3, the gentle crest of *Wind River Pass,* 9,130' elevation (2,783 m), separates Tahosa Valley from the Estes Park Valley.

 TWIN SISTERS TRAILHEAD ✿

Pull right onto the shoulder just beyond the junction with the road to *Twin Sisters Trailhead. For Northbound visitors:* There are two pulloffs on the right beyond the junction.

You can see Twin Sisters Mountain on the skyline to your left. This name refers to the whole massif; but "Twin Sisters Peaks" is used for its two rocky summits located within the National Park.

Rising majestically to the right is the *Longs Peak Complex,* which includes the highest mountains in the Park. Unless you hike to them, the peaks will never be any closer to you than they are now. Morning light illuminates its magnificent vertical rock faces.

Tahosa Valley formed along a fault that trends north-south, parallel to the road. Once seriously considered for the name of the state, Tahosa means "Dwellers of the Mountain Tops." It was the name of a Kiowa who signed a treaty with settlers in 1837. Robert B. Marshall, Chief Geographer of the United States, chose this name in 1916, after evaluating the area for national park status.

272

Mountain man Kit Carson often trapped in Tahosa Valley in the early 1800s. He built a small cabin near here.

The black, organic soil exposed in the meadow is sedge peat that formed when plant litter accumulated in a pond created by the retreat of a recent glacier. Layers of sand and gravel alternate with the black soil, indicating variations in past climate.

Stop 5 is in 0.4 miles

In *0.1+ miles* from Stop 4, a gravel road on your left leads to *Enos Mills's Cabin,* the home of the famous naturalist. Mills was a major proponent of establishing Rocky Mountain National Park. In 1885 Enos Mills exercised claim to this land under the Timber and Stone Act.

 ENOS MILLS HISTORIC MARKER

Pull left into a parking area next to the *Enos Mills Historic Marker.* Mills was a prominent regional naturalist, mountain climber, writer, and photographer. He traveled extensively,

Enos Mills in his homestead cabin that he used as a library circa 1890. Enos Mills Cabin Collection; by permission of Enda Mills Kiley.

and according to his journals, he was "alone by a campfire in every state of the Union." Mills gained national recognition as a conservationist who lobbied citizens and the U.S. Congress for the establishment of Rocky Mountain National Park. He also promoted the founding of other national parks and monuments, including Big Bend in Texas and Indiana Dunes.

Mills was in poor health when he came to Colorado from Kansas in 1884 at age 14. A dietary change and the clear air soon cleared up his discomforts. He built the small cabin across the creek in 1885. Summers were spent working for his uncle, Elkanah Lamb, on a farm near Fort Collins. In winter he earned his way mining in Colorado and as far north as Butte, Montana. Mills was introduced to his first national park when he helped Colonel Chittenden survey the roads in Yellowstone.

Although schooled only through eighth grade, Mills had an insatiable thirst for knowledge. Each trip from a mine to a library took him ". . . from madness to reason. . ." He also nurtured a love for nature instilled in him by his mother and augmented by his wandering through the mountains. So high was his regard for life that he eventually ceased hunting, trapping, and cutting timber.

With a passion, he learned everything he could about the wilderness that was to become Rocky Mountain National Park. Observing plants, wildlife, and their interactions with the environment, he became increasingly interested in adaptations living things have for surviving in this harsh, changeable climate. For Mills "Nature was filled with entertainment, refreshment, and surprise."

At age 21 he had a chance meeting with the California naturalist, John Muir, who soon became his mentor. With Muir's inspiration and encouragement, Mills channeled his energies into preserving natural resources. He also wrote fervently about his philosophy and ideas with the intent of sparking curiosity and excitement in others.

In 1901 Mills bought Carlyle Lamb's Longs Peak House once located just across the road. Four years later, he built the Longs Peak Post Office and a new inn on the same site after the old structure was razed by fire. The new building provided comfortable lodging, with running water, electricity, and steam heat.

Enos Mills was an outgoing person who enjoyed educating his guests about the wonders of nature. He guided many groups up Longs Peak and led them on outings throughout the region on foot, horseback, and by auto. Drinking, smoking, and card-playing were discouraged at the inn, in the belief that they would prevent guests from immersing themselves in the Great Outdoors.

In spite of his intensity and sense of purpose, Mills was a good-natured man. On days when clouds obscured the mountains, he would respond to inquiries about Longs Peak by saying, "You must be in the wrong place!" He also chuckled about the weary hiker who, upon hearing Mills's jubilation over the view from Longs Peak, retorted: "If its so beautiful down there, why did you bring me all the way up here to see it?"

In 1909 Enos Mills proposed the establishment of a national park along the Front Range of the Rockies, extending from Estes Park to south of Pikes Peak. The concept received the enthusiastic endorsement of the Estes Park Protective & Improvement Association and the Colorado Mountain Club. President Theodore Roosevelt commissioned Mills to travel across the country as a persuasive spokesperson for the idea.

Rocky Mountain National Park became a reality in 1915, including about one-quarter of the land in the original proposal. Mills wrote that the campaign for the Park's founding was ". . . the most strenuous and growth-compelling occupation I have ever followed."

As his responsibilities grew, Mills established the "Trail School" to train nature guides in his philosophy. This mode of environmental education was pioneering in its time. In Rocky Mountain National Park's first summer, the school attracted Esther Burness and her sister from Cleveland. They worked at the inn and became the Park's first licensed guides. Eventually Esther became Mills's bride.

Mills died unexpectedly in 1922 from complications resulting from an abscessed tooth. The inn remained under

Longs Peak Inn built in 1905 by Enos Mills. Believing that buildings should look as natural as possible, he arranged the logs vertically instead of horizontally. Mills incorporated fire-cured trees with branches protruding from them to include their natural beauty in the building. Longs Peak, Mt. Meeker, and Mills Moraine can be seen beyond the inn. Enos Mills Cabin Collection; by permission of Enda Mills Kiley.

Interior of Longs Peak Inn. The Inn was a registered post office. Enos Mills Cabin Collection; by permission of Enda Mills Kiley.

PEAK-TO-PEAK HIGHWAY

Enos A. Mills with his only child, Enda, in front of the original cabin about two years before he died in 1922. Enos Mills Cabin Collection; by permission of Enda Mills Kiley.

Esther Mills's management until it was sold in the 1940s. She also wrote a biography about her late husband entitled *Enos Mills of the Rockies.* The lodge across the road from the historic marker was built after Mills's second inn was destroyed by fire.

Enos Mills's daughter, Enda Mills Kiley, and her husband Bob, have opened her father's first cabin as a museum displaying Mills's books, photographs, and other objects related to his life. The Kileys share their love of nature with visitors, including school children, whom they encourage to walk a short nature trail to the museum at any time of year.

From the Mills Memorial, you view the Longs Peak Complex, just as Mills often did. To the right is *Estes Cone,* 11,006' elevation (3,355 m), a non-volcanic feature that is a local landmark. *Twin Sisters Mountain,* 11,413' elevation (3,476 m), is prominent on the skyline behind Mills Marker. On its flank is the 1925 Butterfly Burn, now densely forested with lodgepole pine and aspen.

A long forested ridge curves east from the base of Longs Peak. This is the *Mills Moraine* deposited by the most recent glacier that flowed from the cirque basin at the foot of the east face of Longs Peak. The *Eugenia Mine,* staked in 1905, is on Battle Mountain just north of Mills Moraine. Its productivity was a disappointment to its owners.

Longs Peak has fascinated climbers for many hundreds of years. Intrepid Arapaho Indians ceremonially captured eagles on its flat summit by sitting patiently under blinds baited with coyote or wolf carcasses. They awaited opportunities to pluck feathers from a curious eagle.

The next people to reach the summit of Longs Peak were a group led by Major John Wesley Powell on August 4, 1868. Powell, a geology professor from Illinois, was soon to become famous for his pioneering exploration of the Grand Canyon of the Colorado River. He was accompanied on his ascent by several of his geology students and William Byers, founder and editor of Denver's *Rocky Mountain News.*

In her book *A Lady's Life in the Rocky Mountains,* Englishwoman Isabella Bird tells of climbing the peak in 1873 with "Mountain Jim" Nugent, an early Estes Park settler. Abner Sprague, pioneer rancher in Moraine Park, and his friend, Alson Chapman, ascended the peak on July 24, 1874. Sprague led numerous groups of guests there over the next 60 years. Longs Peak was called the "American Matterhorn" by eastern climber Frederick Chapin, who wrote *Mountaineering in Colorado—The Peaks about Estes Park* in 1889.

After completing several ascents, Reverend Elkanah Lamb decided to descend Longs Peak by its sheer East Face, ". . . where no man had gone before. . ." Upon surviving a near-fatal slide down an ice field, he wrote: "I immediately fell on my knees and thanked God for deliverance."

Earl Harding wrote of his friend, Enos Mills's encounter with an avalanche on "Lamb's Slide:" ". . . springing 20 feet from the cliff, (he) was hurled away—to death or safety?

278

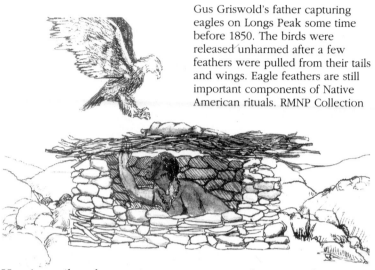

Gus Griswold's father capturing eagles on Longs Peak some time before 1850. The birds were released unharmed after a few feathers were pulled from their tails and wings. Eagle feathers are still important components of Native American rituals. RMNP Collection

Here's peril and sensation new, even to the man whose only stimulant is danger, mad racing down a mountainside, riding on the very wings of death."

Longs Peak's East Face continues to be the focal point of daring climbers to this day. In September 1922 Professor J. W. Alexander climbed it alone in one day from Chasm Lake, using ropes and pitons. During the 1930s Swiss mountaineer and botanist, Walter Kiener, studied the peak's alpine tundra and also explored a route up its East Face that now bears his name.

Since the early 1950s, the *Diamond*—a 1,000-foot cliff on the East Face—has been considered the most challenging climb in the Colorado Rockies. It was opened to climbing parties in 1960 and was first ascended that year by David Rearick and Bob Kamps of California, who preceded a Colorado team preparing to make the ascent the same season. Coloradan Bill Forrest accomplished the first solo climb of the Diamond that same year, spending one night in a hammock bombarded by rock falls.

An important climbing event on the Diamond was the first "free-climb" of its face. This climbing technique requires that an ascent be completed without placing body weight on fixed ropes.

Wayne Goss and Jim Logan began this feat one morning in July 1975. Upon reaching the ledge called

"Broadway," half way up the face, they encountered Stephanie Atwood, Molly Higgins, and Laurie Manson intent on making the first women's ascent of the Diamond. The five shared a hamburger dinner, anchored themselves in for the night, and completed their climbs the next morning.

Stop 6 is in 2.7 miles at Meeker Park Picnic Area

From Longs Peak Inn to Wild Basin, patches of rusty yellow-brown, sandy-pebbly debris are visible in roadcuts. Some geologists conjecture that these are remnants of moraines left by the ancient and elusive Pre-Bull Lake glaciers dating back somewhere around 750,000 years ago. Other geologists propose that these deposits are remains of old landslides and mudflows that may be even older. In either case, they are intriguing deposits for their age and location.

In *0.5+ miles* from Stop 5, an unpaved road that joins Peak-to-Peak Highway on the right leads to *Longs Peak Ranger Station, Campground, and Trailhead.* A Park ranger stationed there can advise climbers about routes and weather conditions on Longs Peak. Permits are required for any backcountry overnight stays. The campground is for tent camping only. An emergency telephone and restrooms are available.

This side road passes the *Rocky Ridge Music Center,* a summer camp founded by Beth Miller Harrod in 1942 in the former Hewes-Kirkwood Inn and Resort. The music center has a distinguished faculty offering instruction in voice and instruments. Public concerts are given during the summer months.

On the right in *2.3+ miles* from Stop 5, *St. Catherine's Chapel* sits perched on an ancient glaciated granite knob overlooking Cabin Creek. Majestic Longs Peak and Mt. Meeker rise behind it. Wetlands along Cabin Creek are dominated by willows and alders that provide excellent habitat for birds. The chapel is on the grounds of St. Malo Center, a summer retreat and conference center owned by the Catholic Archdiocese of Denver. It is named both for a patron saint and for the donors of the property—Mr. and Mrs. Charles Malo, Denver residents.

6 MEEKER PARK PICNIC AREA

Turn left into a large picnic area managed by the U.S. Forest Service. This is an excellent place to examine plants you have been seeing along the way. Four different kinds of trees grow here: aspen, Douglas-fir, and two species of pine—lodgepole and ponderosa.

The ground here supports carpets of *kinnikinnik,* a low-growing, evergreen shrub related to the California manzanita. Its leaves were smoked by Native Americans.

Around the parking area you may see other plants with light green, unbranched stalks two to five feet in height. For at least 40 years, these *green gentians* grow close to the ground as large rosettes of greyish-green leaves before producing tall flower stems bearing star-shaped pale green blossoms. Green gentians bloom once, then they die.

The trees growing behind the wooden map demonstrate the hardiness of Rocky Mountain plants. They have great tenacity to survive and grow on shallow, rocky soils, buffeted frequently by drying winds. Trees become established in small bedrock cracks where soil and water are trapped, sustaining the young seedlings. As roots grow and expand in the narrow fissures, the bedrock literally is pried apart.

You may find yourself in the company of several *birds* that keep a watchful eye on visitors. Blue Stellar's jays and iridescent, long-tailed, black and white magpies are noisy and notorious scavengers. You probably will also see some quieter relatives—Clark's nutcrackers with their grey, black, and white plumage and the more plainly feathered gray jays. Black-capped and mountain chickadees together with white-breasted nuthatches search the trees for food. Dark-eyed juncos forage on the ground. Ruby-crowned kinglets sing melodiously from trees during summer months.

In contrast to the National Park Service policy that prohibits collecting firewood, the U. S. Forest Service issues permits for selective harvesting of firewood and Christmas

Green gentian. Ann Zwinger

281

trees in designated areas. Few forests in this part of the Rockies are suitable for commercial timbering.

Stop 7 is in 0.6+ miles

 MEEKER PARK

You may pull onto the highway shoulder where convenient. Meeker Park Lodge is across the road, and *Mt. Meeker* rises on your right. To its left and closer to you, knobby *Horsetooth Peak,* 10,344' elevation (3,153 m), and *Lookout Mountain,* 10,715' elevation (3,266 m), protrude above the forest.

Nathan C. Meeker, for whom the mountain and Meeker Park were named, came to Colorado from the East where he was agricultural editor for the *New York Tribune.* With well-known newspaper publisher Horace Greeley he founded a farming community in 1870 on the eastern plains called the Union Colony of Greeley, Colorado.

While serving as an Indian agent on the White River Ute Indian Reservation in western Colorado, Meeker was killed in 1879 by his wards, infuriated that he tried to convert them into farmers. His fatal error was plowing an irrigation ditch across the open field where the Utes raced their ponies.

Since it was homesteaded in 1888 by Franklin Horn-baker, *Meeker Park* has been different things to different people. A dairy was developed to supply food to miners in the vicinity. Later it became a center for summer homes, many still used today. Meeker Park Lodge was opened in 1934.

Stop 8A begins in 0.3 mile

 WILD BASIN GLACIAL REMAINS
(no sign)

Stop 8 is divided into three parts to emphasize a highly significant group of glacial features. The valley of North St. Vrain Creek is unique in this region: only here can you see moraines of three consecutive Great Ice Age glaciations in

Model A Ford driving the Longs Peak Road in 1922. NPS

clear sequence—Pre-Bull Lake, Bull Lake, and Pinedale. The three exposures are grouped as a single stop to emphasize their spatial and chronological relationships.

Stop 8A: After making a broad curve to the left and crossing a ravine, pull off to the right onto the highway shoulder. Examine the slope across the road where *glacial deposits* of Pre-Bull Lake age are exposed by road excavation. This debris is so old that the heap-like moraine form is gone and the iron minerals in it has been oxidized to a rusty color. Most fine materials have been removed by wind and water.

If you wish to see another Pre-Bull Lake glacial deposit, drive through Olive Ridge Campground, which is *0.6+ miles* beyond North St. Vrain Creek. The Pre-Bull Lake moraine there is from one to six feet thick and spread throughout the campground. Large, rounded boulders outlining the roadways and campsites were brought down valley and scattered by recent Pinedale glaciers. They have been rearranged neatly in the campground by the U.S. Forest Service.

Stop 8B: In *0.3 miles* from Stop 8A the road is a cut into a more recent glacial deposit left by a Bull Lake glaciation. *Bull Lake glaciers* occupied the valley of North St. Vrain Creek from 200,000 to 130,000 years ago. They overran and obliterated most evidence of the earlier glaciers. This second glacial period is named after the Bull Lake site in the Wind River Mountains of Wyoming where deposits of this age were first identified.

This Bull Lake glacial debris still retains some of the ridge-like shape typical of a moraine. It contains many large boulders and cobbles. The light yellow-grey stain is caused by only partial oxidation of iron and is indicative of its relative youth.

Stop 8C: In *0.1+ miles* from Stop 8B on your right, the road cuts through an even larger and younger moraine deposited between 22,000 and 20,000 years ago by a more recent Wild Basin Glacier. This kind of glacial material is called a Pinedale-age moraine after its type locality in the Wind River Mountains of Wyoming.

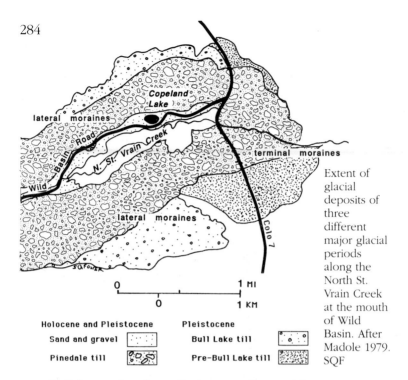

Holocene and Pleistocene   Pleistocene

Sand and gravel   [ ]   Bull Lake till

Pinedale till   Pre-Bull Lake till

Extent of glacial deposits of three different major glacial periods along the North St. Vrain Creek at the mouth of Wild Basin. After Madole 1979. SQF

Pull forward a short distance until you drive onto a sizeable turnout on the right. In front of you is part of the north lateral moraine left by the Pinedale-age glacier. Across the road is a cut in the glacier's terminal moraine.

Notice the grayish-white soils in these moraines. They have not been in place long enough to oxidize and turn rusty. In another 200,000 years, the large boulders, cobbles, and pebbles scattered through these moraines will weather into smaller materials such as you saw in the Pre-Bull moraine.

Stop 9 is in 0.6 miles from Stop 8C at Copeland Lake

In less than *0.1 miles* beyond Stop 8C and on the right is the *junction of Peak-to-Peak Highway with Wild Basin Road*. Turn right onto this road and drive past Wild Basin Lodge.

In *0.3+ miles* from Peak-to-Peak Highway, turn right again onto the gravel road signed *Wild Basin Trailhead*. It will deliver you to the threshold of one of the most beautiful and remote portions of Rocky Mountain National Park.

285

⑨ COPELAND LAKE
(no sign)

Pull left into a parking area just past the Sandbeach Lake Trailhead. You are overlooking *Copeland Lake,* a water source for the City of Longmont down on the plains. The treeless peak dominating the head of Wild Basin valley is *Mt. Copeland,* 13,176' elevation (4,016 m), John B. Copeland, after whom it is named, was an early settler in the region.

Copeland Lake photographed by Enos Mills in 1900 before water was diverted into it by the City of Longmont. Mills gave the name "Wild Basin" to this remote valley that retains much of the wilderness character that he knew. Enos Mills Cabin Collection; by permission of Enda Mills Kiley.

Draped on the valley wall to the right of Mt. Copeland and extending down valley across the Peak-to-Peak Highway is *Copeland Moraine*—the same north lateral moraine of the Wild Basin Glacier you inspected at Stop 8C. Its southern counterpart forms the hill across the valley.

Visualize the cavity occupied by Copeland Lake when it was filled by a massive block of ice that broke from this most recent glacier. As the ice chunk melted, its burden of rock and gravel collapsed into the hole, creating a *kettle lake*.

A stand of mature ponderosa pine grows around the lake. The lateral moraine above the lake is forested with a mixture of ponderosa pine and Douglas-fir. Many Douglas-fir are infested with the western spruce budworm, a native insect that devours needles and eventually kills the trees.

The moraine across the valley is covered with a mixed forest of aspen and Douglas-fir. To its right in the distance is a scar from a forest fire ignited by lightning in fall 1978. Another burned patch can be seen at the base of Mt. Copeland. The National Park's present policy is to suppress all forest fires within the Park boundary, whatever their cause.

Stop 10 is in 0.6 miles

When you leave Stop 9, look to your left as you cross the small earthen dam. *North St. Vrain Creek* can be seen flowing through a *willow wetland*, also called a *willow carr*. This wetland is a Colorado Natural Area. In early summer, it has a higher density of breeding birds than surrounding forests because of its abundant food and dense shrubbery. Beaver and muskrat also frequent this area. Wetlands cleanse water of sediments and heavy metals, and slow floodwaters.

After the road descends the ridge, it crosses a large, flat, forested area that is a *glacial outwash terrace* extending nearly a mile upriver.

10 GLACIAL OUTWASH TERRACE
(no sign)

The road beyond this point is too narrow to accommodate large *recreational vehicles* (RVs). They should be parked on the gravel pad.

North St. Vrain Creek's *U-shaped valley* was transformed from its original narrow, river-cut V-shape to a broad U-shape by the scouring of several glaciers over the last million years.

A large *braided stream* flowing from the snout of the most recent glacier wandered back and forth, picking up and redepositing mounds of glacial debris. It washed away much of the fine material and redistributed the pebbles, cobbles, and sand into this flat *glacial outwash terrace*.

Immense boulders scattered over the terrace were transported by the glacier from as far up valley as the Continental Divide. Once dropped here, they were too large to be dislodged as North St. Vrain Creek formed the outwash terrace.

Growing on the cool, moist, north-facing surfaces of rock outcrops you will find dense mounds of green moss.

Stop 11 is in 0.6 miles

In *0.1 mile*, you cross *North St. Vrain Creek*. Its cold, clear water cascades over large boulders left by glaciers. The stream is lined with Colorado blue spruce, narrow-leaved cottonwoods, river birch, and willows.

The creek and a trading post on the eastern plains bear the name of two Frenchmen, Ceran and Marcellin St. Vrain, who trapped and traded fur along the Front Range. The Fort St. Vrain Trading Post, located near the confluence of St. Vrain Creek with the South Platte River, was built by the two brothers in 1837.

---

11 NORTH ST. VRAIN CREEK and GLACIALLY POLISHED BEDROCK

Pull into one of the picnic areas next to the creek. You may see an *American dipper,* a dark grey, robin-sized bird that dives into the stream to catch small insects. Between its insect-hunting forays, the dipper bobs up and down repeatedly on rocks only inches from the water.

Dippers build moss and grass nests several feet above the stream on cliff faces or on the sides of large boulders. They feed their fledglings in late June and early July.

This is also the habitat of the *belted kingfisher.* They are conspicuous for their noisy chatter emitted when flying to a perch above a pool. From there they watch for small fish, which they take with a sudden head-long dive into the water.

Native greenback cutthroat trout live farther upstream above waterfalls, where their habitat is inaccessible to other trout species. Once the only native trout species in the Colorado Front Range, greenback cutthroat trout cannot survive with introduced trout species that compete with them for food and interbreed with them. These two forces have destroyed all but a few isolated populations of greenbacks.

The rounded *granite outcrops* to the left of the road were sculpted by glaciers. Granite in the Rocky Mountains does not hold a glass-like glacial polish as do the rocks in California's Sierra Nevada. Moister summer weather in the Rocky Mountains causes rapid weathering of rock surfaces. ***Beware of this stream and its slippery rocks in spring and early summer.***

Stop 12 is in 0.6 miles

Guests at the English Hotel near Lake Estes in the early 1880s. The Earl of Dunraven entertained Buffalo Bill Cody, Kit Carson, General Sherman, Albert Bierstadt, and many other notables of the era at this hotel. Initially called the English Hotel in recognition of its foreign clientele, mostly the Earl's hunting friends, its name eventually became Estes Park Hotel. It operated until 1911 when it burned to the ground. NPS

From here to the next stream crossing, you will see aspen with beautifully smooth, white bark. Elsewhere in the park, the lower trunks of aspen are dark grey or black in color. Wherever elk and deer are over populated, they must eat aspen bark to survive in winter, leaving trees with telltale scars.

In *0.2 miles,* you come to *Finch Lake Trailhead* on your left. It goes up and over the *South Lateral Wild Basin Moraine* to lovely and tranquil Finch Lake.

12 WILD BASIN RANGER STATION and TRAILHEAD

You are on the threshold of a beautiful and remote section of Rocky Mountain National Park. Hiking trails lead from here to glacial lakes, waterfalls, and wilderness.

Wild Basin is on a route used by *prehistoric Native Americans* traveling across the Continental Divide. These people pursued trade, hunting, food-gathering, and social activities via this and three other routes across the Park.

A large grove of Rocky Mountain maple shrubs outlines the upper end of the parking lot. Subalpine fir trees, scattered through the area, display silvery, smooth

290

bark quite distinct from the darker, scalier bark of most other evergreen trees.

To the right as you enter the parking area are the *Wild Basin Ranger Station and Residence.* This architecture is a prime example of the policy set by Director Stephen Mather in 1918 to "have all structures in national parks blend with the natural surroundings as much as possible." The buildings have been recommended for inclusion on the National Register for Historic Places.

SIDETRIP FROM WILD BASIN

You may wish to take an alternative route on your return to Estes Park. To do this, return to the junction between Stops 2 and 3, *2.3 miles north of Lily Lake, Stop 3 in this guide. On this broad curve, turn a sharp right onto Fish Creek Road and follow it down into the valley. At the first paved junction, turn left and continue to Stop 13,* 4.6 miles from Peak-to-Peak Highway.

Looking north from Fish Creek Road, you have expansive views northwest of Lumpy Ridge and sections of northern Estes Park valley. The Griff Evans homestead is in foreground. This photo was probably taken from near the English Hotel in the 1880s. NPS

Fish Creek Road was used by the earliest settlers traveling into the Estes Park region. It joined the Lamb Toll Road at the fork where you turned left.

Fish Creek Road passes the site of the English Hotel in three to four miles. This hotel was built in 1877 on an attractive site with a view of the high peaks chosen by Albert Bierstadt, renowned American painter, who also designed the structure. He was commissioned by Englishman Windham Thomas Wyndham-Quin, who held the Irish title of fourth Earl of Dunraven and several other titles.

The Earl acquired much of Estes Park Valley and adjacent lands now within the National Park. He created a private hunting reserve on these lands for his European hunting cronies. Wyndham-Quin proclaimed publicly in the *Rocky Mountain News* that "admission to Estes Park, his game preserve, was by invitation only."

The Earl failed to establish exclusive rights to this preserve and was repeatedly challenged by other early settlers about the legality of his claim to the land. He ceased visiting Estes Park in 1881, leasing his land and hotel to Theodore Whyte, his property manager. The land was purchased by Freelan O. Stanley in 1904.

Stop 13 is in 4.6 miles

13 JOEL ESTES MONUMENT

Turn left to park next to Lake Estes just before the intersection with U.S. Highway 36. Across the road on a low hill is a slender, granite boulder with a bronze plaque mounted on it honoring the *Joel Estes family*, the first homesteaders in the Estes Park valley.

Joel Estes and his son Milton happened onto this glorious valley in 1859 while they were hunting. Joel had sought gold in California in 1849 and the rumors of gold strikes in Colorado lured him to the Rocky Mountains.

The Estes built two rustic cabins near the confluence of Fish Creek and the Big Thompson River in 1860. For five years they survived the challenges of homesteading in the mountains, but the wretched winter of 1865-66 finally drove

Joel Estes's homestead about 1872 when owned by Griff Evans. This site is under the small bay of Lake Estes. Isabella Bird, early English traveler, spent the winter of 1872 in one of these buildings. NPS

Joel Estes

Joel out of the valley. He sold his claim and cattle in 1866 for a yoke of oxen and left for southern Colorado.

Another early visitor at the Estes homestead was William Byers, an avid mountaineer and editor of Denver's *Rocky Mountain News.* Aspiring to be the first person to climb Longs Peak, Byers came to this area with a group of friends in the summer of 1864. He succeeded in reaching the adjacent summit of Mt. Meeker, but was unable to continue on to Longs. Writing about this climb in his newspaper, Byers described the lovely valley of "Estes Park"—the first published use of this name.

Longs Peak, the Mummy Range, and Lumpy Ridge are mirrored in Lake Estes in the early mornings. Created by the 70 foot earthen Olympus Dam, the lake holds waters from Big Thompson and Fall rivers, together with water diverted from the Colorado River by tunnels of the Colorado Big Thompson Project.

Turn left onto U.S. Highway 36 just north of the parking area to continue this side trip.

Stop 14 is in 0.6+ miles at the Estes Park Area Historical Museum

PEAK-TO-PEAK HIGHWAY

293

14 ESTES PARK AREA HISTORICAL MUSEUM

On your left at the intersection of U.S. Highway 36 and Fourth Street is the *Estes Park Area Historical Museum*. Its exhibits contain many interesting mementos of the region's colorful history, including photos and statues of Joel Estes, his wife Patsey, and their fourteen children.

In 1987, the first building that housed the headquarters of Rocky Mountain National Park was relocated to the museum site. It is being restored and will eventually contain exhibits about the establishment of the National Park.

On the Museum grounds is the former home of the MacDonald family who established a business in Estes Park in the late 1800s. It was moved to this location in 1983, as part of the downtown redevelopment following the Lawn Lake Flood. MacDonald Bookstore on Elkhorn Avenue is still in the family.

Stop 15 is in 0.1+ miles

15 ESTES PARK POWER PLANT
7,504' (2,287 m)

Just before the junction of Colorado Highway 7 and U.S. Highway 36, use the right turning lane to drive into the parking area at the Estes Park Power Plant, operated by the Bureau of Reclamation. The building contains exhibits about the Colorado Big Thompson Project. Tours may be taken through the power plant.

The primary purpose of this project is to transport water from the West Slope via a thirteen mile tunnel through the Continental Divide to Lake Estes where it is stored. The water is released down the Big Thompson River to ranches and cities on the Great Plains.

Electricity is generated at several hydroelectric plants in the Big Thompson Project. Power at the Estes Park plant is produced by water from Marys Lake surging downhill

294

The road to the museum continues to the *Stanley Park Fairgrounds,* where the Rooftop Rodeo and other events are held every year. Freelan O. Stanley donated this land to the Estes Park community.

In *0.5+ mile,* two access roads on the right lead into *Lake Estes Recreation Area* where there are several picnic areas, boat ramps, and restrooms. Fishing and boating are allowed, but camping is prohibited.

View from Mt. Olympus taken by Enos Mills in 1895. The Big Thompson River meanders east from the Continental Divide across land now occupied by Lake Estes. Enos Mills Cabin collection; by permission of Enda Mills Kiley.

through a penstock and tunnel. The Estes Park plant generates 45,000 kilowatts when operating under average water intake.

As you exit the parking area, turn right.

Stop 16 is in 0.8+ miles at the Stanley Hotel

In *0.3+ miles* from Stop 15, a road on the right descends to the parking area for the *Estes Park Tourist Information Center.* This is an excellent place to obtain more information about the region.

The *junction of U.S. Highway 36, U.S. Highway 34, and U.S. 34 By-Pass* is at the stoplight in *0.1+ miles* more. To continue this tour, drive straight through this intersection and up the hill onto U.S. 34 By-Pass. Turn right into *Stanley Center* shopping area and follow the main road through the center to the *Stanley Hotel.*

STANLEY HOTEL

Enjoy the view of Estes Park and its mountain backdrop from the porch of the Stanley Hotel; explore the grounds of this renowned institution. Its buildings are listed on the *National Register of Historic Places.*

Freelan O. Stanley came to Estes Park in 1903 after being told he had six months to live. He stayed on to build this impressive Victorian hotel that opened in 1909 on land he purchased from the Earl of Dunraven. The Earl might have been its namesake, had it not been for his unpopularity in Estes Park. The hotel was named instead for Stanley, its civic-minded owner.

Stanley and his identical twin, Frances, were outstanding inventors. Best known for the Stanley Steamer, an automobile they designed, they also developed a machine to coat dry photographic plates with light-sensitive emulsions, a device they sold to Eastman Kodak Company in 1904.

In June 1903, Stanley brought a Steamer to Denver by train. He drove the vehicle to Lyons, where he tried to recruit an assistant to help him keep water in the auto's boiler while en route to Estes Park. No one accepted his invitation, so Stanley flogged his Steamer up the harrowing route by himself. He reached Estes Park in one and one-half hours, where he gleefully telephoned news of his accomplishment back to the incredulous residents of Lyons. The Steamer was not the first automobile to be driven into Estes Park. It was preceded a month earlier by a product of the Chicago Motor Vehicle Company.

As his health improved in this western environment, Freelan Stanley became actively involved in many Estes Park affairs. He was responsible for building the town's first electric plant and water system. He also donated land for the town's first wastewater treatment plant.

This side trip leads from the Stanley Hotel to the MacGregor Ranch north of Estes Park and terminates at the scenic head of Devils Gulch. Return to U.S. Highway 34 Bypass and turn right. In *0.6+ miles* from this junction, turn right onto MacGregor Avenue and continue another *0.9 miles* until you see the gate to MacGregor Ranch on a sharp right hand curve.

Stop 17 is in 1.5 miles

F.O. and F.E. Stanley in the first Stanley Steamer, 1897. NPS

17 MacGREGOR RANCH

7,616' (2,321 m)

After going through the large wooden gate to MacGregor Ranch, turn right immediately into a small pullout.

The densely forested valley to your left is *Black Canyon*, the watershed for the Estes Park community. Three mountains in the Mummy Range frame Black Canyon: *Mount Fairchild*, 13,502' elevation (4,115 m), at its head; *Dark Mountain*, 10,859' elevation (3,310 m), to the right; and *McGregor Mountain*, 10,486' elevation (3,196 m), to the left, named for Alexander MacGregor, despite its incorrect spelling.

To the right, *Twin Owls* loom against the sky on the ridge. So-called for its resemblance to two owls perched side by side, the granite outcrop is part of *Lumpy Ridge*, a name borrowed from the Arapaho Indians. Although it is within the boundary of Rocky Mountain National Park, Lumpy Ridge forms the northern boundary of Estes Park Valley, which is outside the National Park.

The knobs on Lumpy Ridge are granite *exfoliation domes* that were once buried thousands of feet deep beneath layers of metamorphic and sedimentary rock. As the weight of the overburden was removed by erosion, the rock in these domes responded to the release from pressure by cracking parallel to its surface. Concentric slabs of granite were created that appear like shells on a gigantic onion. This *exfoliation* process also produced the arches you will see along Lumpy Ridge a little later on this tour.

Turn around to view the stacks of immense boulders above the forest across the road. They are composed of the same type of granite as the domes in Lumpy Ridge, yet a very different process has created their distinctive form called a *tor*. This Celtic word means 'mound' or 'heap,' and refers to high, craggy rock outcrops surrounded by parkland.

The tors are angular blocks created by rock cracks or *joints*. Weathering along the joints has reduced the surface of the hard, crystalline granite to iron-stained, pea-sized grains called *gruss*.

Over several million years, this weathering process has left the large, resistant *corestones* stacked one on another. Acres of gruss cover the gently rolling land around the crags. A well-drained soil forms on the gruss that supports grasslands. Ponderosa pines root and grow in the cracks of the tors. It is still a mystery to geologists why identical granite material has formed domes on Lumpy Ridge and tors in Estes Park Valley.

At the base of Lumpy Ridge are the buildings of *MacGregor Ranch* on one of the oldest working cattle ranches in Estes Park. The *MacGregor Museum* is housed in one of these buildings *0.3 miles* from the gate. It is open Tuesdays through Saturdays, 11 AM to 5 PM, from Memorial Day through Labor Day. You can explore the ranch environs from several established trails.

Alexander Quinter MacGregor, a young attorney from Milwaukee, Wisconsin, first came to Estes Park on a hunting trip in 1872. MacGregor fortuitously met Maria Clara Heeney, who was among a group of University of Wisconsin art students visiting the area with Clara's mother, Mrs. Georgiana Heeney serving as chaperone.

Diagram of tor formation. SQF after Linton 1955

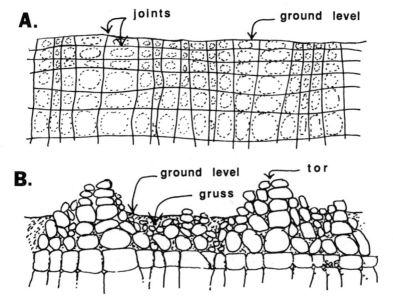

The young couple fell in love with each other and
with Estes Park. Alexander laid claim to this land in 1873.
After he and Clara were married in 1874, they returned with
Clara's mother to found Black Canyon Ranch, now known
as the MacGregor Ranch.

Both MacGregors were civic-minded, a trait that was
passed on to their heirs. Their home became Estes Park's
first post office, where Clara served as postmistress. Alexander engineered the construction of a toll road from Estes
Park to Lyons, but found it hard to collect tolls from the
independent settlers. He met an untimely death in 1896
from lightning while hunting on Fall River Pass.

Muriel MacGregor, a grand-daughter and last surviving
member of the family, died in 1970. Her will specified that
the ranch was to continue operating and that its profits
were to be used for educational and charitable purposes.
The preservation of the 1,200-acre ranch as open space and
a working ranch serves to commemorate the MacGregor
family's generosity and sense of community.

In order to preserve its untrammeled beauty for future
generations, the federal government purchased critical
scenic easements on the ranch in the mid-1970s. These
easements will keep this portion of Estes Park much as it
was when the MacGregors settled here in 1874.

After Muriel's estate was settled, the family home was
reopened as a museum in May 1973. Exhibits, including
photographs, personal belongings, and other memorabilia
convey the family's experiences on an early western cattle
ranch.

Across MacGregor Avenue on your right is a fence
with an odd-looking, overhanging top (the part on the
corner has recently been replaced). This fence was built in
1913 to prevent 49 transplanted elk from roaming away
from their new range in the Estes Park area.

The elk were brought from Yellowstone National Park
by the Estes Park Protective and Improvement Association
to replace native herds obliterated by hunting in the late
1800s. Most elk in the National Park today descended from
these transplanted animals.

300

Early days at MacGregor's Ranch. NPS

Early settlers supplemented their living by killing elk and deer, and hauling the carcasses by the wagonload to Denver where they found an excellent market for fresh meat. This practice, in addition to competition on the range with cattle, had reduced the elk numbers to near zero by 1880.

As you leave MacGregor Ranch, turn left at the gate onto Devils Gulch Road, an extension of MacGregor Avenue.

Stop 18 is in 2.2 miles in Northern Estes Park.

In *0.8 miles*, a parking area for a second trail to *Gem Lake* is on your left. This trail to Gem Lake—a sparkling jewel set in an immense *solution pothole* on Lumpy Ridge—treats hikers to sweeping views of the peaks along the Continental Divide.

In *1.8 miles* from Stop 1, a graded road appears straight ahead just as the Devils Gulch Road veers to the right. This *McGraw Ranch Road* provides access to the eastern side of the Mummy Range in Rocky Mountain National Park via the Cow Creek and West Creek trails. The original McGraw Ranch was purchased by the federal government in September 1988.

18 | NORTHERN ESTES PARK
(no sign)

In *0.4 miles* beyond the McGraw Ranch Road, graded *County Road 61* goes straight ahead, while Devils Gulch Road angles left. Take County Road 61 and pull over onto its right shoulder as soon as possible. This road leads to H Bar G Ranch Hostel, originally homesteaded by Shepherd "Shep" Husted, a rancher, ranger, and guide who moved to Estes Park in 1898.

Husted's reputation as an expert guide and naturalist resulted from his astute observation of the natural world and his receptivity to the ideas of the many educated tourists he guided. Among those who appreciated his services were Chief Justice Oliver Wendell Holmes, writer Edna Ferber, and the Doctors Mayo. Husted climbed Longs Peak 350 times during his years in Estes Park, a record as yet unmatched.

In June and July, the grasslands surrounding you resemble a Van Gogh painting splashed with blue penstemon, yellow wallflowers and arnica, pale lavender and magenta locoweed, silver fringed sage, and many other flowers. This parkland is a microcosm of what Estes Park was like when first settled in this valley, well over 100 years ago.

Ranchers and homeowners have placed bird houses on many fenceposts to encourage mountain bluebirds to nest here. Watch for these vivid cobalt blue birds swooping over the grasslands and descending into them to feed.

To reach the next stop, return to the paved Devils Gulch Road and turn right.

Stop 19 is in 0.9 miles

After you make the turn, look across the meadow to your right and a little behind you to see *Eagle Rock*, a large granite dome silhouetted against the sky. From some sides, this imposing dome looks very much like the head, beak, and shoulders of an immense perched eagle.

Beyond Eagle Rock is Skyland Ranch, the mountain home of *Ruth Ashton Nelson*, pioneer botanist of the Estes Park area. During her years as a Park Naturalist in the 1920s, she collected plants throughout the region. Her book, *Plants of Rocky Mountain National Park*, is still the definitive work on this subject.

HEAD OF DEVILS GULCH
7,980' (2,469 m) (no sign)

At the upper end of Estes Park Valley, just before the road drops steeply into *Devils Gulch,* pull right into a small turnout next to a private driveway.

You are at the northern edge of Estes Park, the broad, gently sloping valley after which the community was named. The view from here of its mountain backdrop is stunning.

The word "park" throughout Colorado comes from the French word "parque." French explorers gave the name to large, grassy areas like this one that are surrounded by mountains. Colorado's mountain parks provide important, but increasingly threatened, winter range for deer and elk. A century ago, large herds of wild animals grazed on their abundant grasses.

Soils in parks are so deep that trees and shrubs are crowded out by the vigorous growth of grasses. The scattered ponderosa pines in this valley grow from bedrock outcrops, their roots probing deep along cracks where water accumulates.

This site is within the area affected by the devastating storm that caused the Big Thompson Flood on July 31, 1976. The flash flood drowned at least 140 people. Yet, many residents of western Estes Park, where only four inches of rain had fallen, knew nothing of the event until the next morning.

The circumstances for this flash flood were created when two warm, moist air masses were held stationary for two days by a very slow-moving cold front. Gentle rain fell on the region for several days. On the evening of July 31, without warning or mercy, eight to twelve inches of rain fell in about four hours. The precipitation gave rise to more than 100 times as much water as normal in the canyons of the Big Thompson River and the North Fork of the Big Thompson.

Devils Gulch Road winds down a steep grade through *Devils Gulch*. 'Gulch' is a western word for a steep, narrow canyon. The 1877 Hayden Survey's *Atlas of Colorado* called this gulch "Devils Canon," perhaps describing the way clouds rise from it almost as steam does from a boiling caldron.

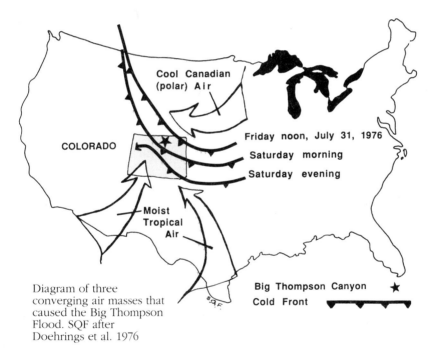

Diagram of three converging air masses that caused the Big Thompson Flood. SQF after Doehrings et al. 1976

USEFUL INFORMATION ABOUT THE AREA

FACILITIES IN ROCKY MOUNTAIN NATIONAL PARK

Visitors Centers and Museums

The following visitor centers and museums contain exhibits, sell literature and maps about the Park, and are staffed with Park Naturalists who will answer your questions about the Park. Slide programs are given in some of these facilities, as well as in amphitheatres in some campgrounds. There are numerous interpretive signs and nature trails throughout the Park; some of these are mentioned in the Roadside Guides.

ROCKY MOUNTAIN NATIONAL PARK VISITOR CENTER is located in Park Headquarters on U.S. Highway 36, *1.2 miles* outside the Beaver Meadows Entrance and *2.5 miles* from downtown Estes Park. This visitor center is at Stop 1 in *Deer Ridge Roadside Guide*.

ALPINE VISITOR CENTER is at Fall River Pass on Trail Ridge Road, *20.4 miles* from Beaver Meadows Entrance Station and *20.5 miles* from the Grand Lake Entrance Station. It is at Stop 17 in *Trail Ridge Roadside Guide*, Stop 1 in *West Slope Roadside Guide*, and Stop 24 in *Old Fall River Roadside Guide*.

KAWUNEECHE VISITOR CENTER is on West Slope Road *0.3 miles* south of the Grand Lake Entrance Station. It is at Stop 20 in the *West Slope Roadside Guide* and Stop 1 on the *Grand Lake Loop Roadside Guide*.

MORAINE PARK MUSEUM is found just off Bear Lake Road in Moraine Park, *1.3 miles* from the Beaver Meadows Entrance Station. It is at Stop 1 in *Bear Lake Roadside Guide*.

305

NEVER SUMMER RANCH MUSEUM is adjacent to West Slope Road in the Kawuneeche Valley, *7.9 miles* from Grand Lake Entrance Station. The museum is at Stop 14 in the *West Slope Roadside Guide.*

MacGREGOR MUSEUM is located on MacGregor Ranch on MacGregor Avenue, *0.8 miles* from U.S. 34 By-Pass and *0.2 miles* beyond Stop 17 on the *Peak-to-Peak Roadside Guide.*

Campgrounds

There are five campgrounds within Rocky Mountain National Park. In the summer season, it is advisable to obtain reservations for campsites. These reservations can be procured in advance of your trip by writing Ticketron, Department r-401, Hackensack Avenue, Hackensack, N.J. 07601, or by going to the Campground Office in the Headquarters Building, or the Kawuneeche Visitor Center.

Camping in the backcountry is strictly regulated by permits issued for specific sites and dates at no cost. These permits are obtained by writing to the Backcountry Office, Rocky Mountain National Park, Estes Park, Colorado 80517-8397. For information, call 303-586-4459 or 586-2371. There are backcountry permit offices east of the Park Headquarters Building and in the Kawuneeche Visitor Center.

National Park Service campgrounds on the East Slope of the Park are:

ASPENGLEN CAMPGROUND, located across the river from Fall River Entrance Station just off U.S. Highway 34, *Deer Ridge Tour.* Sites are obtained on a first-come, first-served basis; the campground is open year round.

GLACIER BASIN CAMPGROUND, located on Bear Lake Road *5.1 miles* from Beaver Meadows Entrance Station. Sites are obtained only by reservation during the summer season; it is closed during the winter.

LONGS PEAK CAMPGROUND, reached by a road that connects with Colorado Highway 7, outside the National Park. The junction is *9.1 miles* from Park Headquarters and *6.0 miles* north of Allenspark on Peak-to-Peak Highway. Sites are for *tent camping only* on a first-come, first-served basis year round.

MORAINE PARK CAMPGROUND, located on Moraine Park Road, *0.5 miles* from its junction with Bear Lake Road, and *1.6+ miles* from Beaver Meadows Entrance Station. Sites are obtained only by reservation during the summer season; it is closed during the winter.

National Park Service campground on the West Slope of the Park is:

TIMBERCREEK CAMPGROUND, located *8.1 miles* north of Grand Lake Entrance Station on West Slope Road; it is *34.4 miles from Park Headquarters*. Sites are obtained on a first-come, first-served basis; the campground is open year round.

Picnic Areas

Picnic areas are found throughout the Park, many with restroom facilities and fire grills. Small clusters of picnic tables placed along roads in the Park offer solitude.

Transportation and Tours

There are several tour options available for visitors who do not wish to drive. Check with the Tourist Information Center or the U.S. Forest Service Information Office in Estes Park or the Grand Lake Chamber of Commerce for details.

National Park shuttle buses run from the bus terminal near Glacier Basin Campground to Bear Lake at frequent intervals during July, August, and early September. Drivers describe points of interest and stop at several points along the route. Visitors are encouraged to make use of this opportunity.

Hiking and Riding Trails

There are more than 355 miles of hiking trails within the Park, some of which are short and easy, while others are more challenging. Various written trail guides are available at the Park visitor centers.

Horses and guides can be hired during the summer from livery stables at both Sprague Lake and Moraine Park, reached from the Bear Lake Road. You can obtain information about trails that may be closed to livestock from the Backcountry Offices, where permits needed for the use of privately owned pack animals within the National Park can also be obtained.

Skiing

Hidden Valley Ski Area, a downhill ski facility, is located adjacent to Trail Ridge Road on the East Slope of the Park. It is open from November through April.

Opportunities for all abilities of cross country skiers abound in the Park. The best snow conditions for cross country skiing are often on trails found around Bear Lake, Sprague Lake, upper Moraine Park, lower Wild Basin, and along Kawuneeche Valley.

Fishing

Fish and berries are the only natural objects that may legally be removed from the National Park without a National Park Service scientific research permit. You may fish in all waters of the Park, unless they are specifically designated "closed." Special regulations are in force and posted at Colorado greenback cutthroat trout habitats. All persons over the age of 12 must follow fishing regulations and hold a current Colorado State Fishing License.

Facilities for the Handicapped

Restrooms accessible to the handicapped are located along Trail Ridge Road at Park Headquarters, Rainbow Curve, Rock Cut, and the Alpine Visitor Center.

Several trails are also accessible to people in wheel chairs:

- A gravelled trail goes around part of Sprague Lake, Stop 6 in *Bear Lake Roadside Guide*

- A boardwalk provides access to trout fishing and wildlife observation points at the Beaver Ponds, Stop 2 in *Trail Ridge Roadside Guide*.

- A boardwalk goes along the edge of Many Parks Curve, Stop 4 in *Trail Ridge Roadside Guide.*

- Two paved trails are available on Trail Ridge:

One leads to spectacular views at Forest Canyon Overlook, Stop 9 in *Trail Ridge Roadside Guide;* the other—the Tundra World Trail—goes one-half mile along the ridgetop at Rock Cut, Stop 12.

A backcountry camping area for up to ten campers or five wheelchairs is available near Sprague Lake. Call (303) 586-2371 for details on its location and reservations.

FACILITIES AND SERVICES OUTSIDE THE NATIONAL PARK

Tourist Information Centers

Communities near the east and west entrances to Rocky Mountain National Park maintain tourist information centers where you can obtain advice and pamphlets about motel accommodations, camping facilities, visitor activities, restaurants, day care, and entertainment.

ESTES PARK TOURIST INFORMATION CENTER is adjacent to U.S. Highway 34, U.S. 36, and U.S. 34 By-Pass, *0.3 miles* beyond Stop 15 in the *Peak-to-Peak Roadside Guide.*

GRAND LAKE CHAMBER OF COMMERCE is located at the junction of U.S. Highway 34 and Colorado 278 west of Grand Lake Village, Stop 2 on the *Grand Lake Loop Roadside Guide.*

The U.S. FOREST SERVICE provides information through its District Office in Estes Park, located just north of Colorado Highway 7 on Second Street. It is reached by turning onto Colorado Highway 7 from U.S. Highway 36 and driving two blocks, then turning left on Second Street. This is just beyond Stop 15 on the *Peak-to-Peak Roadside Guide.*

Museums

ENOS A. MILLS HOMESTEAD CABIN is located on
Colorado Highway 7—the Peak-to-Peak Highway—
8.5 miles from Park Headquarters between Stops 4 and
5 on the *Peak-to-Peak Roadside Guide.*

ESTES PARK AREA HISTORICAL MUSEUM is on the
corner of U.S. Highway 36 and 4th Street near the
Stanley Fairgrounds, across from the Lake Estes Recreation Area. It is Stop 14 in the *Peak-to-Peak Roadside
Guide.*

KAUFMAN HOUSE MUSEUM is on Pitkin Street one
block south of Grand Avenue, *0.4 miles* from Stop 3
on the *Grand Lake Loop Roadside Guide.*

Campgrounds

OLIVE RIDGE CAMPGROUND is located just off
Colorado 7 south of Wild Basin, *13.6 miles* from Park
Headquarters. It is managed by the U.S. Forest Service.

STILLWATER CAMPGROUND is located just off U.S.
Highway 34 south of Grand Lake village and is
managed by the U.S. Forest Service. It is on the shore
of Shadow Mountain Lake in Shadow Mountain
National Recreation Area.

Several private campgrounds are operated near both
Estes Park and Grand Lake. Information about them can be
obtained from the Information Center and Chamber of
Commerce.

View from Park Hill of Estes Park and Lumpy Ridge. L.C. McClure 1910

INDEX

314

315

Lookout Mountain, 281
Louisiana Purchase, 22
Lulu City, 22, 188, 190-1; Lulu Mountain, 193, 195
Lumpy Ridge, 46, 266, 290, 292, 297-8

MacGregor, Alexander Q., 260-1, 297-8; Mac-Gregor Avenue, 296, 299, 300; MacGregor Museum, 298, 305; MacGregor Ranch, 297-9, 300; Muriel MacGregor (daughter), 299; McGregor (sic) Mountain, 297
Magpie, 49, 280
Many Parks Curve, 44, 123-6
Maple, Rocky Mountain, 86, 104, 124, 235, 289
Maps of: Rocky Mountain National Park, xii-xiii; individual roads, 35, 74, 114, 167, 211, 229, 262; former glaciers in Rocky Mountain National Park, 14; weather patterns, 177, 303; Colorado Big Thompson Project, 222, 268
March, D. J. and Minnie, 231, 235, 239
Marmot, yellow-bellied, 149, 152, 250-1; Marmot Point, 248
Marys Lake, 123, 266, 294; Marys Lake Power Plant, 266; Marys Lake Road, 262-3, 267. *See also* Mary I. Fleming Estes
Mather, Stephen T., 25, 148, 214, 246, 290
Mayfly, 236
Mayo, Doctors, 301
McGraw Ranch Road, 300
McLaren, Fred, 197
McPherson, Imogene, 76
Meadow vole, 147, 152
Meander, 106, 198-9
Medial moraine. *See* glacial moraines
Medicine bow, 171; Medicine Bow Curve, 169-171; Medicine Bow Forest Reserve, 24; Medicine Bow Range, 170
Meeker, Nathan C., 281; Mount Meeker, 63, 258, 279, 281, 292; Meeker Park, 281; Meeker Park Picnic Area, 280-1
Metamorphic rock, 4, 140, 159, 183, 187, 266; metamorphic mica schist, 166
Middle Fork and Grand River Mineral and Land Improvement Co., 190
Mill Creek, 85-7
Mills, Enos A., 24-6, 260, 266, 268, 272-7, 285, 293; Enos A. Mills Cabin Museum, 272, 309; Enos A. Mills Historic Marker, 272; Mills Moraine, 277; Enda Mills Kiley and Bob Kiley (daughter and son-in-law), 270, 276; Esther Burness Mills (wife), 274, 276. *See also* Elkanah Lamb (uncle)
Milner, T. J., 176; Milner Pass, 157, 176-8; Milner Pass Glacier, 177-8
"Miner Bill's" Cabin. *See* Bill Currance
Mining, 1, 22, 102, 190
Montane life zone, 18-19, 37; montane plants, 37, 41, 44-5, 64
Monument rocks, 152
Moraine Avenue, 36
Moraine lake, 12, 63, 77, 177-8, 214, 217, 220

Moraine Park, 13, 76, 79, 107, 123; Moraine Park Campground, 105, 306; Moraine Park Museum, 76, 78, 304; Moraine Park Post Office, 81; Moraine Park Road, 80, 105
Moraines. *See* glacial moraines
Moss, 287
Moss campion, 142, 154
Motor Nature Trail, 226, 230, 235
Mountain ash, 102
Mountain building cycle, 3-8
Mountain finders, 42, 46, 78, 88, 96, 124, 128, 130, 140, 156, 158, 170, 182
Mountain lion. *See* lion, mountain
Mountain wetland. *See* wetland
Mudflow breccia, 172-4
Muir, John, 1, 24, 273
Muledeer, 37, 41, 60, 75, 86, 133, 149, 152, 233, 269, 289, 300
Mummy Range, 10, 82, 123, 130, 154, 156, 236, 254, 266, 292, 297
Museum, 304-5, 309; Enos A. Mills Cabin, 272, 309; Estes Park Area Historic Museum, 261, 294, 309; Kaufman House, 309; Moraine Park Museum, 76, 78, 304; Never Summer Ranch Museum, 196, 305. *See also* Visitor center

Narcissus-flowered anemone, 144
National Park concept, 25-6
National Park Service, operational policy, 27, 67-8, 99, 280, 286; rustic style architecture policy, 68, 179, 214, 290
National Register of Historic Places, 76, 82, 115, 169, 185, 191, 196, 230, 257, 290
Native Americans, 1, 17, 21-3, 41, 81, 95, 110, 133-5, 154, 164, 168, 171, 177-8, 179, 190, 201, 208, 213, 219, 223, 226, 230, 241, 266, 278, 280, 289
Nature trail, 58, 91, 118, 123, 141, 148, 276
Nelson, Ruth Ashton, 53, 260, 302. *See also* Willard H. Ashton (father)
Never Summer Mountains, 8-9, 16, 141, 154, 157-8, 170, 173-4, 181-3, 185, 187, 189, 193, 198, 200; Never Summer Ranch, 196-7; Never Summer Ranch Museum, 196, 305
Nimbus, Mount, 181, 195
Ninebark, 236
Nitrate lichen. *See* lichen
Nivation depression, 146-8, 152
North Inlet, 214, 217, 219; North Inlet Lateral Moraine, 220; North Inlet Trailhead, 219
North St. Vrain Creek, 260, 281, 283-4, 286-8
Northern Estes Park. *See* Estes Park
Northern harrier, 151
Nugent, "Mountain Jim," 277
Nutcracker, Clark's. *See* Clark's nutcracker
Nuthatch, 280

Old Faithful Snowslide. *See* snowslide
Old Fall River Road ("Continental Road"), 57, 115-6, 161, 177, 184, 232-3, 235-6, 246, 249-50, 255-277, 226-257; construction of, 233;

316

318

Visitor center: Alpine, 161, 304; Kawuneeche, 206, 212, 304; Rocky Mountain National Park, 36, 304
Volcanic rocks, 172-4, 189, 217; volcanic ash-flow tuff, 157, 159, 160. *See also* Mudflow breccia; Troublesome Formation

Water diversion, 184-6, 200, 210, 221-2, 266-7, 292, 294; Water Supply and Diversion Company, 185-6. *see also* Colorado Big Thompson Project; Grand Ditch
Water ouzel. *See* American dipper
Water pipit, 147, 151
Waxflower, 49, 236
Way, L. Claude, 214, 233
Weasel, 152
Weather, xvii, 14-16
Weathering pits. *See* solution pits
Welded ashflow tuff. *See* volcanic tuff
Wescott, "Judge," 223; Mount Wescott, 223
West Creek Trail, 300
West Portal Road, 219-20
West Slope, 166, 201, 220, 266, 294; West Slope aqueduct, 184; West Slope climate, 172-3, 204; West Slope Road, 164-207; West Slope streams, 186; West Slope water, 185, 208
Western sagebrush, 43
Wetland, 19, 193-5, 203, 235, 279; alpine, 147, 254; hillside, 52, 63; mountain, 86, 241; willow, 54, 286
Wheeler, H. M., 24
Wheeler, "Squeaky" Bob, 166, 178, 187, 189-90
White, William Allen, 82-4; William Allen White Cabin, 82-3
White-tailed ptarmigan. *See* ptarmigan, white-tailed

Whyte, T., 291
Wild Basin: 22, 223, 260; Glacier, 283, 286; glacial remains, 281; moraine, 289; ranger residence, 290; Ranger Station, 289-90; Road, 284; Trailhead, 284, 289; valley, 285
Wildflower gardens, 28, 52, 64, 75, 95, 107, 124, 126, 133, 141-2, 144, 149, 154, 173, 176, 188, 196, 203, 236, 241, 249, 254, 301
Willard, B.E. Dr., 99, 150, 250
Willow, 41, 106-7, 119, 133, 171, 279; Willow Park, 248, 253; Upper Willow Park, 253. *See also* wetland
Wilson, President Woodrow, 25
Wind River Mountains of Wyoming, 13, 283-4. *See also* aging moraines
Wind River Pass, 271
Wind velocity, 15, 135, 159
Windy Gap, 135
Wintergreen, 200
Wolverine Mine, 200
Wolves, 268
Wood frog, 192, 194
Woodpecker, 60, 204
Woodtick, xix-xx
Wren, 60
Wright, Frank Lloyd, 54; Frank Lloyd Wright Taliesen Associates, 36
Wyndham-Quin, Windham Thomas. *See* Dunraven, Earl of

Yard, Robert S., 26
YMCA of the Rockies, 263
Ypsilon, Mount, 54, 108